The
South
Atlantic
Quarterly
Fall 2005
Volume 104
Number 4

Visit Duke University Press Journals at www.dukepress
.edu/journals.

Subscriptions. Direct all orders to Duke University Press,
Journals Fulfillment, 905 W. Main St., Suite 18B, Durham,
NC 27701. Annual subscription rates: institutions, $140;
e-only institutions, $126; individuals, $35; students, $21.
Add $12 postage and 7% GST for Canada. Add $16 postage
outside the U.S. and Canada. Back volumes (institutions):
$140. Single issues: institutions, $35; individuals, $14. For
more information, contact Duke University Press Journals at
888-651-0122 (toll-free in the U.S. and Canada) or 919-687-
3602; subscriptions@dukeupress.edu.

Permissions. Photocopies for course or research use that
are supplied to the end user at no cost may be made
without explicit permission or fee. Photocopies that are
provided to the end user for a fee may not be made without payment of permission fees to Duke University Press.
Address requests for permission to republish copyrighted
material to Permissions Coordinator, Duke University
Press, 905 W. Main St., Suite 18B, Durham, NC 27701;
permissions@dukeupress.edu.

Advertisements. Direct inquiries about advertising to
Journals Advertising Specialist, Duke University Press,
905 W. Main St., Suite 18B, Durham, NC 27701;
journals_advertising@dukeupress.edu.

Distribution. The journal is distributed by Ubiquity
Distributors, 607 DeGraw St., Brooklyn, NY 11217; phone:
718-875-5491; fax: 718-875-8047.

The *South Atlantic Quarterly* is indexed in *Abstracts of
English Studies, Academic Abstracts, Academic Index, America:
History and Life, American Bibliography of Slavic and East
European Studies, American Humanities Index, Arts and
Humanities Citation Index, Book Review Index, CERDIC,
Children's Book Review Index (1965–), Current Contents, His-
torical Abstracts, Humanities Index, Index to Book Reviews in
the Humanities, LCR, Middle East: Abstract and Index, MLA
Bibliography, PAIS,* and *Social Science Source.*

The *South Atlantic Quarterly* is published, at $140 for insti-
tutions and $35 for individuals, by Duke University Press,
905 W. Main St., Suite 18B, Durham, NC 27701. Periodicals
postage paid at Durham, NC, and additional mailing offices.
Postmaster: Send address changes to *South Atlantic Quarterly,* Box 90660, Duke University Press, Durham, NC
27708-0660.

ISSN 0038-2876

Thinking Politically

SPECIAL ISSUE EDITOR: ALBERTO MOREIRAS

The
South
Atlantic
Quarterly
Fall 2005
Volume 104
Number 4

Alberto Moreiras

Introduction

The "Thinking Politically" Conference, held in Durham, North Carolina, on October 24–26, 2003, was the inaugural event of the Duke University Institute for Critical Theory. Fredric Jameson, the institute's director, invited colleagues and outside guests to discuss "the problem of whether interpretive strategies of broadly defined 'classical' texts provide the coordinates for a reconceptualization of the sites, stakes, and agencies of the political that could rescue it from seemingly irreversible obsolescence."[1] Jameson's call referred simultaneously to the waning of the political, "erased by the logic of the market," and to the insistent calls for its restoration. But Jameson noted that "most of this discourse devolves into ethical, theological, and civic republican motifs. . . . For the Left, the present conceivability of any strategic orientation to state power has arguably imparted an abstract character to its various affirmations of 'the political' as an agenda in its own right." Jameson urged conference participants to reflect on key texts of political thinking in the modern European tradition, at the same time engaging "the problematic status today of the semantics of decision, commitment, and denunciation" and

The *South Atlantic Quarterly* 104:4, Fall 2005.

addressing "the question of what constitutes the specifically political dimension of texts in this tradition, and whether this can ever be distinguished
from mere partisan ideology, however stirring."[2]

Here I will briefly focus on a theme that was arguably at the very basis
of Jameson's questions and that became a substantial subject of debate at
the conference: the vexed notion of the autonomy of the political, so often
denied by Left thinking. Could any possible primacy of politics over history
(including economic history) be considered absolute or relative? If relative,
then politics would still be subordinate to history in the last instance. If
absolute, then politics would be the norm of action. But an absolutely primary politics would have to rely on the total immanence of its own conditions and would in fact be normless: that is, it would provide something like
a normless norm for action. A politics without a norm—that is, a politics
that would itself be the normative standard, without recourse to alterity or
to a heterogeneous grounding—can only be a politics of force, and it would
have become an ontology (as in the Nietzschean case).

Or is it possible that a norm for politics can be found outside history itself,
and thus also outside force? That norm would not yet be an ontology, but it
would register at some infraontological level, perhaps at the level of desire: a
normative affect regulating something like what Bruno Bosteels calls in his
essay for this issue, quoting Alain Badiou, the "communist invariant," or,
from an altogether different tradition, what Jacques Derrida would call the
undeconstructibility of the call for justice. Would it be necessary to conclude
that every possible understanding of the political as a primary motivator for
human action that would not immediately reduce politics to force would
still have to be automatically partisan? Can politics be thought without partisanship? Is partisanship an unconditional, irreducible determinant of any
theory of the political?

The Spanish philosopher María Zambrano stated in her 1958 book *Persona y democracia* that a democratic politics is bound to a very precise determination: the abandonment of "sacrificial history." If the abandonment of
the sacrificial structuration of history defines democratic politics, by the
same token the practice of democracy defines an antisacrificial perspective on action. A democratic politics, regardless of what politics could be
in itself, is always bent on the suppression of the divide between, on the
one hand, what Zambrano called "idols" and, on the other, "victims."[3] This
cuts across other divisions of the political field, such as the Schmittian
friend/enemy division, or the division of the social between the part of the
whole and the part of no-part recently proposed by Jacques Rancière.[4]

If politics is exhaustively contained in the friend/enemy division, then politics is defined by power: politics seeks power—its acquisition or its continued possession—as the power of one group over other groups, and it is therefore always already partisan politics. If politics marks the fundamental act of appearance of a claim to existence by the part of no-part, that is, of those who are negated by the ideological articulation of social totality, then politics is defined by recognition: the part of no-part wants to be recognized as such by the social totality, or it wants to be recognized as the social totality (the proletariat as universal class, or the people as general will). If politics is understood as the practice of abandoning the sacrificial structuration of history, then politics appears as specifically democratic politics. Through any of those determinations there emerges the thought that the only possible nonpartisan understanding of the political is precisely the understanding of the political as always already partisan.

We can imagine a complex interaction between demands for power, for recognition, and for the end of sacrifice in any concrete situation. At their limit, however, the three definitions are incompatible, and in their mutual excess, they organize something like an aporia of the political. Politics would finally be the infinite negotiation between those three demands: for power, for recognition, and for an end to social sacrifice. But if this is true, then only democracy can organize, even if aporetically, the simultaneous pursuit of the three demands, as no other system can countenance the end of the sacrificial structuration of history. Democracy can, however, authorize unconditional demands for power and recognition. Not any demands for power and recognition, of course—just some: the absolute power of the people, for instance; or the total recognition of the proletariat as class, which is the political abolition of class; or the total recognition of gender, which is the political abolition of gender. Only in the horizon of democracy is it possible to think of the total subsumption of power, recognition, and the end of sacrifice. But this would be the end of the political, and thus necessarily also the end of democracy, and the end of the end of sacrifice.

The essays that follow openly thematize the political *within* the democratic horizon. They represent a contribution to a Left thinking of the political that, while refusing its total subsumption into economic history, still remains thoughtful as to its limitations and constraints. They resist the ontological horizon, even in the fallen sense of political culturalism that pervades so many of the contemporary academic discussions. Their differences, however, must for the moment remain unspecified: simply to be read.

Notes

1   The conference included papers by Warren Montag on Spinoza, Anne Garréta on Carl
Schmitt, Fredric Jameson on Rousseau, Srinivas Aravamudan on Hobbes, Stathis Kouvélakis on Marx, Ken Surin on Balibar, Alberto Moreiras on Donoso Cortés, and Malcolm
Bull on John C. Calhoun. A keynote address by Gopal Balakrishnan concentrated on
Machiavelli. Grant Farred, *SAQ*'s general editor, invited me to prepare this special issue
on the basis of the conference papers, to which a number of essays were to be added that
no longer concentrated, as those papers did, on "classical" texts on the political. For various reasons some of the conference papers (Balakrishnan, Surin, Moreiras) have not been
included in the present collection. But Stella Sandford was invited to write on the status
of sex in Greek political thinking, Peter Hallward on transformational politics, Teresa
Vilarós on the Cold War, and Bruno Bosteels on the "communist invariant."
2   Fredric Jameson, "Thinking Politically" conference introduction. See the complete text at
www.duke.edu/literature/institute/thinkingpolitically.htm (accessed February 21, 2005).
3   María Zambrano, *Persona y democracia: La historia sacrificial* (1958; reprint, Barcelona:
Anthropos, 1988), 42.
4   Jacques Ranciére, *Disagreement: Politics and Philosophy*, trans. Julie Rose (Minneapolis:
University of Minnesota Press, 1999), 13–14.

Stella Sandford

Thinking Sex Politically:
Rethinking "Sex" in Plato's *Republic*

This essay is concerned with the category of
sex, where *sex* means "sex difference," as distinct from "sexual difference" (a psychoanalytic
category), "gender" (a category describing historical, cultural, and institutional demands or
norms), and "sexuality" (which refers to sexual
desire and/or its orientation). Its aim is to
show that we cannot adequately think about
"sex" politically without also thinking about it
philosophically. "Thinking philosophically," in
this essay, means thinking through a text from
the history of philosophy—Plato's *Republic*—and
critically examining the assumptions of some of
the English translations of and commentaries
on it, in the light of recent theoretical debates.
The aim is to make a general point about the
thinking of sex that holds across disciplinary
boundaries.[1]

Sex is usually understood to be a natural
"given," and the question of identifying what sex
is is still usually presumed to be one that can be
settled empirically, probably by biologists. However, recent work in both biology and philosophy
has shown that "sex" is not merely an empirical
issue but, rather, a more complex categorical and
therefore philosophical one, though some of the

The *South Atlantic Quarterly* 104:4, Fall 2005.

reasons for thinking this are themselves empirical.[2] Briefly, at the level of anatomy, genital morphology, chromosomal configuration, and hormone distribution, the assumption of a clear binary sex difference is not confirmed.[3] The incidence of human intersexuals suggests that it is the category of binary sex difference itself, not the empirical distribution of its characteristics, that demands investigation. The existence of the intersexed reveals that sex is an epistemological and ontological problem and that the presumption of its justification on the basis of an appeal to allegedly straightforwardly perceptible facts is mistaken.[4] Transsexualism poses further philosophical problems in relation to the concept of sex. The fact that one can *change* sex raises the existential question of what it is to *be* sexed, and not just to be sexed as this or that but to be sexed at all, as well as the ontological question of what sex itself *is*.

Despite the intelligibility of these questions, however, the presumption of binary sex difference is enduring, and resistance to the philosophical questioning of the category is strong. To understand this we need to investigate how the concept "sex" functions in relation to other concepts. When we are careful to distinguish it from related concepts like "gender," "sex" is used as an abstract noun of classification referring to "the sum of the characteristics that distinguish organisms on the basis of their reproductive function," and also to "either of the two categories, male or female, into which organisms are placed on this basis."[5] As such, the specificity of the concept concerns the status attributed to its two terms, male and female. As a distinct concept, "sex" involves the idea that being-male and being-female are the natural, determining bases for the definition of what it is to be a girl or a boy or a man or a woman. "Sex," that is, is generally conceived as a concept that signifies something about the immutability and essential nature of its terms, such that they signify as foundational and not themselves susceptible to determination. ("Male" and "female" are treated as natural kinds.) With regard to human existence, the function of the concept of sex has largely been to define being-male and being-female as foundational to, and to a great extent determining of, the social and psychological being of men and women.

To the extent that it thus functions ideologically, as a structuring part in a pattern of beliefs related to the social forms of gendered existence, sex is an eminently political concept. Hoary old presumptions about the universality, neutrality, or purity of the practice of the discipline of philosophy may continue to allow some to believe that it has nothing to do with politics. But even where philosophy has become overtly political by becoming feminist, thinking politically about sex has rarely involved the critical philosophical analysis of the concept itself. Such an analysis requires an investigation of the function of "sex" in its conceptual constellations in different linguistic and historical contexts and can begin only with specific examples from which we might hope to draw more general conclusions.

This essay focuses on one such example: the function of the concept of sex in the English translations of and commentaries on the arguments for the proposals concerning the role of women in Plato's *Republic*. The main claim in this essay, based on a strict textual analysis, is that there is in fact no concept of "sex," as the general term for the categories of male and female, in the classical Greek text of Plato's *Republic*. On the basis of this claim, a new interpretation of the relevant passages of the *Republic* becomes possible and causes us to call into question the apparent "givenness" of the concept of sex and to appreciate its historical contingency, to see that it is a distinctively "modern" concept.[6] In what follows I shall first examine Plato's main argument for the second and third of three proposals concerning the role of women in the *Republic* from the standpoint of some of the most familiar English translations and feminist responses, where the concept of sex is freely employed. I shall then attempt to justify the claim that there is no concept of sex in the *Republic*, reexamining the argument and some related passages from the *Laws* accordingly. Finally, I shall consider some of the broader philosophical consequences of this claim and its implications for contemporary feminism as an indication of what it might now mean for us to think "sex" politically.

The Relevance of Sex

In what is conventionally numbered book 5 of Plato's *Republic*, Socrates[7] makes three proposals concerning the ruling "guardian" class of the *Republic*, proposals which seem radical and shocking to his interlocutors: (1) that wives and children should be held in common; (2) that men and women should receive an equal education; and (3) that women should participate in all aspects of governance. Disagreements in the feminist literature have largely centered on the second and third proposals.[8] As the second (a radical transformation of education in its broadest sense of upbringing and acculturation) is the condition of possibility of the third (participation in governance), these two proposals are part of a single program of social and political transformation which, *mutatis mutandis*, is recognizable in the actual transformations of the nineteenth and twentieth centuries—regional, national, and continental variations notwithstanding.

Whatever Plato's intentions in its initial presentation, various forms of one crucial aspect of his main argument in favor of these proposals have been central, either implicitly or explicitly, to both liberal and socialist feminism. The argument, insofar as it has interested Plato's feminist readers, may be summarized as follows. According to Socrates in Plato's *Republic*, the difference between the sexes (which is not, in itself, denied) is not such that men or women, *qua* men or *qua* women, are suited to any one kind of work or any distinct social or cultural existence. Rather, the difference between the sexes is reduced to the different roles of men and women in reproduction and is said to be *irrelevant* to their capacities for work. Despite Plato's generalized sexism—his apparent belief that men are superior to women in all things—the argument seems to support the view that it is the different treatment and cultural expectations of boys and girls and men and women that produce many of the differences in capacity and character that people are wont to ascribe, erroneously, to the "natural" differences between the sexes.

Despite profound differences in the various feminist interpretations of Plato's position and its wider implications, there has been a common assumption that the concept of "sex" plays a central role in it. This assumption is, of course, not unmotivated by the terms of the text itself, and in particular by the references throughout to "male" (*arren*) and "female" (*thēlus*). Having earlier compared the military wing of the guardian class to watchdogs, Socrates argues for the equal education of men and women by extending his comparison into an analogy (here Socrates reports his questions and his interlocutor's answers):

> "Ought female watchdogs [*tas thēleias tōn phulakōn kunōn*] to perform the same guard-duties as male [*hoi arrenes*], and watch and hunt and so on with them? Or ought they to stay at home on the grounds that the bearing and rearing of their puppies incapacitates them from other duties, so that the whole burden of the care of the flock falls on the males?" "They should share all duties, though we should treat the females as the weaker and the males as the stronger [*hōs asthenesterais chrōmetha, tois de hōs ischuroterois*]." "And can you use any animal for the same purpose as another," I asked, "unless you bring it up and train it in the same way?" "No." "So if we are going to use men and women

for the same purposes, we must teach them the same things?" "Yes." (451d–452a)[9]

For Socrates, this argument establishes that men and women should receive the same education if they are to be used for the same purposes, but it does not establish that they can and should be so used. In the elaboration of his case, the two questions of the possibility and the desirability of Socrates' proposals are condensed into the question of whether or not they are contrary to nature, as the major objection to them will claim that they are. Because of the limitations of the guard dog analogy, Socrates is aware that most of the work in the argument is still to be done, a point that, at first sight, Aristotle's surprisingly literal objection ("It is absurd to argue, from the analogy of animals, that men and women should follow the same pursuits, for animals have not to manage a household")[10] seemingly fails to acknowledge. According to Socrates:

> The first thing we have to agree on, then, is whether these proposals are feasible [*dunata*] or not. For, whether it's asked in joke or in earnest, we must allow people to ask the question, Is the female of the human species naturally capable of taking part in all the occupations of the male [*poteron dunatē phusis hē anthrōpinē hē thēleia tē tou arrenos genous koivōnēsai eis hapanta ta erga*], or in none, or in some only? (452e–453a)

As the question is introduced with the interrogative particle *ara*, a negative answer is expected. The implication, then, is that the capability of the female is "in question," in the sense of "in doubt."[11] Accordingly, Socrates formulates a serious objection to his own proposals, on behalf of the doubters, by referring back to the previously agreed-upon principle that "each man was naturally [*kata phusin*] fitted for a particular job of his own" (370b):

> "Well," he [the doubter] will continue, "isn't there a very great natural difference between men and women [*estin oun hopōs ou pampolu diapherei gunē andros tēn phusin*]?" And when we admit that too, he will ask us whether we ought not to give them different roles to match these natural differences [*oukoun allo kai ergon hekaterō prosēkei prostattein to kata tēn hautou phusin*]. When we say yes, he will ask, "Then aren't you making a mistake and contradicting yourselves, when you go on to say that men and women should follow the same occupations, in spite of the great natural difference between them [*pleiston kechōrismenēn phusin echontas*]?" (453b–c)

Socrates' answer to this objection, which aims to clear away the appearance of internal inconsistency, constitutes the main argument for both the second and the third proposals. It is the objection, he says, that is faulty, in not being able to distinguish between merely verbal oppositions and more important "distinctions in kind" (*mē dunasthai kat' eidē diairoumenoi*) (454a) and in not considering "what kind [*eidos*] of sameness or difference of nature we mean, and what our intention was when we laid down the principle that different natures should have different jobs, similar natures similar jobs" (454b). "We never meant," Socrates says,

> "that natures are the same or different in an unqualified sense [*ou pantōs tēn autēn kai tēn heteran phusin etithemetha*], but only with reference to the kind of sameness or difference which is relevant to various employments. For instance, we should regard a man and a woman with medical ability as having the same nature [*hoion iatrikon men kai iatrikēn tēn psuchēn ontas tēn autēn phusin echein elegomen*]. Do you agree?" "Yes." "But a doctor and a carpenter [*iatrikon de kai tektonikon*] we should reckon as having different natures."[12] "Yes, entirely." "Then if men or women as a sex [*to tōn andrōn kai to tōn gunaikōn genos*] appear to be qualified for different skills or occupations," I said, "we shall assign these to each accordingly." (454c–e)

Given the previous agreement on the "very great" natural difference between men and women, the situation is now that the interlocutors are agreed both that men and women have different natures (as men and women), and that some men and women have the same nature (as doctors, for example). This is not a contradiction in Socrates' argument, but the exposition of an apparent contradiction in the beliefs of his interlocutors, due to the same mistake that Socrates identified earlier: failure to ask in what the difference between the natures of men and women consists and how that difference is relevant. The next step will be to determine just this:

> "Then if men or women as a sex [*to tōn andrōn kai to tōn gunaikōn genos*] appear to be qualified for different skills or occupations," I said, "we shall assign these to each accordingly; but if the only difference apparent between them is that the female bears [*to men thēlu tiktein*] and the male begets [*to de arren ocheuein*] we shall not admit that this is a difference relevant for our purpose, but shall maintain that our male and female Guardians [*tous te phulakas hēmin kai tas gunaikas*] ought to follow the same occupations." (454d–e)

According to Julia Annas, the "crucial point" in Plato's argument is not whether there are differences between men and women—indisputably, there are—but whether these sex differences, which are certainly relevant in procreation, have any bearing on men and women's professional capabilities.[13] For Annas and many other feminist readers, Plato was able to see that these differences are only illegitimately cited as the justification for women's exclusion from participation in education, administration of the state, governance, and so on. For others still, this insight extends to Plato's ability to see that what women currently are and do is not what women *could be* and *could do* under different, more favorable conditions (principally, with more favorable educational opportunities).[14]

Given the conservative or reactionary role that "sex" tends to continue to play in discussions of the capabilities, characteristics, and proper pursuits of men and women, it is not surprising that feminists should emphasize the general irrelevance of the fact (if such it is) of sex difference to professional capability and argue that the fact of sex difference does not translate into necessarily determined intellectual or psychological differences. To the extent that readers have found book 5 of the *Republic* to contain arguments congenial to feminism, it is therefore also not surprising that Plato's position is couched in these terms.[15] According to this interpretation, Socrates' argument is pitted against his interlocutors' assumption that sex difference—the fact that women bear and men beget—is a valid basis for doubting that women are capable of sharing in men's work (most specifically in governance). Despite their varying degrees of sympathy for Plato, most feminist commentators thus agree that the crucial point in his argument is the shift in emphasis away from "sex" as an explanatory category in the social and political existence of women toward "gender," the set of socially determined behaviors and characteristics prescribed for and—to a greater or lesser extent—lived out by women. It is thus generally assumed that the modern category of "sex" is somehow operative in, or can be read back into, the arguments in book 5 of the *Republic*.

The Relevance of *Genos*

However, from the modern perspective there is a conceptual lacuna in Plato's text which most English translations and interpretations—including the feminist interpretations—do not merely miss but in fact conceal. Moreover, this lacuna occurs in precisely that passage in which, according to Annas and others, the crucial point is made, namely:

"Then if men or women as a sex [*to tōn andrōn kai to tōn gunaikōn genos*] appear to be qualified for different skills or occupations," [Socrates] said, "we shall assign these to each accordingly; but if the only difference apparent between them is that the female bears [*to men thēlu tiktein*] and the male begets [*to de arren ocheuein*] we shall not admit that this is a difference relevant for our purpose, but shall maintain that our male and female Guardians [*tous te phulakas hēmin kai tas gunaikas*] ought to follow the same occupations." (454d–e)

What is perhaps most interesting about this—the crux of Socrates' argument—is obscured, I shall now argue, by the translation of *genos* as "sex," and by the use of the English terms "male" and "female" in the final line.

In classical Greek there is no distinct word for "sex." The word *genos*, which is sometimes translated as "sex," primarily means "race," "stock," and "kin," as well as "offspring," "tribe," "generation," and "kind." In the passages under consideration, every time Plato's *genos* is translated into English as "sex," the more general "race" or (better) "kind" would make equally as much sense. What, then, justifies the translation of *genos* as "sex"?

In modern English, "sex," as we have said, is an abstract noun of classification referring to "the sum of the characteristics that distinguish organisms on the basis of their reproductive function," and also to "either of the two categories, male or female, into which organisms are placed on this basis." "Sex" as a conceptually distinct term is aligned with nature itself, in contrast with the conventional attributes of "gender." As such, "sex" functions conceptually (and also allegedly empirically) as the basis for, but *is not identical with*, the categories "man" and "woman" (a species-specific version of the adult forms of male and female) and the characteristics of gender. If "sex" is a *general* term referring to the two categories "male" and "female," the category according to which the "nature" of men and women is ultimately determined, there is no concept of sex in Plato's *Republic*. For each time *genos* is used in the *Republic* in relation to men or women or male or female, it is attached *to one or the other* in order to specify men or women or male or female as a class in distinction from this or that man or woman or male or female animal. The word is never used (indeed, it *cannot* be used) as a singular term to refer to a distinction in kind covering both men and women or male and female. That is, it is never used as the general term "sex" is used in English.[16] And although the concepts of "male" and "female" seem to be unproblematically recognizable in the Greek *arren* and *thēlus*, the absence of any concept of sex as a general term that designates what kind of categories "male" and "female" are would suggest that *arren* and *thēlus* are *not* identical with the English "male" and "female."

The fact that there is no distinct word for "sex" in classical Greek and the—empirically verifiable—fact that the word *genos* is never used in the *Republic* as a singular term to refer to a distinction in kind covering both male and female (because it cannot be used thus) are important for the claim that there is no concept of sex in Plato's *Republic*. However, it does not by itself offer conclusive support for the claim. Rather, the claim is made, very specifically, with reference to the precise context and function of the word *genos* in Plato's dialogue, in comparison with the function of the modern English "sex." Any objection to the claim must therefore be made at the same level. The fact that generations of highly respected classical scholars have routinely employed the category of sex in commentary on and interpretation of Plato's text does not *demonstrate*, but merely *presumes*, that the modern concept is an appropriate translation, and it is precisely this presumption that this essay aims to question. This contemporary context should make it clear, further, that I do not mean to suggest that there is an "objective truth" of "sex" revealed by the modern English word but hidden to Plato. Rather, one of the consequences of the claim that there is no concept of "sex" in Plato's *Republic* is that the contingency of its modern function is revealed. If the claim is taken seriously, it will have implications not only for how we read the *Republic* and other texts of the period, but also for how we understand the status of our *own* concepts of "sex" and "gender." For it would be mere presentist prejudice to imagine that our conceptual divisions must be the right ones and that the absence of any exact parallel with the modern concept of "sex" in classical Greek is a lack.

Reading the *Republic* without the presumption of the modern category of sex entails a shift of interpretive emphasis and warrants the reexamination of several main concepts. In the crucial passage at 454d–e there is a noticeable shift from "man" and "woman" to "male" and "female." In Lee's translation:

> "if men or women as a sex [*to tōn andrōn kai to tōn gunaikōn genos*] appear to be qualified for different skills or occupations," [Socrates] said, "we shall assign these to each accordingly; but if the only difference apparent between them is that the female bears [*to men thēlu tiktein*] and the male begets [*to de arren ocheuein*] we shall not admit that this is a difference relevant for our purpose, but shall maintain that our male and

female Guardians [*tous te phulakas hēmin kai tas gunaikas*] ought to follow the same occupations."

According to the presumption of a determining concept of sex as a baseline
supporting and regulating the characteristics of men and women, the move
from "man" and "woman" to "male" and "female" is interpreted as a descent
to the bottom line, a movement downward on a vertical plane. The destination of this downward movement is already presupposed in the translation of *genos* as "sex" and consolidated in Lee's translation of *tous te phulakas
hēmin kai tas yunaikas*—literally, "our guardians [masculine gender] and the
[or 'their'] women [or 'wives']"—as "our male and female Guardians": that
is, according to the categories of sex.

However, without the presumption of the category of sex predetermin-
ing the interpretation, the move from "man" and "woman" to "male" and
"female" might be seen as a movement, on a horizontal plane, to alternative designations, not foundational descriptions. Without the presumption of the foundational category of sex, "man" and "woman" and "male"
and "female" could represent different ways of conceiving the difference
between groups or kinds (Plato uses *genos* in relation to the terms of both
conceptual pairs) across which the distinction of conditioned/conditioning
is not distributed. Indeed, one might even see the primarily adjectival forms
of *arren* (male) and *thēlus* (female) as determinations or attributes *of anēr*
(man) and *gunē* (woman), a position which, however unorthodox or counterintuitive, does have the merit of making sense of their almost complete lack
of relevance to Plato's argument in contrast to the role played by descriptions of the possibilities for men and women.

The common assumption that the modern category of sex is central to
Socrates' argument also involves the assumption that it drives the position
that Socrates *opposes*. According to this assumption, what is contentious and
radical in Socrates' argument is his claim that the fact that females bear and
males beget is irrelevant to employment and governance. But if the presumption of the modern category of sex—which we tend to equate with
"the natural"—is removed, then Socrates' assertion of "a very great natural
difference between men and women"—the first real stumbling block to his
proposals—need not be read as a reference to the fact that one begets and
the other bears. Indeed, Socrates' argument makes much more sense (and
is certainly much more interesting) when it is *not* read in this way. The objection is, rather, a much more far-reaching assertion of a difference between
men and women *in every aspect of their existences*, an assertion governed

by the assumption of a set of "natural" characteristics peculiar to women, including (as Socrates emphasizes) a generalized inferiority and weakness.

The question is, what is the presumed basis of this set of characteristics peculiar to women? With the ready availability of the concept of sex, the answer is easy: the basis of the characteristics peculiar to women is their sex, their being-female. But if the availability of the modern concept of sex is not presumed, then what women *are* as a *genos* is constituted by this collection of characteristics, this totality of the set of womanish characteristics themselves, just as much as by their being-female. Without the presumption of the modern concept of sex to carry the explanatory burden, the "nature" of women is not attributable to a singular "essence," in the modern sense, but is composed of a unified multiplicity of behavioral and other characteristics, including their being-female, the totality of which bears the (now historico-)ontological weight. In modern terminology, the greater significance of the set of womanish characteristics and attributes here would amount to the greater significance of "gender" than of "sex"; sex would be just one of these characteristics. This is not just the claim that social and political conditions, rather than differences in capability emanating from the natural fact of sex, determine in any given culture what women can and cannot *do*. It is the claim that the whole of the set of womanish characteristics and attributes, including being-female, constitutes the basis of what a woman *is*. They—and not the modern category of sex—define what it is to *be* a woman in the strong sense.

As has often been pointed out, Plato's dialogues are littered with casual references to women defined according to a set of (wholly negative) characteristics, and they are historically typical in that respect. To the extent that this is also presupposed as the background to the *Republic*, it is what Socrates tries to put into question. What Socrates (unlike modern feminists) must oppose is thus not the presumption of the determining role of sex difference, but the presumption that women as a race (*genos*) are different—indeed opposite—to men in *every respect*, in *every aspect* of their "nature." Accordingly, Socrates' contentious move in the relevant passages in the *Republic* is *not* the claim that the different roles of the male and the female in reproduction are irrelevant to the matter at hand. It is the *reduction of* "the very great natural difference between men and women" *to* the fact that one begets and the other bears. Philosophically, that is, Socrates' contentious move is the metonymic definition of the nature of men and women in terms of being-female and being-male, the metonymic *substitution of* different roles in reproduction *for* the "very great natural difference." To the extent that being-male and being-female do not have the determining function given them by the modern concept of sex, Socrates' reduction amounts to denying the relevance of "the very great natural difference" as it is usually understood while seeming to acknowledge it. Substituting a part (function in reproduction) for the whole (social and political being), Socrates reduces differences that would be seen as specifically human to a kind of difference that is common to all animals (his use of the verb *ocheuein* for the male role in reproduction emphasizes this, as does the example of the guard dog). According to this interpretation of Socrates' argument, Aristotle's objection to it is not so literal after all. That is, Aristotle objects to the reduction of the very great differences between men and women—differences in every aspect of their social and political existences—to the relatively unimportant difference between bearing and begetting as bare animal functions.

As this may be thought to be a contentious interpretation, it is worth reiterating the point to make it clear. The logic of Socrates' argument, and the logic of Aristotle's objection to it, suggest that what needs to be opposed is *not* the idea that being-male and being-female (the fact that the one begets and the other bears) determines all aspects of the social, psychological, and political existences of men and women. Aristotle, it seems, objects to the reduction of men and women to their being-male and being-female precisely because these latter *cannot* be seen to determine one aspect of their social existences (broadly speaking, the division of labor) that for him is crucial to the definition of the existences of men and women.

Thus the target and the rhetorical tenor of Socrates' argument look rather different when it is not presumed, a priori, that the modern concept of sex is operative in the text: when it is not presumed, that is, that what it is to be a man or to be a woman—what constitutes a man as a man and a woman as a woman—is primarily determined by their being-male and being-female. The text suggests, rather, that what constitutes a man as a man and a woman as a woman is equally or even chiefly the sociohistorical norms of what we now call "gender," where this includes the attributes of masculinity and femininity and the normative social and political roles prescribed for each. This is not to deny, of course, that Socrates and his contemporaries were aware of the anatomical differences between men and women. But it is to suggest that the anatomical differences between men and women were not necessarily understood—as they tend to be today—on the basis of a foundational category of sex.[17]

Becoming Women, Becoming Men

The idea that—in the absence of a concept of sex—it is the set of woman-ish characteristics and attributes, quite as much as their being-female, that define what it is to *be* a woman sheds an interesting light on the social prohibition of "womanish" behavior for men in ancient Athens and illuminates the arguments in Plato's *Republic* and *Laws* against certain forms of poetry and against men taking women's parts in dramatic performance. These arguments are, in part, the extension of the familiar social prohibition taken to its limit. "The gravest charge against poetry," in book 10 of the *Republic*, concerns "its terrible power to corrupt even the best characters, with very few exceptions" (605c). Even the best of us, Socrates says, on hearing Homer represent the sufferings of a hero, will be carried away by our feelings and, moreover, praise the poet who can affect the listener most powerfully in this way (605c–d): "Yet in our private griefs we pride ourselves on just the opposite, that is, on our ability to bear them in silence like men [*hōs touto men andros on*], and we regard the behaviour we admired on the stage as womanish [*gunaikos*]" (605d–e). Admiring this behavior, feeling sympathy with this behavior, entails a loosening of the control of the best part of the soul over the lowest and *leads to* this kind of behavior itself (606a–d). It leads to becoming womanish.

This also explains why, in an earlier section of the *Republic* before the introduction of the idea of female rulers, it is said that the guardians, being men (*andras ontas*), will not be allowed to take the parts of or imitate women (395d). For if the set of womanish characteristics, quite as much as being-female, defines what it is to be a woman, a man for whom these characteristics, through repeated imitation, have become natural will, to some degree, *become* a woman. If it is not the case that men and women are defined solely according to their being-male or being-female, the set of behavioral characteristics and attributes that contribute to the definition of what it is to *be* a woman are not mere predicates: they have existential status, a state of affairs that is no doubt encouraged, if not explained, by the lack of linguistic distinction in classical Greek between what we now call the existential and the predicative senses of the verb "to be." These womanly characteristics in a man are not therefore just accidents attached to a determining male substance; they entail an existential transformation.

This existential transformation is possible, moreover, despite the fact that males are always male. As has been pointed out, the modern identification of sex with what is natural leads us to think of the idea of a "woman's nature" in terms of the determining role of her being-female. If, however, as Socrates' argument suggests, a woman's or a man's nature is equally determined by the set of behavioral characteristics and attributes that we now call "gender," we can see how it is possible to conceive of the idea that womanliness and manliness can commute across male and female. At the end of the *Laws*, Plato's Athenian protagonist imagines the ideal punishment for a man who, in the face of his enemy, deliberately abandons his weapons, "preferring a coward's life of shame to the glorious and blessed death of a hero."[18] This is a man who lacks *andreia*, "courage" or "manliness," the chief virtue of the hoplite. It is not, he says, within mortal power to change such a man into a woman (*eis gunaika ex andros metabalousa*) as a god once changed Kaineus the Thessalian into a man—that is, it is not within mortal power to effect the physical transformation from male to female. But the decreed punishment shall be the next best thing, "the closest possible approximation to such a penalty: we can make him spend the rest of his life in utter safety" (944e), never being appointed to any soldierly position, as he has, because of his own nature, given up on or been debarred from the risks that only men can run (*apheisthai tōn andreiōn kindunōn kata phusin*) (945a). The man who lacks manliness shall be treated like the woman he really is by nature,[19] a nature that his male anatomy does not override. In this case, indeed, anatomy *contradicts* nature. His being-male cannot ensure that he is a man when his behavior has proved him to be a woman.

Para doxan

The possibility for womanishness, understood in this way, to commute across male and female is recognized in the *Republic* and the *Laws* in the prohibition of behaviors that would encourage it. To some extent, this same commutability of womanishness and manliness is also the ultimate basis for the possibility of Socrates' proposals concerning women in the *Republic*. For Plato and his contemporaries, the set of characteristics and attributes that contribute to the definition of women as women includes flightiness, untrustworthiness, secretiveness, lack of self-control, and tendency to extremes of emotion (the list could be much longer). As these are the precise opposites of the characteristics of the guardians, and as Socrates argues that some women have the nature befitting a guardian, his argument must imply that some women do not have the characteristics and attributes that contribute to the definition of women as women. All that remains of this set in Socrates' argument—and this is the sole concession to the imaginary opponent's objection—is the idea that women are, in all respects, weaker than men. It is only this remainder that prevents the implication of his argument leading to the *explicit* conclusion that some women (those with the nature of a guardian) are, to all intents and purposes, men.

But this *is* the implicit conclusion: some women are, or could be, to all intents and purposes, men, although they remain incontrovertibly female. This conclusion seems very odd and contradictory in relation to the function of the modern concept of sex, according to which being female would determine that one was a woman, but not in the context of the equal significance of the set of womanish and manly characteristics and attributes in the definition of what it is to be a woman or a man. To the extent that this conclusion intensifies, rather than contradicts, the assumptions of Socrates' interlocutors, it is "paradoxical" (*para doxan*, as Socrates frequently says): not contrary to logic or possibility, that is, but contrary to *convention* and to what is taken to be desirable. In this context it is always possible that women might become men—a possibility that is both feared and socially prohibited.[20] Socrates' innovation is to endorse and promote this possibility as an alternative to the womanly woman with the set of conventional characteristics and attributes described elsewhere in Plato's dialogues.

The idea that some women might—indeed, ought to—become men has been the target of one form of the feminist critiques of Plato, articulated most vigorously, perhaps, by Arlene W. Saxonhouse, who speaks of the "de-sexed and unnatural females" of Socrates' imagination, repeating the objection of Socrates' imaginary opponent in a modern form:

> As Socrates attempts to turn women into men by making them equal participants in the political community, he ignores the peculiar natures of each and thus undermines the perfection of the political society in the *Republic*. . . . If one's *phusis* [nature] is defined by that which one does better than anyone else, then Socrates has disregarded the *phusis* of the female.[21]

Saxonhouse makes this argument in the context of a defense of what she sees as the "natural role" of women, determined by their "peculiar biological qualities."[22] It is based on the unexamined modern concept of "sex" functioning as both the "real property" securing the arguments and the thing secured by them, the thing mortgaged and the loan itself. Although

Saxonhouse is by no means representative of the many feminist readings of book 5 of the *Republic*, this concept of sex is the common assumption that cuts across them all. Without this assumption, I have argued, the context of the discussion of Socrates' proposals is realigned, and the specificity of his argument—its simultaneous immersion in and divergence from the assumptions of his contemporaries—emerges more clearly.

This specific analysis reveals a general point, relevant across the various disciplinary attempts to think sex politically. It reveals the historical specificity of the modern concept of sex, a concept whose general, conservative ideological function, in its association with the idea of a fixed, immutable "nature," is to mark a universal and unchallengeable difference, located now at the level of the biological, with reverberations throughout the social and political spheres. Thinking sex politically thus means questioning not just assumptions *about* sex, but the assumption of the givenness of the concept of sex itself.

Notes

1   This essay is a shortened version of the first chapter of my forthcoming *Plato and Sex* (Polity Press, 2006).

2   Perhaps the best-known philosophical critique of assumptions concerning the category of sex is Judith Butler's *Gender Trouble: Feminism and the Subversion of Identity* (New York: Routledge, 1990). Almost all of the philosophical work in this field, however, is indebted to Michel Foucault, *The History of Sexuality: An Introduction*, trans. Robert Hurley (New York: Pantheon, 1978).

3   See, for example, Anne Fausto-Sterling, *Sexing the Body: Gender Politics and the Construction of Sexuality* (New York: Basic Books, 2000).

4   See, for example, Suzanne J. Kessler, *Lessons from the Intersexed* (New Brunswick, NJ: Rutgers University Press, 1998).

5   These are the definitions given in the Collins English Dictionary.

6   I use the term "modern" in a broad sense here in distinction from the "ancient." I leave open the question as to when, exactly, "sex" came to have the meaning that we tend to ascribe to it today. Thomas Laqueur suggests that "sex" began to take on this meaning in the seventeenth century. See Laqueur, *Making Sex: Body and Gender from the Greeks to Freud* (Cambridge, MA: Harvard University Press, 1992), 8.

7   For the purposes of this essay, "Plato" refers to the author of the *Republic* and other dialogues, "Socrates" to a character in these dialogues.

8   See, for example, Susan Moller Okin, *Women in Western Political Thought* (Princeton, NJ: Princeton University Press, 1992).

9   Unless otherwise stated, quotations are from Desmond Lee's translation of Plato's *Republic* (Harmondsworth, UK: Penguin, 1987). References in the text cite the Stephanus numbers of Plato's dialogues.

10   Aristotle, *The Politics* and *The Constitution of Athens*, trans. Jonathan Barnes (revising
      Benjamin Jowett) (Cambridge: Cambridge University Press, 1996), 39 (1264b, 4–7).

11   So, Waterfield's translation (*Republic*, trans. Robin Waterfield [New York: Oxford Univer-
      sity Press, 1993]): "Shouldn't we allow that there is room for doubting . . . whether women
      do have the natural ability to cooperate with men."

12   The English phrase "a man and a woman with medical ability" translates the two Greek
      words *iatrikon* and *iatrikēn*, which are masculine and feminine forms, respectively, of the
      same adjective, here meaning "skilled in the medical art." The words "doctor" and "car-
      penter" translate *iatrikon* and *tektonikon*, both masculine forms of different adjectives.
      Thus the Greek emphasizes, more than the English translation can, the sameness of the
      man and woman with medical ability and the difference between the man who is a car-
      penter and the man who is a doctor.

13   Julia Annas, "Plato's *Republic* and Feminism," in *Feminism and Ancient Philosophy*, ed.
      Julie K. Ward (New York: Routledge, 1996), 4, 3. See also Janet Farrell Smith, "Plato, Irony,
      and Equality," in *Feminist Interpretations of Plato*, ed. Nancy Tuana (University Park: Penn-
      sylvania State University Press, 1994). Farrell Smith's argument draws on that of Gregory
      Vlastos, "Was Plato a Feminist?" also in Tuana, *Feminist Interpretations of Plato*.

14   See, for example, Susan B. Levin, "Women's Nature and Role in the Ideal *Polis*: *Republic* V
      Revisited," in Ward, *Feminism and Ancient Philosophy*.

15   See, for example, Elizabeth V. Spelman, "Hairy Cobblers and Philosopher-Queens," in
      Tuana, *Feminist Interpretations of Plato*, esp. 89, 94.

16   For example, in book 5 of the *Republic*: 453a, *tou arrenos genous*, "of the male race"; 454d, *to
      tōn andrōn kai to tōn gunaikōn genos*, "the race of men and the race of women"; 455c, *to tōn
      andrōn genos . . . to tōn gunaikōn*, "the race of men . . . the [race] of women"; 455d, *to gunai-
      keion genos*, "the race of women," "the womanish race"; 455d, *to genos tou genous* (genitive
      of comparison), "the race of [men] [in comparison with] the race [of women]"; 457b *dia
      tēn tou genous astheneian*, "because of the weakness of the race [of women]."

17   In a recent article, Chloë Taylor Merleau has argued something very similar to this in rela-
      tion to Aristotle. See Chloë Taylor Merleau, "Bodies, Genders and Causation in Aristotle's
      Biological and Political Theory," *Ancient Philosophy* 23.1 (2003): 135–51.

18   Plato, *Laws*, trans. Trevor J. Saunders (Harmondsworth, UK: Penguin, 1975), 944c. All
      quotations from the *Laws* use this translation by Saunders.

19   The passage reads: "ho de ophlōn tēn dikēn pros tō apheisthai tōn andreiōn kindunōn
      kata phusin tēn hautou prosapotisatō misthon . . ." Saunders translates: "and in addition
      to being thus permitted, like the woman he is by nature, to avoid the risks that only men
      can run, the guilty man must also pay a sum of money . . ."

20   Indeed, despite the function of the modern concept of sex, the contemporary anxiety
      that females might, to all intents and purposes, become men is regularly revealed in
      the antifeminist discourses that still warn of the "de-sexing" of modern women and
      the feminist "perversion" of their natural roles. In a recent (July 2004) statement of
      doctrine on gender issues, Pope John Paul II's chief theological spokesperson, cardi-
      nal Joseph Ratzinger (now himself Pope Benedict XVI), accused feminists of "blurring
      the biological difference between man and woman" with dangerous claims about the
      constructed nature of gender roles—claims that cause women to "neglect their family

duties." See John Hooper and Tania Branigan, "Pope Warns Feminists," *The Guardian*, July 31, 2004, available at www.guardian.co.uk/international/story/0,,1273102,00.html (accessed March 26, 2004).

21 Arlene W. Saxonhouse, "The Philosopher and the Female in the Political Thought of Plato," in Tuana, *Feminist Interpretations of Plato*, 68, 70. See also Saxonhouse, *Fear of Diversity: The Birth of Political Science in Ancient Greek Thought* (Chicago: University of Chicago Press, 1996), especially 147–57.

22 Ibid., 72, 71.

Srinivas Aravamudan

"The Unity of the Representer":
Reading *Leviathan* against the Grain

The concept of state sovereignty as laid out in Thomas Hobbes's *Leviathan: Or, The Matter, Forme and Power of a Common-Wealth Ecclesiasticall and Civill* has had immense influence on various Enlightenment theories. Readers of Hobbes need to address some central conundrums. Does Hobbesian sovereignty actually guarantee the rights of the political subject, or does it eviscerate that subject even while claiming to protect its rights? When does political philosophy actually assist politics, and when does it preempt its appearance? What is the relevance of theories of language, representation, and impersonation to theories of power, violence, and rights? Reading Hobbes can prompt a larger inquiry about the nature and limitations of sovereignty and its theory, and the manner in which considerations of the political often elude sovereignty's grasp.

The rest of this article will consider influential critiques of *Leviathan* and its implications. Reading others' readings of Hobbes allows us to follow the trajectory of sovereignty theory in a number of contemporary instances, if only to measure whether and to what extent new ground has been broken.

The *South Atlantic Quarterly* 104:4, Fall 2005.

Carl Schmitt's Rightist Critique of *Leviathan*'s Confused Tropology

In *Leviathan*, we see the development of a constituting subject of history freed from a presumptive State of Nature, rather than just the historical subject who is always in history and constituted by it. The radical nature of Hobbes's natural law argument brought a materialist and potentially athe-istical flavor to questions of power, right, and subjectivity, even if some prominent scholars such as Aloysius Martinich hold that this long-standing interpretation is a fundamental refusal to acknowledge the prominent role played by Hobbes's insistence on religious conformity. What Hobbes called "the mutuall Relation between Protection and Obedience" inaugurates a radical break from stories of divine right toward suggesting a countervail-ing secular notion of sovereignty and subjection as twin concepts, born out of force through the myth of a departure from the State of Nature.[1] *Leviathan* puts forward some of the following suggestive ideas: (1) sovereignty begins with a crucial moment of first surrender to escape the unending war of *bellum omnium contra omnes* (or the war of every man against every man); (2) subjection emerges from submitting oneself to overwhelming force; (3) the only alternative to the covenant with the sovereign is immi-nent death; (4) political agents (for which Hobbes uses the term *authors*) are constituted by various exclusions, whereby idols, children, fools, or madmen cannot be authors; (5) the sovereign is not subject to the same laws as subjects are but, rather, is extralegal and unbeholden to the laws; (6) through a watertight logic of "blaming the victim," the subject is the author of whatever the sovereign does and therefore always has the govern-ment he deserves and, by definition, cannot therefore suffer injury at the hands of the state; (7) the two main principles of political dominance in society are force and fraud; and (8) a multitude of peoples and voices are always represented in the singular person of the sovereign, again by defini-tion, because "it is the *Unity* of the Representer, not the *Unity* of the Repre-sented, that maketh the Person *One*" (114, fig. 1). While these eight points proceed in the direction of a narrative of absolute State dominance, it might also be suggested that the notion of subjection is not as absolute as is some-times believed. The subject submits, and "every Subject is Author of every act the Soveraign doth," but the subject is also at liberty to be a coward, or disobey commands against the laws of nature, such as those that expect him to kill himself or deprive himself of food or the fulfillment of natural instincts (148, 485). If attacked, the subject is free to resist, even though the sovereign has every right to kill him nonetheless. At stake is whether the glimmer of a parity covenant is present, even if the account largely matches that of a suzerainty covenant—returning to Hobbes's final formula of the "mutuall Relation between Protection and Obedience" (491).

Mostly reviled and/or misunderstood in his time by both Royalists and Parliamentarians, and inviting further opprobrium from the religiously inclined as a materialist and atheist, Hobbes was read with hostility (despite notable exceptions, such as Spinoza) until his partial resurrection by nineteenth-century utilitarians. His first great modern reader was Ferdinand Tönnies, at the turn of the last century, who saw in him resources for socialism but who also ultimately turned on him as the initiating architect of *Gesellschaft* against *Gemeinschaft*, or the contractual against the communitarian. This analysis anticipates later Marxist critiques, such as C. B. Macpherson's.[2]

The aspects of State dominance are taken up by one of the most notorious twentieth-century exponents of right-wing Hobbesianism. Carl Schmitt's decisionist take on the theory of sovereignty is summed up by his famous opening dictum of *Political Theology*: "Sovereign is he who decides on the exception." The suspension of the state of nature as a state of war by the Hobbesian sovereign leads him to occupy both the inside and the outside of the legal order he promulgates. Picking up on this crucial constitutive element of sovereignty in the context of the failure of emergency powers under the Weimar Republic, Schmitt proposes two kinds of dictatorship for the sovereign's last resort to the State's constitutive outside. One is the commissarial dictatorship of the ordinary state of exception, which suspends the law of a polity for a given period of time, only to return to the norm when the presumptive emergency is over. The other is the sovereign or revolutionary dictatorship of a moment such as the French or Russian Revolution (or perhaps that of the Nazi seizure of power), when the previous constitution is abolished and a revolutionary dictatorship holds power outside all existing political norms. At first Schmitt appears to appreciate this authoritarian stand in Hobbes, one that allows legitimacy to trump legality and authority to trump truth in the creation of law (or the doctrine of *auctoritas non veritas facit legem*); but in a later reading of Hobbes influenced by the young Leo Strauss, he also faults Hobbes for making possible the reverse. For Schmitt and Strauss, Hobbes is also the spiritual forefather of bourgeois law and the constitutional state. Hobbesian theory has also paradoxically led to modern liberal states in which legality substitutes for legitimacy. Liberalism dangerously hides the fact that legitimacy and ruling force can never be derived from legality except in banal circumstances. States of emergency are therefore much clearer indications of the State's extralegal and extra-constitutional authority.[3]

Schmitt's *The Leviathan in the State Theory of Thomas Hobbes* is an efficient place to encounter the creation of a twentieth-century Hobbes, credited with being the progenitor of both the totalitarian state and the liberal-administrative one. Schmitt locates this Hobbesian paradox in the complex mythological center of the text: the symbol of the Leviathan. In Hobbes's frontispiece the Leviathan is figured as a *macros anthropos* or *magnus homo*. The myth of Leviathan is taken from the Book of Job and elaborated in medieval metaphysical and cabalistic texts, variously featuring the image of a sea monster, whale, fish, dragon, or serpent. Hobbes's Leviathan arises as if he were a god protecting his fellow human beings (*homo homini deus*) from the state of nature, in which everyone can in fact be a wolf to his fellows (*homo homini lupus*). Leviathan, therefore, takes the form of a gigantic artificial construct (even though here it is artifice in the baroque sense, which includes notions of mechanism, organism, and work of art, rather than later conceptions of artifice, which emphasize the inhuman or techno-logical machine). Leviathan is a Greimasian rectangle whose corners can be designated as Man, God, Beast, and Machine. However, this artificial body, according to John Pocock, is also a mask or impersonator of each and every subject that sees Leviathan as acting in his name.[4] The "Mortall God" operates under the logic of his immortal equivalent. Hobbes is just as obsessed with the animal as with the god. According to him, animals share the moral passions with man: "[T]his alternate Succession of Appetites, Aversions, Hopes and Fears, is no lesse in other living Creatures then in Man: and therefore Beasts also deliberate. [. . .] And Beasts that have *Deliberation* must necessarily also have *Will*" (44).[5]

As a result, Leviathan is sometimes referred to by Hobbes as a mortal God (combining two of these attributes) and at other times as Artificial Animal (combining the other two attributes). The mortality of the God in the State suggests that the State can be overthrown and that sovereignty thus has a finite and defeasible historical life; all the same, the State's godlike function suggests that during its life the State hovers above society as a qualitative total State. However, the State's subsequent and indiscriminate immersion in every realm of society makes its artificial and mechanical agency also that of a quantitative total State for readers such as Schmitt, suggestive of the nightmare in which a supposedly nonpolitical society experiences lib-

eral saturation through a command apparatus that dominates the mecha-
nization of man. The co-presence of Man, God, Beast, and Machine in the
attributes of the State makes it irrational and rational, terrestrial and extra-
terrestrial all at once. As the Latin motto over the frontispiece says, quoting from the Book of Job: *Non est potestas Super Terram quae Comparatur ei*
(Upon earth there is not his like).

Most of Hobbes's metaphors regarding the Leviathan posit a mechanism-
organism. The State, according to Hobbes, is an "Artificial Animal," with
Sovereignty the equivalent of its "Artificiall *Soul*." The Magistrates are its
"artificiall Joynts," and Reward and Punishment are the "*Nerves* and ten-
dons"; "*Wealth* and *Riches*" are this body's strength, "*Equity* and *Lawes*" its
artificial reason and will. Sedition is this body's sickness and civil war its
death (9). These metaphors multiply throughout the text and include corporeal diseases such as bulimia, wounds, wens, lethargy, pleurisy, inflamma-
tion, fevers, worms in the digestive tract, and consumption, also figurally
applied to diseases of State (229–330).

Against the idea of the whale-like Leviathan is the idea of the bull-like,
ox-like, or elephant-like Behemoth that it holds down. Behemoth stands
for revolution or civil war, as Hobbes's later text of that name emphasizes
in its discussion of the English Civil War. According to Schmitt, who sub-
titles his book on Leviathan *The Meaning and Failure of a Political Symbol*,
Hobbes cannot handle the multiple mythical connotations of Leviathan,
which is ultimately "a half-ironic literary idea borne out of good English
humour."[6] Schmitt, whose interest lies in the territorial and continental
European State, would rather Hobbes have used the terrestrial Behemoth
than the marine Leviathan as the symbol of State. However, he also acknowledges that there is a brilliant counterintuitive aspect in the English context for Hobbes's choice. The year when *Leviathan* was published, 1651, also
saw the passage of Cromwell's Acts of Navigation, which helped establish
England as the globe's preeminent maritime and commercial power for the
next three centuries. In England, the sea and global commerce were the
mechanisms by which the bourgeoisie defeated the landed and territorial
aristocracy, and therefore the Leviathan prefigures that defeat even as it also
(somewhat unhelpfully for Schmitt) leads to England's identification of non-
State enemies, and her development of total war in the maritime context.[7]

For Hobbes, commonwealths are formally created by the mechanism of
"institution" or "acquisition." The theory of compact in Hobbes functions
as a logical construction that is indifferent to the historicity of questions of

custom, usage, and tradition. When we put aside the constructionist myth of commonwealths created by institution, we are left with the historically determined categories of commonwealths created by acquisition and paternal right, and the submission of subordinates to that right. And when we take those models further, the colony is not so much the exception where a different, less liberal regime exists: rather, it is the rule.

When Hobbes fleetingly discusses the New World, he suggests a state of nature: "[F]or the savage people in many places of *America*, except the government of small Families, the concord whereof dependeth on naturall lust, have no government at all; and live at this day in that brutish manner, as I said before" (89). When he explicitly invokes colonies in *Leviathan*, he opts for the reproductive metaphor: "[T]he Procreation, or Children of a Common-wealth, are those we call *Plantations*, or *Colonies*; which are numbers of men sent out from the Common-wealth, under a Conductor, or Governour, to inhabit a Forraign Country, either formerly voyd of Inhabitants, or made voyd then, by warre" (301). Once this colony is settled, Hobbes goes on, the polity from which it originated "was called their Metropolis, or Mother, and requires no more of them, then Fathers require of the Children, whom they emancipate, and make free from their domestique government, which is Honour and Friendship" (175). Otherwise, these colonies remain provinces if they are not licensed or decreed as free by "their Soveraign [who] authorised them to Plant" (176). The fleeting reference to colonies hides an intriguing personal involvement: in the 1610s and 1620s, Hobbes was secretary to Lord Cavendish, Earl of Devonshire, and tutor to his son for a period of over two decades, during which time he was a very active shareholder in the Virginia Company and in the Somer Islands Company, which had an interest in the Bermudas. Hobbes had a greater knowledge of Native American polities than he let on, and Noel Malcolm has suggested that he chose to ignore evidence he had that there might be acephalous but relatively peaceful societies in the world and also that colonists such as Sir Edwin Sandys were using natural law contractarianism against absolutist right of the king in these territories.[8]

While the Hobbesian state would never be realized in England, according to Schmitt it would remain a genuine historical option in France and Prussia. Acknowledging with Strauss that Hobbes had already opened the door to a liberal outcome, Schmitt's virulent anti-Semitism would lead him to suggest that the Leviathan was actually caught, castrated, and killed by the theories of Jews such as Benedict Spinoza, Moses Mendelssohn, or Friedrich Stahl-Jolson, as well as those Jews benefiting from the opening of trade enabled by the British Empire. For Schmitt the history of sovereignty is inextricable from the history of its failure as a myth, and also a lamentation of its actual failure to sustain the Weimar Republic. Schmitt's unhappiness with the semantic excess of the Leviathan myth that undermines its use for political authoritarianism is exacerbated by what he considers the efficaciousness of the Sorelian myth of the general strike for inspiring the Marxist imaginary. Schmitt's reading of *Leviathan* emphasizes Hobbes's role as a theorist of absolute state power (that we can see as an outcome of the suzerainty covenant) and untrammeled individual rights (that we can see as an outcome of the parity covenant). Hobbesian power could not trump liberal rights because of liberalism's successful covering over of the sovereign's extralegal legitimacy by accounts of empty legality. Schmitt's solution is for conservative authoritarianism to recapture the status of the exception and thereby hold the line of the unity of the political against liberal obfuscations. In other words, though the political subject was attenuated but barely present in Hobbes, it could be grown into formidable stature later. Therefore, Schmitt decides to dispense altogether with the question of the elicitation of political consent. Schmitt's rightist Hobbesianism therefore goes beyond even Hobbes, affirming only the most authoritarian and obscurantist myths regarding the origin of sovereignty in the fictitious State of Nature. It remains to be seen whether in the United States' current war on terror we are currently witnessing the development of an "ordinary commissarial emergency" in Schmittian terms, or a rarer "state of exception" that sees the emergence of a new form of sovereignty.

Foucault's Critique of Hobbesian Formalism

In his course of lectures given at the Collège de France in early 1976, collected in the volume "*Society Must Be Defended*," Michel Foucault reads Hobbes's sovereignty theory as rationalizing political acquisition through a dehistoricized notion of the institution of commonwealth. By way of this reading, Foucault also makes the point that race is not, as is often believed, just a late modern pseudoscientific construction but is, rather, a formation that goes back to the late medieval and early modern period, where it is inextricably linked to the emergence of a division at the heart of society between nation and state, between history and politics, and between a subject people and a conquering people. To quote Foucault, "[T]here are no battles in Hobbes's primitive war, there is no blood and there are no corpses. There are presentations, manifestations, signs, emphatic expressions, wiles, and deceitful expressions; there are traps, intentions disguised as their opposite, and worries disguised as certainties."[9] Hobbes is presented not so much as the theorist of war, but as the traumatized refugee of the English Civil War who wishes to eliminate its contestation of right and construct a theory that forgets the historical facts of conquest. Even now there is still considerable debate in the literature as to whether Hobbes is an unconventional Royalist, a de facto theorist, or a consent theorist, and Foucault is somewhat inaccurate on the details of this crux, as Hobbes actually seems unashamed about describing the Norman Conquest as proof of William's acquisition. Hobbes had also likely read Algernon Blackwood on the manner in which Charles V subjugated the West Indies and the New World. The larger stakes of Hobbes's argument, however, emphasize that the developing Whig account of sovereignty as based on "immemorial custom and usage" is unpersuasive, as custom lacks binding force. Hobbes, therefore, shifts from historicism to spatialism and uses Euclidean deduction rather than Baconian induction.

Hobbes's justification of sovereignty through a mixture of force and covenant, almost immediately criticized by Robert Filmer, is anathema to Royalist and Parliamentarian alike. As many historians of the English Revolution have suggested, it is during the English Civil War in the 1640s that the Norman conquest of the Saxons in 1066 reemerges as a bone of contention for historical and political interpretation. During this period, the separation of the gentry from the aristocracy is reinscribed in a way that puts the question of sovereignty at the heart of a profoundly ethnonational or racial demarcation. John Pocock's book *The Ancient Constitution and the Feudal Law* charts this development in great detail with reference to its prehistory. The mid–seventeenth century is also the moment when the first Parliamentarian Whigs develop the notion of the Norman yoke, relying on Sir Edward Coke's history of the dual traditions of law and land-tenure as an "artificiall reason" so complex that only legal scholars could understand it completely. Against this philological and nomological argument that projects ideals into a distant past, Hobbes proposes a radical presentism combining "natural reason" with the sovereign's will.

While Parliament attempted to reestablish "Saxon" priority through the gentry and restrict the "Norman" dominion of the monarchy, Coke's jurisprudence independently develops the notion of parliamentary empowerment on the basis of Saxon rights as adumbrated in thirteenth-century medieval law. Hobbes eliminates the utopian Saxon historicism that the Parliamentarians were using to restrict the king's prerogative and that the Levellers and Diggers were expressing in their desire to move toward much more radical goals such as the elimination of property, the dismantling of the expropriating legal apparatus, and the return of the commons. What *Leviathan* does very efficiently, according to Foucault, by introducing a natural law philosophical and juridical discourse, is to change the discourse from political historicism to that of bureaucratic administration. In his own analysis of the Civil War in *Behemoth*, Hobbes identifies five different groups as contesting sovereignty during the English Civil War: the Presbyterian ministers who argued from conscience; the democratic gentlemen of Parliament who had read too much Aristotle; the lawyers of common law carrying forward Coke's legacy and wishing to restrict taxes and armies; the merchants who opposed taxes altogether; and the men of wasted fortunes and opportunities who wished to profit from a splintering of sovereignty.[10] Hobbes is silent about the masterless men, but from the perspective of the Diggers and Levellers, the English Civil War was a continuous war of possessors and dispossessed. According to that logic, the war was an outbreak of military hostilities within an ongoing permanent war, not a return to the frightful State of Nature that Hobbes was mythologizing.

Hobbes's frontispiece of 1651 (fig. 1), when compared to the frontispiece of William Atwood(?)'s *Argumentum Anti-Normannicum* of 1682 (fig. 2), visually emphasizes for us the radical difference between two very different kinds of discourses. In Hobbes's frontispiece the gigantic figure of the Leviathan, looming in the background with sword and crosier, dominates an agrarian and an urban landscape. He is an artificial person; his body is covered by the much smaller profiles of his many subjects (it has been suggested that the subject-multitude comprises more than three hundred individuals). The Leviathan's looming presence is dehistoricized and nightmarish, leading to the paradigmatic panels of the lower half of the plate, where the left side features fortifications, a crown, cannons, weapons, and a battle scene, and the right side a church, a bishop's miter, divine thunderbolts, syllogisms, and academic disputations, all juxtaposed as symbolically sustained by the dominant background figure. The sovereign power of the state sustains civil society, which in turn submits to its overlord. Critics have identified this gigantic emblem of the state with the practice of creating royal effigies that were carried in procession on ritual occasions. These

Figure 1. Frontispiece to *Leviathan* (1651)

Figure 2. Frontispiece to *Argumentum Anti-Normannicum* (1682). Photo courtesy of the Newberry Library, Chicago.

effigies were especially important during burials and coronations of monarchs to emphasize the continuity of sovereignty even during the hiatus created by the mortality of the individual and embodied the need for an orderly transition and succession to the designated heir. The theory of personation, representation, or substitution of the author/sovereign by his person/representative is highly elaborated in chapter 16 of *Leviathan*, which contains the key to Hobbes's concept of the political. This unity of the figure of the representer is reiterated through ideas such as the representative, the lieutenant, the vicar, the attorney, the deputy, the procurator, or the actor. The normative elaboration of sovereignty binds the person or Actor, who makes a covenant that in turn binds the sovereign or Author. The state of exception, on the other hand, unbinds the Author from the Actor. All personation—indeed, all fiction—proceeds from this foundational connection of Author and Actor. All the Subjects of the Sovereign are Authors of the Leviathan, even if the Sovereign Person is the Soul of this Mortal God. This baroque theatrical idea of personation can be interpreted as Hobbes's coded insistence on the space of the discourse of the political. One could read this coding against the grain as also suggesting at some points the absence of real power behind the state mask, especially if seen through the lens of Walter Benjamin's reading of the failure of baroque sovereignty in his book on the *Trauerspiel*.[11]

The frontispiece of the *Argumentum Anti-Normannicum* (fig. 2), a book that has been misattributed to Coke but is now deemed to have probably been authored by William Atwood, makes a claim to political historicism through its description of the construction of sovereignty as always that of a transitional handoff from an old regime to a new one. In contrast to that in *Leviathan*, the *Anti-Normannicum*'s frontispiece represents a battlefield between two identifiable armed forces, Normans and Saxons, in relation to which a peace is being concluded not through the fait accompli of a domination from the background but through a coronation at the foreground, where William is inheriting Harold's crown and also agreeing to uphold Edward the Confessor's laws, within which the rights and duties of both Saxon and Norman subjects are protected. William's accession received unanimous consent from the English assembly before he took his coronation oath. Even as he takes the oath, William declares, "[N]o illegal or ARBITRARY ACTS, under pretence of the *Prerogative Royal*, will I suffer or permit to the *oppression* of my ENGLISH *Subjects*, between *whom*, and my *Normans*, I will administer EQUAL RIGHT."

According to this pamphlet, the English state is the result of a transaction between two peoples that ensures a hybrid system of laws and duties after a conquest as these people are forged into one. According to Hobbes, the Leviathan springs up fully armed, without any explanations except those afforded by moral psychology, and rules over a multitudinous aggregate that does not have to be a single people. Behind the surface of proto-utilitarianism, Hobbes relies on a natural law justification, and the ethical obligations theorized through books 2–4 are in excess of the physiological egoism explored in book 1. If the imperatives of natural law discourse, then, are to suppress the history of conquest, as Foucault argues, Hobbes is already responding with a theory of sovereignty that symptomatically preempts and displaces revindication by subject peoples, whether Saxons, or the colonized subjects of Charles V in the New World, or the supposedly politically incoherent "Savage peoples of America." Hobbes dismisses these natives as not wanting to build houses because they hadn't seen any, a charge he takes as an analogy for those who do not wish to explore his political theory of sovereignty even though it was so effective (232). Hobbes's dismissal of the Indians as incapable of understanding political sovereignty, on the one hand, and his suppression of the binational theory of the English state being elaborated by other political theorists, on the other, is a dismissal of the discourse of political historicism itself and, along with it, the subordinate if vanquished agency of the subjects who do not accept the legitimacy of the sovereign. Majoritarian rule leads to absolute rule, and winner takes all in Hobbes's commonwealth, where, if "the Representative consist of many men, the voyce of the greater number, must be considered as the voyce of them all" (114).

The comparative sovereignty of political historicism runs counter to the natural law fiction of political formalism. This is not so much to argue that the account of the Norman yoke is less ideological than Hobbes's. It could be argued that the Whig pamphlet is a convenient political rewriting of medieval history. The pamphlet strains credulity when it suggests that William's accession to the throne of England was accompanied by the unanimous acclaim of the Saxon gentry. However, it affords very different consequences from Hobbes's covenant theory that would be maintained in essence by Locke's liberal and resolutely antihistorical consent-oriented counterbalance, and an entire Enlightenment tradition of political philosophy that looked for a new form of sovereignty liberated from history.[12] Rousseau's republicanism (based on laws and a civic virtue and religion), the form of republicanism that so motivated the French Revolutionaries, also relies on a representation of the people through a *volonté générale* or general will and ultimately shares a lot with Hobbes, even though Rousseau famously criticizes obligations incurred under the condition of the State of Nature, which by definition is a situation free of all social obligation. As Étienne Balibar has suggested, Rousseau's desire to keep refreshing the legitimacy of the people outside the State-form leads to an oscillation between moments of constitution and insurrection, whereas Hobbes wants a single constituting founding fiction and no more.[13]

From Sovereignty to Governmentality

To reiterate, political historicism concerning sovereignty, however mythical, is the most efficacious means of attack against political formalism—whether of the Hobbesian variety, relying on egoistic moralism, ethical duties, and scientific reason, or of the Schmittian variety, relying on the friend/enemy distinction as characteristic of the political, and the state of exception as constitutive of sovereignty. Jacques Rancière suggests that as a "royal-empiricist" Hobbes realizes acutely what Foucault accuses him of suppressing: that the reading of old histories foments rebellion. The history of historiography creates a fictional scene of politics challenging the king. The generation of sovereignty theory under Hobbes is itself a reaction formation to this "power, abuse, and malfeasance of words without referents" that constitute irreverent historical speech. The revolution of paperwork under political historicism generates the first death of the king; the viewpoint of science and royal empiricism makes Hobbes generate a State discourse that attempts to stave off the inevitable death of the king by modern means.[14]

In his later work, Rancière will go on to sound the externality of politics to state sovereignty as the noise of the part that has no part. Politics or democracy interferes in relation to the police function of the ordering of bodies in space—whether according to Platonic authoritarianism or liberal managerialism. Hobbesian "metapolitics," according to Rancière, identifies equality and freedom at the very start—that is, as the State of Nature—and annihilates it then and there through the ushering in of sovereign order. In other words, where Schmitt reads Hobbes in order to riff that "sovereign is he who decides on the exception," Rancière's reading if reduced to an equivalent aphorism would be something like "political is she who is excluded by the sovereign norm." However, it is not the mere fact of exclusion that makes politics into the utopian outside of bare life, as it might for Giorgio Agamben. Rather, the part that has no part has to insist that it is the real totality; but by speaking from the constitutive outside of the existing one, it also has to insert its discourse into the false universal that until then constituted the whole as police function. Politics is therefore the moment of the deregulation of the counting of parts and a momentary collapse of business as usual. The political is a radical questioning of what until then were the stable boundaries of the police function. When politics is absent, the smooth functioning of the sovereign policing apparatus takes place by way of the geometrical distribution of instances such as Platonic or communitarian archipolitics, Aristotelian or liberal parapolitics, or, indeed, Hobbesian or authoritarian metapolitics. The notion of the mask behind which Hobbes's sovereign functions will be brilliantly inverted by Marxism, which will argue that politics itself takes place elsewhere, in the metapolitical realm of the socioeconomic, even though the acting out of the ideological game of parliamentarism is supposedly a playacting of politics. (Leo Strauss's and Schmitt's reading of Hobbes makes him out to be acting out a version of liberal parapolitics rather than Hobbesian metapolitics—but in their respective categorizations, they enact something like an authoritarian ultrapolitics in the name of a Hobbesianism-beyond-Hobbes.) Rancière's analysis of the contemporary age of the postpolitical, laboring (like our current age) under the shadow of liberal and cosmopolitan governmentality, consensus democracy, and Habermasian communicative action, is relevant to our understanding of sovereignty. According to Rancière, consensual postdemocracy is the nihilistic polishing off of metapolitics and the realist absorption of all reality and truth into the category of the possible. The political—in contrast, for Rancière—is that which is poetic and communicative at the same time, simultaneously employing all three grammatical persons rather than just the first- and second-person dialogue involved in rational communicative action. There is no politics without the play of the grammatical third person of describing one's externality to norms as well as one's silencing or disregarding by those very norms. Liberal governmentality organizes a play only between first and second persons in order to arrange globally inclusive participation that will always leave out many of those who will still be the part who play no part.[15]

The return to Hobbesianism and a renewed critique of it by Foucault in relation to the new social wars of the twentieth century had many predecessors between the two World Wars, including Carl Schmitt, Leo Strauss, and R. G. Collingwood, all of whom in different ways found the doctrine of force and subjection to correspond much better to contemporary reality than liberal progress narratives did.[16] Schmitt's reliance on the "state of exception" for his account of political theology was also much admired by Walter Benjamin in his attempt to describe the evacuation of sovereignty in German tragic drama. The history of empathy around Hobbesianism between Benjamin and Schmitt has been told elsewhere. In these Weimar texts, Benjamin and Schmitt explore two very different uses of the notion of a Hobbes-derived "state of exception" against the mechanisms of liberal democracy — but they ended up in very different camps of Jewish messianic Marxism and National Socialism respectively. While Schmitt positions himself even to the right of Hobbes, seeing the decision of the state of exception as the crucial guarantee hanging behind even the figure of the Leviathan, Benjamin wants the sovereign to make conditions such that the state of exception would never be used.[17]

A more recent intervention on the state of exception, by Giorgio Agamben, reads the abjected figure behind the political will of sovereign power as that of naked or bare life. This naked life "is kept safe and protected only to the degree to which it submits itself to the sovereign's (or the law's) right of life and death"; at the same time, though, this naked life is "the ultimate and opaque bearer of sovereignty." The "state of emergency" — which Agamben sees in the extrajudicial form of the concentration camp — is increasingly, for him, the exception rather than the rule. Agamben symptomatically essentializes the Holocaust through a historical foreshortening that ignores the circuit of slavery and colonialism by which Western sovereignty turns and returns to generate its own normative exceptionality. In Agamben's reading, a fetishization of the notion of abject, bare, or naked life is conceived as necessarily disconnected and severed from the social processes of civil society as underwritten by this absolutism, which needs that figure to underwrite the exceptionality of the norm. By emphasizing the continuity of the Roman figure of the *homo sacer*, or the man who can be killed but cannot be sacrificed, Agamben creates a continuous Holy Roman or crypto-Christian genealogy that elides the contestation of Roman sovereignty from the Middle Ages that existed even within the confines of Europe. Agamben thereby recognizes a figure of naked "human" existence as a unity of the represented that he discerns behind what Hobbes argued was only the artificial unity of the representer, which has as many disaggregated Authors as it has subjects. The artificial unity of the represented notion of naked life in Agamben's reading relies on the industrial or military rendition of the camp as the generative exception. What was, in Hobbes, the notion of the protected but completely beholden socially active subject corresponds to the sentimentalized trope of the unprotected outcast, the banished refugee, or the socially expelled, who are politically inactive in Agamben's reading except as voiceless victims. Such a rendition uncannily reflects and compounds Hobbes's flight from contestations of historicity, whereas Foucault's or Rancière's account of what Hobbes was suppressing to come up with natural law theory seems more compatible with an excavation of the historical underpinnings of sovereignty and subjection in conquest, acquisition, and the extension of paternity.[18]

We should also note the reemergence of religious messianism at the outer edge of sovereignty—whether in Schmitt's political theology, Benjamin's Marxism, Agamben's naked life, or even Ranajit Guha's history of peasant revolts in nineteenth-century Bengal.[19] These developments can help contextualize the lengthy religious expositions of books 3 and 4 of *Leviathan*. John Pocock argues that Hobbes combines two structures of authority in the work—through an ahistorical justification based on, in the first two books, moral psychology and natural law of the Leviathan and, in the last two, an anti-Papal, anti-enthusiastic, and anti-sectarian apocalypticism and mortalism that relegate all decisions about faith to the sovereign who is the "one chief Pastor" (322).[20] The genealogy from St. Peter to Constantine suggests to Hobbes the devolution and synthesis of religious into secular authority; the subject has to obey the Civil Sovereign whether he is Christian or infidel. Suffice it to say that religion becomes a matter of state in Hobbes, divested of the doctrinal disputes that ravaged the seventeenth century, and entirely controllable, presaging the later use of civic religions for social adhesion since the French Revolution and after: for instance, in Kant's theorization of a synthesis between morality and the State that keeps the transcendental function of sovereignty intact and the State unsurpassable, keeping what Étienne Balibar has called the twin legitimation of a juridical presentation alongside a mystical presentation.[21] This explains, to some extent, R. G. Collingwood's *New Leviathan*, written during the height of World War II, which updates the Christian Commonwealth of book 3 of *Leviathan* with a discourse on civilization and extends the attack on the Kingdom of Darkness in book 4 of *Leviathan* to a new attack on barbarism. While Hobbes attacked spiritual darkness, demonology, and reliance on vain philosophy and fabulous traditions, he reserved his most excoriating invective for a frontal assault on Catholicism and the Pope himself, whom Hobbes regarded as the Antichrist. Today the discourse on civilization and barbarism is being refashioned to combat radical forms of Islam.

Turning the dictum of absolute force on its head, Howard Warrender suggested that Leviathan ultimately demonstrated, if somewhat counterintuitively, "*the appalling weakness of the sovereign*," because force is all too blunt an instrument to motivate subjects efficiently.[22] In such a reading, the sovereign turns into Gulliver in the land of the Lilliputians, bound down by hundreds of skeins of almost invisible threads that we could liken to the myriad effects of nonteleological discipline. The hidden supplement to Hobbesian sovereignty, then, is that which Foucault doesn't find in Hobbesian juridical discourse: the polymorphous mechanisms of disciplinarity and then ultimately biopower that are irreducible to questions of public right. This nonsovereign power of discipline and biopower could ultimately perhaps be recuperable to sovereignty through a new pastoralism, or what Foucault later called governmentality, but initially the end-oriented discipline of politics and civil philosophy is radically separated from all other nonteleological physical sciences in Hobbes's positivistic demarcation of the separate disciplines.

Science, according to *Leviathan*, is divided between "Consequences from Accidents of Bodies Naturall" and "Consequences from Accidents of *Politique* Bodies" (61). While passion and self-love are the "notable multiplying glasses" of men, these very men are "destitute of those prospective glasses, (namely Morall and Civill Science)" (129). Hobbes seeks a synchronic contemporaneity whereby a political theory or science that was based on notions of time gets rearticulated in terms of a politics of mechanistic space (geometry and optics, it must be remembered, were Hobbes's favorite scientific preoccupations): "[T]he skill of making, and maintaining Common-wealths consisteth in certain Rules, as doth Arithmetique and Geometry; not (as Tennis-play) on Practise onely" (145).[23]

Conclusion

Before returning for a final moment to Hobbes, it might be worth attending to two recent approaches that claim the atrophying or hypertrophying of sovereignty. Jean-Luc Nancy provides a vision of sovereignty beyond sovereignty when he suggests, by way of a reading of Georges Bataille, that the space of the presentation of sovereignty is that of an archaism, untreatable in its essence even as it is currently exhausting itself through brilliant and incandescent display. At the same time of this exhaustion or atrophying of sovereignty, the sphere of ecotechnics (*l'écotechnie*, Nancy's version of economic and mediatic globalization) inexorably expands into a "barely sovereign role of regulative, juridical, and social administration"—which we may gloss by way of Rancière's parapolitical or Foucault's governmentality. In this version, sovereignty haunts the administered world at either end of the principle and enactment of law, even as ecotechnics and its attributes are sovereignty beyond sovereignty. Sovereignty dwindles into nothing (and also everything) over the course of elaborating political economy through globalization.[24]

The second is that of a vision of "necropolitics" by Achille Mbembe, whose account represents the hypertrophying of sovereignty. Mbembe argues that sovereignty is even more deadly than Hobbes suggests: in Mbembe's elaboration, sovereignty is sheer and unlimited power to kill. For Mbembe, the Schmittian state of exception rules to the degree that even Agamben's spatialization of the camp is a small and gingerly attempt at establishing a provincial enclave, at least when compared to the gray zones of Africa, the plantation societies and Middle Passages of slavery, or the obscene deliriums of postcolonial dictatorships and their necropolitical expenditures amid the generalized destitution and dismemberment of the populations these regimes control. Both Palestine and South Africa represented new experiments in geographical and territorial manipulations of sovereignty, whether by way of the pass law and bantustan system in apartheid South Africa or the continuing elaboration of "vertical sovereignty" in the Palestinian Occupied Territories, as discussed by Eyal Weizman.[25] While it has become fashionable for those such as Agamben and Mbembe to suggest that sovereignty has hypertrophied so that the exception has become the rule and that therefore sovereignty is now simply the power to kill orgiastically, there is a complete collapse of the technical power of mass destruction and the political power to enforce and legitimize these acts in these various conceptions. Hobbes will insist in the conclusion to *Leviathan* that "he therefore that is slain, is Overcome, but not Conquered." Therefore, sovereignty desires the obedience of "he [who] hath his Life and Liberty allowed him, is then Conquered, and a Subject; and not before" (485). Sovereignty, at least in its normative version, is *le droit de glaive*, a mutual recognition between sovereign and subject based on the reprieve, a secularization of the Christian notion of grace. Of course, the greatest current example of necropower is the existence of nuclear weapons under highly technical systems of control evading any forms of popular sovereignty over their jurisdiction except in name.

It is perhaps not a coincidence that Nancy's vision of an atrophying sovereignty is written largely with reference to the first-world location of Europe, even as Mbembe's darker vision keeps in mind the necropolitical exemplarity of third-world postcolonies, mandate territories, and neocolonial theaters such as Palestine or sub-Saharan Africa. The disciplinary is linked with the pastoral in resource-rich contexts, even as the murderous is associated with the genocidal or the fraudulent in resource-strapped situations. While Nancy's hopeful account eliminates or reduces sovereignty by pluralizing its subjects, Mbembe's apocalyptic account hypertrophies sovereignty to the point that it reduces all subjects to the level of the beast that will be killed without consent, warning, or rationality.

So is sovereignty an ideology of state or a political aspiration of subjects desiring freedom? A state of exception that leads to a new sovereignty is also potentially the creation of a new time—indeed, this is what Walter Benjamin hopes sovereignty can make possible, even though this is really a messianic hope that reads history against the grain. Thinking politically, in the manner of Rancière or Benjamin, would involve reexamining the agency of the fractured and multiple subjects of sovereignty who can speak from the position of the part that plays no part and disrupt the rational continuation of business as usual. Rather than reiterating various narratives about the fiat of a single moment of unretractable subjection as theorized by Hobbes, political agency would hereby be understood as that which opposes the police discourse of sovereignty—whether of the total or the liberal state—with a political contestation and redeployment of the discourse of sovereignty into the discourse of politics.

The space of the discourse of the political is present in *Leviathan* (chapter 16) in the theory of personation and its dizzy multiplications that could lead to fraudulent representations just as much as genuine personation, rather than in the somewhat attenuated account of the subject who can provide some kind of bare-bones resistance but who is in a sense already spoken for. In other words, there is the presence of politics in the *Leviathan* as the interanimation of myth and representation, impersonation and incorporation, and this is realized in the space of the sovereign's theatrical personage, finitely unified through the representer but equivalently multiplied by the synonymous descriptions of the representer through the representative functions of the Lieutenant, the Vicar, the Attorney, the Deputy, the Procurator, or the Actor. It is unclear whether Hobbes's notion of consent is direct or what is technically called "interpretative consent"—that is, ascribed, attributed, or presumed consent—but this is a larger question about all liberal theories of consent and parliamentary democracy. The noncorrespondence of agent and author—the space of political speech—makes possible the universe of impersonation, one that is in fact a world of the absence or gap between a stated and an enacted sovereignty. Within this world one can imagine the noise of the political richly intruding on the police function of orderly representation in all three grammatical persons. As Hobbes suggests, quoting Cicero on personation, "*Unus sustineo tres Personas; Mei, Adversarii, & Judicis,* I beare three Persons; my own, my Adversaries, and the Judges" (217–18). In the realm of impersonation lies the political speech containing all three grammatical persons. Between the utopian desires of a democracy to come (Jacques Derrida) and the hard-nosed realities of postpolitical consensual democracy (Jürgen Habermas), the practice and function of impersonation is a Hobbesian topos of the political that makes itself visible within the very language of the police function of *Leviathan* (Rancière).

Impersonation contains all three of the grammatical persons that Rancière deems necessary for political speech, and in this innovation we can regard Hobbes as our most remarkable contemporary—not just the conservative counterrevolutionary theorist of fear as a political idea, in the manner of Thucydides or Machiavelli, but also the social constructionist who realized that representation is necessary for sustainable political discourse. Imagined as composite social animal, the state, as such, goes beyond Man to include God, Beast, and the Machine within the *macros anthropos/magnus homo*. In this sense, the Leviathan is not just the monster of destruction but the engine—and, indeed, the cyborg—of biopolitical survival and regeneration through the continuing and open-ended metaphors of enactment and impersonation.

Notes

1   Thomas Hobbes, *Leviathan*, ed. Richard Tuck (Cambridge: Cambridge University Press, 1991), 491. All parenthetical page references cited hereafter are from this text.
2   C. B. Macpherson, *The Political Theory of Possessive Individualism: Hobbes to Locke* (New York: Oxford University Press, 1964). For the phantasmatic meaning of Hobbesian con-

tractarianism, see Victoria Kahn, *Wayward Contracts: The Crisis of Political Obligation in England, 1640–1674* (Princeton, NJ: Princeton University Press, 2004).

3 See Leo Strauss, *The Political Philosophy of Hobbes: Its Basis and Its Genesis*, trans. Elsa M. Sinclair (Chicago: University of Chicago Press, 1952).

4 J. G. A. Pocock, "A Discourse of Sovereignty: Observations on the Work in Progress," in *Political Discourse in Early Modern Britain*, ed. Nicholas Phillipson and Quentin Skinner (Cambridge: Cambridge University Press, 1993), 398.

5 For the idea of the "rogue" state and its links to the notion of the animal in Hobbes and other thinkers, see the perceptive account in Jacques Derrida, *Voyous: Deux essais sur la raison* (Paris: Éditions Galilée, 2003).

6 Carl Schmitt, *The Leviathan in the State Theory of Thomas Hobbes: The Meaning and Failure of a Political Symbol*, foreword and intro. by George Schwab, trans. George Schwab and Erna Hilfstein (Westport, CT: Greenwood, 1996), 29.

7 See Srinivas Aravamudan, "Carl Schmitt's *The Nomos of the Earth*: Four Corollaries," *South Atlantic Quarterly* 104.2 (Spring 2005): 227–36.

8 Noel R. Malcolm, "Hobbes, Sandys, and the Virginia Company," *Historical Journal* 24 (1981): 297–321.

9 Michel Foucault, *"Society Must Be Defended": Lectures at the Collège de France, 1975–76*, trans. David Macey (New York: Picador, 2003), 92.

10 See Don M. Wolfe, ed., *Leveller Manifestoes of the Puritan Revolution* (New York: Thomas Nelson and Son, 1944).

11 See Horst Bredekamp, "From Walter Benjamin to Carl Schmitt, via Thomas Hobbes," trans. Melissa Thorson Hause and Jackson Bond, *Critical Inquiry* 25.1 (Winter 1999): 255, 247–66; Walter Benjamin, *The Origin of German Tragic Drama*, trans. John Osborne (New York: Verso, 1998).

12 A similar but much more complicated genealogy for French absolutism is traced by Foucault to the shift from the notion of Frankish or Roman rule over ancient Gaul to the idea that Gauls become the fundamental trope of the nation over the Roman justification of public right as represented by the monarchy. The discourse of public administration is invented as an optic through which the monarch can know the kingdom, even as the discourse of political history becomes first a nobiliary reaction, then a weapon that the nobility and later the third estate drives as a wedge between administrative power-knowledge and the executive authority embodied in the sovereign.

13 See Étienne Balibar, "What Makes a People a People? Rousseau and Kant," trans. Erin Post, in *Masses, Classes, and the Public Sphere*, ed. Mike Hill and Warren Montag (London: Verso, 2000).

14 Jacques Rancière, *The Names of History: On the Poetics of Knowledge*, trans. Hasan Melehy (Minneapolis: University of Minnesota Press, 1994).

15 Jacques Rancière, *Dis-Agreement: Politics and Philosophy*, trans. Julie Rose (Minneapolis: University of Minnesota Press, 1999).

16 See R. G. Collingwood, *The New Leviathan: or, Man, Society, Civilization, and Barbarism*, ed. and intro. David Boucher (New York: Oxford University Press, 1992).

17 See Samuel Weber, "Taking Exception to Decision: Walter Benjamin and Carl Schmitt," *Diacritics* 22.3–4 (Fall–Winter 1992): 5–18; and Bredekamp, "From Walter Benjamin to Carl Schmitt, via Thomas Hobbes."

18 See Giorgio Agamben, *Homo Sacer: Sovereign Power and Bare Life*, trans. Daniel Heller-Roazen (Stanford, CA: Stanford University Press, 1998).

19 Ranajit Guha, *Elementary Aspects of Peasant Insurgency in Colonial India* (Delhi: Oxford University Press, 1983).

20 J. G. A. Pocock, "Time, History and Eschatology in the Thought of Thomas Hobbes," in *Politics, Language and Time: Essays on Political Thought and History* (New York: Atheneum, 1971), 148–201.

21 Balibar, "What Makes a People a People?" 127.

22 Howard Warrender, *The Political Philosophy of Hobbes: His Theory of Obligation* (Oxford: Clarendon Press, 1957), 317.

23 The demarcation of disciplines is featured somewhat differently and definitively in Hobbes's *De Corpore*, but for the sake of consistency I will stick to the account provided to us in *Leviathan*, the more influential text by far.

24 Jean-Luc Nancy, "War, Right, Sovereignty—Technē," in *Being Singular Plural* (Stanford, CA: Stanford University Press, 2000), 101–43.

25 Achille Mbembe, "Necropolitics," *Public Culture* 15.1 (Winter 2003): 11–40.

Warren Montag

Who's Afraid of the Multitude?
Between the Individual and the State

Spinoza speaks of the unity that is the state as only *una veluti mente* and we see a real danger in taking these texts in too literal a sense. It is a danger that, in our opinion, leads to an almost Marxist or Hegelian (or at least collectivist) conception of Spinoza's politics which, we insist, fully affirm liberalism and individualism.
—Steven Barbone and Lee Rice, "La naissance d'une nouvelle politique"

Montag resists a "Straussian" reading of Spinoza's relation to the multitude. Spinoza, according to him, delineates no final division between an intellectual elite and the multitude, nor does he finally support an ideal in which a cultural elite feeds the multitude indulgent stories in order to release itself to think higher thoughts and, if lucky, participate in ruling the state. . . . Montag himself participates in an elite of the left, one that claims it will dissolve into the multitude if and as the latter becomes democratized. It is not easy to decide which elite to worry about most: a self-styled permanent elite or a self-styled temporary elite. In the contemporary context, Montag's gang seems less worrisome, though the balance might shift if—to use his language—the existing equilibrium of social forces were to change significantly.
—William E. Connolly, "Spinoza and Us"

The *South Atlantic Quarterly* 104:4, Fall 2005.
Copyright © 2005 by Duke University Press.

It is very rare today to see the word *dangerous* applied to an interpretation of seventeenth-century philosophy. Indeed, it is difficult to imagine the circumstances in which a critic would be led to describe a reading of Descartes or Pierre Gassendi, or even Hobbes (whose theory of the state of nature, it should be recalled, was once cited in support of the strategy of mutually assured destruction), as dangerous.[1] Spinoza, significantly, is the exception; the word *dangerous* has appeared with increasing frequency to describe interpretations of his work, and the danger posed by the interpretations in question is not simply the danger of misinterpretation, the danger that the interpreters have intentionally or unintentionally attributed to Spinoza ideas not to be found in his work. For some critics, the danger is exactly the opposite: the danger of taking Spinoza at his word, that is, of reading him too literally. Of course, the anxiety of interpretation arises only in relation to certain passages, phrases, and words that for the anxious scholars simply cannot or should not mean what they appear to mean.

Louis Althusser was undoubtedly right to describe Spinoza's philosophy as so "terrifying to its own time" that it could only provoke philosophical repression. But is the fear this philosophy provokes today the same fear that it provoked then? Are the passages whose literal existence could be experienced as dangerous the same? The answer is probably no: if, taking the eighteenth-century as an example, we can agree that part 1 of the *Ethics* (summarized retrospectively by Spinoza in the preface to part 4 in the formula *Deus, sive Natura*) appeared to the vast majority of commentators to contain the germ of Spinoza's heresy, it hardly does so for our time. Indeed, it suggests to many readers that Spinoza is another Enlightenment thinker who, for good or ill, for or against Judaism, sought to replace religion with science. It remains, therefore, for us to specify what it is in Spinoza—in the extraordinarily difficult works of a solitary seventeenth-century excommunicant—that is capable of activating the defenses of philosophy at the dawn of the twenty-first century.

At the risk of oversimplification, I believe that it is possible to identify a node through which pass all the strands in Spinoza's thought, whether political, ontological, or metaphysical, that prove disturbing today. I refer not simply to the well-delineated arguments but also to what are often merely ideas, and even images, in various states of completeness or fragmentation: they all seem to converge around the notion (and not simply the word) of the multitude.[2]

The most obvious sense in which the concept of the multitude touches what Althusser liked to call "un point sensible" in contemporary theory is captured in the polyvalence of Étienne Balibar's phrase "the fear of the masses."[3] Even Antonio Negri's work (which must itself be read not simply in relation to Spinoza but also in relation to its own historical and political context) was to a great extent devoted not so much to the idealization of the multitude, as is so often charged, as to a recovery of its productive or constituent power at the very historical moment that "the fear of the masses" had reached its theoretical peak.[4] The fact that the mere recognition of this power was so immediately and universally dismissed as "idealization" must itself be analyzed, of course, even if such an analysis cannot be undertaken here. Nevertheless, perhaps in his desire to avoid the appearance of a dialectical reading, Negri tended to neglect the theoretical element that appeared simultaneously with Spinoza's exposition of the power of the multitude and accompanies it like a shadow to the very last word of the *Political Treatise* (hereafter cited as *TP*): Spinoza's own fear of the multitude. As Balibar has demonstrated, the phrase *the fear of the masses* communicates Spinoza's own ambivalence toward the masses: they inspire fear in the tyrants and despots who are foolhardy enough to provoke their indignation, even as they themselves experience fear; in fact, they are perhaps most fearsome (and not simply to tyrants) when afraid. Alexandre Matheron is even blunter in rendering the conflicts internal to Spinoza's conception of the mass base of all politics: not only is there nothing idyllic in it, but in fact "the elementary form of democracy, according to Spinoza, is the action of a lynch mob."[5]

But behind the charge of an idealization of the multitude that is extended by critics to nearly all those who discuss the function of the concept in Spinoza's work lies a more fundamental fear, one that is consistently and symptomatically absent from the recent critical reception of Spinoza. It is a fear of following Spinoza's path—a path without a fixed destination, and one that Spinoza must open before him as he sets out from the equation of natural right and power in chapter 16 of the *Tractatus Theologico-Politicus* (hereafter cited as *TTP*). Refusing to grant to humanity the status of an *imperium in imperio*, Spinoza begins his discussion not with the human individual in the state of nature but with nature itself: "Nature has the absolute right to do all that it can do, that is, nature's right extends as far as its power." Further, "since the power of nature is nothing but the simultaneous [*simul*] power of all individuals, it follows that each individual has the sovereign right to do all that it can do."[6]

There are a number of important features to note in this passage, and the most important is also the most commonly overlooked: here Spinoza speaks of nature as a whole, and the "individuals" to which he refers are individual things, a class of which human individuals would be only one member. Indeed, the only individual thing we've encountered so far in Spinoza's argument is the big fish that eats the little fish "with absolute natural right."[7] Thus, while Spinoza uses the verb "to have" (*habeo*) to describe nature's relation to right, he has nevertheless transformed right from a possession into the ability to act and has thereby effaced any possible distinction between the right of any thing in nature and that of the human individual. If the human world possesses any specificity, it must consist in the singular forms in which the power of nature (which cannot be transcended or alienated) is there organized. From this perspective, social existence changes only the relations of power, enabling human individuals to accomplish certain things that alone would be impossible, and, in opposition, limiting their ability to perform other acts that alone or in small numbers they would have the ability to perform. The social state retains its usefulness as long as the former outweigh the latter and individuals are able through collective existence to do and think more than they could alone. When the state ceases to be useful to the individuals that comprise it, it will (and not simply "ought to") provoke rebellion. And like everything else in nature, the right of the state extends only as far as its power. The sovereign who faces rebellion has no grounds for appeal. We have reached the threshold of the concept of the multitude at this point in the *TTP*: every ruler has more to fear from his own citizens (*cives*) than from any foreign enemy, and it is this "fear of the masses" (which at this point, the beginning of chapter 17 of the *TTP*, are still *cives*, a juridical category that might well exclude those who make up the multitude)[8] that places an actual limit on the evil a sovereign may do to his subjects. Spinoza, however, abruptly abandons the argument a few paragraphs into chapter 17 to begin his examination of the Hebrew state.

What is most provocative, even today, in this section of the *TTP* is thus left undeveloped, deferred to the later works, both the *Ethics* and the *TP*. First, as a number of commentators have noted, occasionally with alarm, Spinoza has made the indignation of the multitude—or, even worse, the fear of such indignation—rather than law, or even custom, the principal brake on the power of the sovereign or state. This is undoubtedly the element that Gilles Deleuze, in his preface to the French edition of the *Savage Anomaly*, referred to as Spinoza's "anti-juridicism,"[9] the systematic subordination of law to force and a refusal to entertain any notion of the rule of law separate from the causal power that makes any society what it is. Law, however, neither disappears as an object of analysis in political philosophy nor becomes irrelevant to the composition of a society. Rather, the function of law must be reconceptualized as something other than an ideal foundation, a constitution, or a set of norms. Such notions are not simply false, not simply a given society's inadequate idea about itself; they are positively harmful to the peace and stability of the *Civitas*. Thus, it may be true that in a monarchical state, the sovereign must like Ulysses before the Sirens command others to bind him with laws and keep him so bound even if later, carried away by passion, he commands that these laws be broken; but to rely on the "weak assistance of laws" (*TP* 7.2) can only result in ruin. It is "not enough to have shown what ought to be done"; one must show how people "whether led by reason or passion" (*TP* 7.2) will act in accordance with the prescriptions of the law. Although laws serve to codify and make permanently knowable both the set of actions that increase the power and stability of a society and the set of actions that necessarily weaken it and, under specific circumstances, lead to its disintegration, Spinoza places at the center of his analysis the question of the causal processes and power relations that will compel all those living in a domain to act in accordance with the law regardless of their intentions.

But another dimension of Spinoza's antijuridicism has proven even more provocative. What disturbs commentators even today is the fact that, as Hobbes noted in *De Cive*, from a legal point of view (which itself presupposes a certain theoretical anthropology) "a multitude cannot act" (*De Cive* 6.1);[10] therefore from the point of view of law, there is no collective action in the strict sense, merely the simultaneous actions of separate individuals only apparently united into some collective entity. Spinoza's insistence that right equals power displaces the individual from the center of political analysis. The argument begins in chapters 16 and 17 of the *TTP*, pauses, and then resumes only at *TP* 3.2, the point at which Spinoza introduces the concept of the multitude. There we learn that the right of the sovereign is "limited not by the power of each individual but by the power of the multitude." It is at this point, and I am still in the middle of Spinoza's sentence, that he is compelled by his argument to specify, against Hobbes, how it is that a multitude can act. The right of the state (*imperium*) or supreme authorities (*summarum potestatum*) is limited by the power of the multitude precisely insofar as the multitude is not the mere appearance of collective action, which upon reflection is revealed to be nothing more than dissociated individuals acting simultaneously. Instead, Spinoza goes on to argue, the multitude "is guided, as it were, by one mind" (*TP* 3.2). And the sentence does not stop there. As if in anticipation of the reader's skepticism at the idea of the mind of the multitude, Spinoza offers the following analogy: "As each individual in the state of nature, so the body and mind of a state (*imperium*) have as much right as they have power" (*TP* 3.2).

In a recent essay, Balibar has examined at some length the chain of interpretations and counterinterpretations produced by the analogy Spinoza constructs in this passage: just as the individual has a body and a mind, so does the state (*imperium*), so the state itself must therefore be an individual (following Spinoza's lengthy discussion of the individual in *Ethics* 2, part 13), differing only in scale not only from human individuals but also from any other individual thing.[11] It may be wondered why Spinoza's sentence and his suggestion that the state be viewed as an individual possessed of a mind and a body would, even if one disagrees with it, generate an interpretive conflict. The answer lies in Spinoza's use here—and in other passages both in the *TP*, the *Letters*, and the *Ethics* in which he ascribes the status of an individual to a collective entity—of the qualifier *veluti* (translated here as "as it were": "the multitude is guided, as it were, by mind"). The insertion of the qualifier "as it were" or "as if" ("the multitude is guided as if with one mind") suggests, at the very least, some hesitation concerning the notion of the mind of the multitude and perhaps also the notion of the body and mind of the *imperium*. What is the nature of this hesitation? What prevents Spinoza from saying here (and it's here, *TP* 3.2, that he first ascribes a mind and body either to the multitude or to the *imperium*) what he will admittedly say without qualification at a later point: that these collective entities are individual or singular things and as such are irreducible to their component parts? Does the insertion of *veluti* indicate his attitude toward his readership in another form of his general rhetorical strategy of translating or giving new meanings to familiar terms without replacing them, in which case we would read him as attempting gradually to overcome the prejudices of his audience to allow them to break with the form of methodological individualism necessarily imposed on us by the very nature of the imagination (as discussed in the appendix to *Ethics* 1)? Or, in contrast, does the use of the qualifier *veluti* (and in the *Ethics* he will use the term *quasi* to perform a similar function) indicate that Spinoza does not in fact assign, except in a metaphorical sense, the status of an individual to the multitude or to the *imperium*, which would then be "like" individuals or even quasi-individuals, while remaining distinct from any real form of individuality, or at least human individuality (since the *imperium* is said to possess a mind as well as a body)? In his analysis of the controversy sparked by this passage, Balibar groups the responses into two categories, the dogmatic and the critical. The former term is not meant to be pejorative; rather, it signals a desire on the part of the commentators in question to reduce the conflict exhibited in Spinoza's text to what they regard as the text's sole meaning. Thus, Matheron and, in a different way, Negri tend to disregard the discordance introduced into Spinoza's postulation of the *imperium* as individual by the use of the term *veluti*, while Lee Rice and Douglas Den Uyl, in contrast, take the term as a marker of Spinoza's commitment to an early form of methodological individualism for which any collectivity is reducible to the individuals that comprise it, criticizing Matheron's position as organicism.[12] Matheron speaks of the *conatus* of the *imperium*—the sense in which a state, like any other individual, endeavors to persist in its own being.[13] Rice, in opposition, argues that a state cannot possess a *conatus* because it is not an individual thing but a temporary correspondence between the actions of a number of individuals who exist prior to it and to which it must be reduced. Pierre-François Moreau's response, according to Balibar, can be called critical insofar as Moreau insists on restricting himself to Spinoza's actual utterances, very much in the spirit of chapter 7 of the *TTP*.[14] He finds that Spinoza does not always use a qualifier when treating the *imperium* or *civitas* as an individual and therefore cannot be regarded as employing the term *individual* in this context in a metaphorical way.

A number of observations can be made about this debate, and I will begin by expanding on Balibar's general observation that these interpretations, despite their divergences, share an anthropomorphic conception of the individual.[15] In fact, to take it a bit further than Balibar does, I would argue that all the participants in the debate remain committed to what Althusser called, speaking of Feuerbach (who in a sense haunts this entire discussion), a reversible specular relation that itself rests on a centered foundation, that is, an anthropology.[16] Thus, on the one side, the individual and, on the other, the state, society, community, collective, and so on are mirror images of each other. To declare one rather than the other natural or artificial, primary or secondary, in no way allows one to escape the anthropology that remains presupposed without question. The implications of the observation for our understanding of the history of philosophy and Spinoza's place in it are significant: it reveals the ways in which there exists a certain complicity between philosophical traditions often regarded as antagonistic—for example, the methodological individualism of a Hobbes, or even more of an Adam Smith, and the collectivism of Hegel (who, in the preface to the *Phenomenology of Spirit*, reproaches Spinoza for failing to think substance as a subject). From the point of view of this anthropomorphism, it matters little whether the social whole exists by nature or is woven by an invisible hand— by individuals producing a supra-individual possessed of a suprarationality (say, the market) that can and indeed must be understood as endeavoring to persist in its own being and therefore possessed of a *conatus*. In fact, the opposition between the individual and the community, society, system of wealth, and so on is simply another variant of the vicious theological-anthropological circle, a circle that Michel Foucault, from another perspective, captured in his description of the "man" of humanism as an empirico-transcendental doublet, a figure that Spinoza had already analyzed in the appendix to *Ethics 1*.[17] Further, in addition to the theological dimension of this anthropology, it is also, to use a phrase from Moreau's study of Utopian discourse, a juridical anthropology, vacillating between two legal entities, the juridical person or individual and its collective counterpart, the people, the state, the society, and so on.[18]

In order to break the hold of this seemingly inescapable opposition, we can do no better than to return to the passage from the *TP* discussed earlier to note a discrepancy which, to my knowledge, only Balibar has observed: "The right of the supreme authorities is nothing else than natural right itself, limited indeed by the power not of every individual, but the power of the multitude, which is guided, as it were, by one mind–that is, as each individual in the state of nature, so the body and mind of the *imperium* have as much right as they have power" (*TP* III, 2). Spinoza moves from *multitude* to *imperium* almost as if the two terms are synonymous, although this is clearly impossible if the right of the supreme authorities is limited by the multitude. Significantly, all the other commentators have followed him, focusing their arguments on the relation between individual and community or society. Balibar, recognizing the difficulty of taking *imperium* simply as a synonym for *multitude*, attempts to resolve this difficulty by arguing that the relation between the two terms is one not of equivalence but rather of form and content: it is "the *imperium* that gives form and thus body to the multitude."[19] Yet it appears that Spinoza, in other formulations in the *TP*, suggests exactly the opposite: that the multitude gives body to the otherwise empty forms of the *imperium* and, under specific circumstances, may be moved by certain affects (Spinoza mentions indignation) to destroy an *imperium*. Even if we accept Balibar's solution to the problem of the displacement from the multitude to *imperium* or *civitas* in this particular passage, however, we must nevertheless acknowledge that there exists a distinction, if not an irreconcilable antagonism, between *multitude* and *imperium* that has been systematically suppressed in what is otherwise the most important debate to take place around Spinoza (and of course the stakes are far greater than simply the correct interpretation of Spinoza) in perhaps the last century.

I want to argue that this suppression through displacement signals the liminal nature of the multitude as a concept: it is neither an individual, in the meaning that the dominant juridical anthropology assigns to the term, nor *the* collective, *the* community, *the* people having legally constituted themselves as a juridical entity ("a people makes a people"). Rather, emerging precisely out of Spinoza's critique of the constitutive function of law (and here, as elsewhere, Hegel's specification of the contradictions proper to the moment of reason as lawgiver in the *Phenomenology of Spirit* follows Spinoza very closely) and his insistence that right equals power, the multitude calls into question the conceptual antinomies of a certain liberal tradition that began with Francisco Suarez, Hugo Grotius, and Hobbes and continues to thrive in our own time. Neither a mere juxtaposition of separate individuals nor a collective entity that draws its legitimacy and function from its source in the voluntary consent of such individuals, the multitude precisely has no juridical legitimation or political form. It is that excess or remainder that is irreducible to the antinomies of legal and political thought, overdetermining both political theory and practice, the permanent excess of force over law, and a force that no state can monopolize precisely because it is the force no one can alienate or transfer insofar as it is necessary to life itself. And I will agree with Balibar to call this remainder or excess the element of transindividuality.

Of course, however dominant the liberal tradition I spoke of earlier remains, and however compelling or even compulsory its antinomies and dilemmas prove to be, even or especially today, there exist preliberal or antiliberal, perhaps even simply nonliberal, philosophical traditions that offer a number of categories by which to think intermediary forms of human existence between the solitary individual and the state. I cannot begin to enumerate the philosophers, from Aristotle to Hegel to Heidegger, or concepts (family, clan, race, *das Volk*–quite distinct from the People—or even class, which, though irreducible to these categories in certain key respects, has not in its actual historical existence been entirely innocent of them either). Does not the multitude take its place among these other categories of collective existence? If so, it would no longer represent an excess or remainder but would belong in a distribution of social forms according to scale and thereby functionally integrated into the highest unit of social life, the *summum potestas*, however we choose to designate it.

If we turn to Spinoza's texts for an answer to this question, we find only further difficulties and questions, statements that, if built upon, might furnish something like an answer but that remain without issue or development or are even manifestly contradicted by other passages. Let me take as an example Spinoza's well-known response to one of his frequent hypothetical interlocutors, the one who seeks to explain the disobedience and subsequent misfortune of the Hebrew people after the destruction of the Hebrew state (*imperium*) "by the stubbornness of the race [*gentis*]."[20] Because this is a difficult passage and it is far from clear what exactly is at stake in it, I want to follow the precise wording of Spinoza's response: "But this is childish. Why would this nation be more stubborn than others? By nature? But nature does not create nations [*nationes*], but individuals [*individua*] who are not divided into nations except by the diversity of language, laws and custom."[21]

The effect of the sentence is to sweep away in a single gesture all the so-called natural unities to which theories of society have appealed: family, clan, race (and *nationes* can be read as "races"). And while the family posed a number of difficulties for the theorists of the contractual origin of the social bond, they were forced by virtue of the philosophies which preceded them and against which they had to demarcate themselves (from Aristotle to Robert Filmer), in however unsatisfactory a way, to confront the family and the problems it posed: natural love, hierarchy, and so on. It is worth remarking in this context that Spinoza, who, as Francois Zourabichvili has recently noted, exhibits a highly ambivalent fascination with the figure of the child, says virtually nothing about the family.[22] Perhaps, as the passage concerning the Hebrew nation seems to indicate, Spinoza seeks above all to deprive the "essential," "natural" forms of community (those identified as such against the imputation of their artificiality by philosophical doctrines of the naturalness of society) of any theoretical privilege, as if such notions prevent us from imagining other ways, not derived from what is commonly thought of as nature, in which human beings unite. But the passage cited above also poses extraordinary difficulties: it appears to exemplify precisely the kind of methodological individualism that I have previously argued is incompatible with everything else Spinoza has to say, whether in the *TTP* or the *TP*, about political life; indeed, if it only made mention of the contractual origin of the "nation" it could have been taken from chapter 13 of *Leviathan*. But there is no such contract in Spinoza's account and no need for any transition between a state of nature and the social state because these are not moments in a chronology that leads dissociated individuals to unite through the mediation of a contract into a nation; rather, they are two forms of causality that operate simultaneously. Further, unless we reject Spinoza's critique in the preface to *Ethics* 3 of the idea of a human realm that is an *imperium in imperio*, given that God or Nature is all that exists, we must also recognize as equally real—that is, equally natural—what Spinoza here calls nature and the institutions and practices that comprise social life. In fact, it appears here that it is not so much the *contumnacia* or stubbornness of the Hebrews that he contests, and therefore the fact that this nation (and by extension others) may or even necessarily does possess a certain *ingenium* or character, but rather (in addition to discounting the causal power of the *ingenium*) the fact of this *ingenium* being caused by nature instead of what we would today call institutions or apparatuses. But if, according to Spinoza, the human world is a part of nature and even language and law cannot in any way be understood separate from it, how are we to understand the term *nature* in this passage? It appears that the *ingenium* of the Hebrew people can be understood only in relation to that part of nature that has humanity as its adequate cause; therefore this *ingenium* is not determined by the power of causes external to human beings, a power that would then escape their knowledge and control, but rather can be known through its causes. And if the power is known, then under precise circumstances it can be changed.

But such an interpretation, however Spinozist it may be, does not account for or explain what Spinoza actually says, the specific terms he uses, in the passage on the Hebrew people. Above all, it cannot explain away the fact that by opposing individuals created by nature and peoples or nations distinguished (here he uses not the word *created* but the verb *distinguo*) "ex divertate linguae, legum et morum [by different languages, laws and customs]," Spinoza has, in however complicated a way (and I believe I have only touched on the complexities of this passage), reproduced a version of the antinomy of individual and community, individual and state, individual and society.[23] Even if we entertain the argument that Spinoza has adjusted the terminology of his exposition to accommodate his readers, we are still faced with striking inconsistencies in his own treatment of the individual/collective relation in his later texts, signaling the fact that this relation posed insurmountable problems for Spinoza until, literally, the very end of his last, unfinished work, the *TP*. I have had occasion elsewhere to remark on the stark contradiction between Spinoza's dismissal of any notion of a fixed essential "stubbornness" of the Hebrew *gentis* and what, according to his own analysis, must be regarded as a puerile or childish insistence on the natural inferiority of women to men, an inferiority that, he is at pains to say, will persist no matter what the institutional context or the attempts to educate women. Nature, to use the terminology of the earlier passage, clearly has created, not simply individual women, but Woman, whose essence is thus placed beyond the reach of institutions, and of human practice altogether; in no conceivable legal and customary regime can the power of women's mind and body be equal or superior to that of men. It is thus not simply the "organicism" of Spinoza's very brief account of women, or Woman, as a fixed, unchanging, and unchangeable collective entity that should be noted but, just as important, his inability to imagine, at the conclusion of the *TP*, particular women not simply as individuals (which would allow them to be expressions of some underlying essence or nature) but as *res singulares*, singular things expressing singular essences.

Thus, Spinoza's final work leaves off at the point at which he—in order to make absolute the absolute *imperium*, democracy—negatively determines those who have the right (*jus*) to participate in political decision making, by enumerating those who do not have such a right: foreigners (*peregrinos*, which in Roman law was also applied to "resident aliens"), women and servants (*servos*, a category that contains servants in a very broad sense, that is, all those under the authority of another man), children, and criminals (*TP* 11.4). Given that women and servants (those in the employ and thus under the power of another), at least in places like England, France, and the Netherlands (each of which also had significant populations of resident aliens), comprise the overwhelming majority of the population whose power no ruler, according to Spinoza, can afford to ignore, we are forced to acknowledge that Spinoza's last text ends with a spectacular dissociation of right and power, with an attempt to legislate out of existence the very multitude that he has argued throughout the *TP* is the primary force of political life, and with a collapse into a notion of a transcendent identity of the collective category of Woman, that historical becoming cannot change, a notion that implies as its correlate a theory of feminine individuals as individual expressions of their transcendent essence.

Thus, from the inaugural moment of its textual inscription in *TP* 3.2, the multitude as a concept pursues itself, in search of its own true meaning, incessantly fluctuating between *imperium* and *cives*, between the terminal and starting points of political philosophy, as if Spinoza can neither think the concept in its specificity nor reduce it to something other than itself. To leave it at this, however, would be to fail to grasp the full measure of what Negri called Spinoza's savage anomaly and the degree to which Spinoza's philosophy retains a singular capacity to disturb the categories that continue, often without our knowledge or consent, to organize our thought.[24] In this spirit I want to return to Balibar's essay "*Potentia multitudinis*," specifically to its concluding lines, in which Balibar attempts to recast the debate between those who consider the state an artificial entity reducible to individuals and those who, adhering literally to Spinoza's text, regard the state itself as an individual endowed with a body and a mind (according to the theory of individuality developed in *Ethics* 2, part 13): for Spinoza, Balibar argues, philosophy's most urgent task was "to think man outside of any anthropomorphism," as he sought to liberate himself from all the models that man (that is, the multitude of men) has not ceased to propose for himself.[25]

How do we begin to think social and political singularity in terms other than those modeled not simply on the familiar juridical anthropology, the notion of the individual as endowed with a body and a mind which is the idea of the body, or even on the empirico-transcendental doublet of individual and community, citizen and state, and so on? In fact, as we have seen, the very possibility of theorizing the specific existence of the multitude depends on the possibility of our freeing ourselves from all such models, from the point of view of which the multitude remains unthinkable. The first step perhaps consists of recognizing with Matheron that the concept of the multitude only begins to become intelligible on the basis of the analysis of the affects, and, more particularly, the phenomenon of the imitation of the affects developed in *Ethics* 3 and 4.[26]

But Spinoza's theory of the imitation of the affects appears to reproduce rather than resolve the dilemmas we have encountered so far. Thus, for Matheron himself the imitation of the affects constitutes a primary "interhuman life" that in turn provides the foundation for a state or society that can be moved by the affects or passions proper to it.[27] Despite the fears of critics such as Lee Rice, his theory in no way excludes the notion of originally dissociated individuals who remain dissociated even in their imitation of the affects of others.[28] In fact, Spinoza's text contains the basis of a reading according to which affective imitation would become nothing more than an act of projection, which requires only that I imagine that the other feels pleasure or pain in order to imitate what I imagine that other to feel. This is precisely Adam Smith's definition of sympathy in chapter 1, part 1, of the *Theory of Moral Sentiments*. For Smith, there is no crossing the boundary between me and the other; I can never know what or even if another person feels. The operation of sympathy remains internal to what Smith calls "spectators," who imagine what they themselves would feel or have felt in a circumstance similar to the other.[29] Sympathy, for Smith, does not (strictly speaking) require even the existence of the other. It is possible for me to sympathize with the dead, given that there is no communication or transfer of feeling or affect across the infinite distance that separates me from all others, all of whom can be no more than projections of myself.[30]

Indeed, *Ethics* 3.21 seems to authorize just such a reading: "He who imagines that what he loves is affected with pleasure or pain will likewise be affected with pleasure or pain." Or at least seems to authorize it until Spinoza adds, "the intensity of which will vary with the intensity of the emotion of the object loved." What might at first be taken as an act, specifically, the act of imagining, undertaken by and within a single person becomes, with the addition of the qualifying clause, not simply an act that requires the presence of the affect in the other, but a being affected with pleasure or pain that is precisely determined by the force of the other's affect. In its complexity and perhaps even its contradictions, the sentence captures something of the movement of the *Ethics* itself from part 2 to part 3,[31] as the imagination (which to a certain extent mediates between inner and outer, between self and other, acting as a conduit between my body considered as a singular thing and other equally singular bodies) gives way to an unmediated imitation that is less a reduplication of one person's affect in another than, as we see in part 21, a perpetuation or persistence of affect without the mediation of the person. The affect thus is not contained in me or the other but lies between us; the production of affects both individualizes and transindividualizes. But Spinoza will go even further: it is not simply that affects, pleasure and pain and their various secondary forms, are communicated like a contagion. There can even be the imitation or communication of desire, which Spinoza calls emulation (*emulatio*): desire is "engendered" (*ingenuratur*) when we "imagine" that others have this desire (*Ethics* 3, def. 33). But given that Spinoza has, earlier in *Ethics* 3 (part 9, Sch.), defined desire as the consciousness of the *conatus* whereby a thing endeavors to persist in its own being, the fact of the transindividual engendering of desire compels us to pose the question of the "thing" whose *conatus* is expressed in consciousness. If desire is the consciousness of the *conatus* and I share a desire with another person, do I share the *conatus* of which the desire is the expression? In other words, what would allow us to be thought of as separate individuals, rather than as parts of a singular thing whose *conatus* (and therefore "interest") is expressed in us both? Nothing at all: "When two individuals of the same nature are combined, they compose an individual twice as powerful as each one singly" (*Ethics* 4.18, Sch.).

This passage from the *Ethics* sheds light on the content of one of Spinoza's most controversial and troubling letters, letter 17 to Pieter Balling, dated June 20, 1664, following the death of the latter's young son. This letter, full of beauty and sorrow, of pleasure as well as pain, the pleasure of under-standing one's own sorrow and, in the act of understanding it, increasing one's force, can or must itself be read as a transcription of imitated affects, of identities, not just those of Balling and his son, or Spinoza and Balling, or even the three together, so intermingled that we can no longer clearly demarcate the pain of the one from the others. Balling, otherwise a follower of Spinoza, "recalls" in his grief that he once while sleeping was awakened by groans like those his son would later utter on his deathbed, at a time when the boy was still healthy and fit. Can we not call these groans, he asked Spinoza, "omens," portents of the fate awaiting his beloved son?[32] Spinoza's response, even taking into account the fact that the letter comes early in his philosophical career, is surprising: he maintains that while "the effects of the imagination which are due to corporeal causes" can never be omens, "the effects of the imagination, or images, which have their origin in the constitution of the mind can be omens of some future event because any mind can have a confused presentiment of what the future is [*quia Mens aliquid, quod futurum est, confuse potest praesentire*]. So it can imagine it as firmly and vividly as if such a thing were present to it."[33]

Here, of course, Spinoza dissociates mind and body to a greater degree than he does in the *Ethics*, but his willingness to preserve the term "omen," by defining it in a way that does not correspond exactly to the meaning attributed to it by the superstitious, is another early example of the philo-sophical strategy that would mark his entire career. Thus, images that arise in the mind may express what is feared—for example, the death of one's young son—and what is feared may indeed come to pass. One's fear may be rational, rather than irrational—a calculation of probabilities, accompanied by an image of what might come to pass but which has not yet done so. What is surprising is what follows Spinoza's description of the firmness and vividness of the image of what was not yet present to the mind: "Let us take (to adduce an example similar to yours), a father who so loves his son that he and his beloved son are, as it were, (*quasi*) one. . . . the father through his union with his son is a part of his son, it being necessary that the soul of the father participate in the ideal essence of the son, and in its affections and in what follows from them."[34] Is it possible to see in this passage the beginnings of a theory of the imitation of the affects and of desire, and therefore the beginnings of a theory of transindividuality? If we take "ideal essence" to be the "actual essence" which in part 3 of the *Ethics* is the *conatus*, the father/son couple possesses an affective unity: each participates in the affect or desire that marks their composition as a single individual whose actual essence is lived by them as desire, and this affect or desire cannot be apportioned to one or the other. Images fluctuate between them without proprietorship or fixed origin.

Can we not now begin to see what constitutes the danger of the multitude in Spinoza's philosophy?—the unthinkable residue of a philosophical tendency that begins with Hobbes and includes, but does not end with, Adam Smith? It is not simply the right or power of mass movements beyond law and property but the transindividualization of desire and affect, and therefore of the *conatus* itself, in a movement that overflows and exceeds the confines imposed by the rituals and apparatuses that govern us. The calculable self-interest of the juridical individual, the foundation upon which rest the hopes and promises of an epoch, is fractured by the eruption of desires and pleasures that cannot be contained by either the individual as constituted in law or the state, the incalculable and incessantly changing forms, from dyads to multitudes, in which individuality and transindividuality are one and the same thing.

Let us recall that letter 17, the letter devoted to the question of omens, includes an example from Spinoza's own life, an image that Spinoza insists was, unlike the groans that Balling recalls having heard before the death of his son, not an omen. It is of course that dream image, an image that persisted, beyond the dream, into the clarity of the morning light: "the image of a black, scabby Brazilian whom I had never seen before."[35] We can say today with perfect assurance that even if Spinoza did not recognize it as such, it was indeed an omen of the hatred and fear that his philosophy would inspire in others and that he could not entirely escape himself, if we take seriously the theory of the imitation of the affects. Further, we may see in the image of that "Ethiopian" (to use the other term Spinoza applies to the image of the black man) another omen: the omen of new compositions, of trans-Atlantic transindividualities making worlds even as they are made by them, of a destiny he cannot escape but is not yet willing to embrace, of multitudes to come whose power is the limit of Empire.

Notes

1   See Gregory S. Kavka, *Hobbesian Moral and Political Theory* (Princeton, NJ: Princeton University Press, 1986).

2   I realize that in choosing to focus on the multitude, I will be accused of giving in to fashion, especially now that Michael Hardt and Antonio Negri's *Empire* has introduced this once obscure term into such general currency that even *Time* magazine has deemed it appropriate for its readership. Those familiar with Spinoza will hasten to point out that the multitude as a concept appears only in Spinoza's last and unfinished work, the *TP*, and does not appear perhaps even under another name in the *Ethics* or the *TTP* and therefore cannot serve the task I seek to assign to it: the task of designating what is most disturbing about Spinoza's work as a whole in the current theoretical conjuncture. I will respond to these perfectly reasonable objections by insisting that while Hardt and Negri's use of the term "multitude" in *Empire* and in some subsequent essays is undoubtedly derived from Spinoza and therefore exists in a certain as yet unspecified relation to the concept as it appears in the text of the *TP* (after all, Negri himself was the first to explore this aspect of the *TP* in detail: see Negri, *The Savage Anomaly: The Power of Spinoza's Metaphysics and Politics* [Minneapolis: University of Minnesota Press, 1991]), it remains in essential ways distinct from it, conditioned as much by the history of Marxism and communism, both theoretically and practically, as by the work of Spinoza. To the second objection, that is, to the charge that I have made central to Spinoza a concept that only appears in his last unfinished text, I would respond by citing Matheron's argument that the theoretical conditions of possibility of the multitude are established not in the *TP*, where these conditions are presupposed, but only in the *Ethics* (particularly parts 3 and 4); see Alexandre Matheron, *Individu et communauté chez Spinoza* (Paris: Editions Minuit, 1969) and "L'inignation et le *conatus* de l'état spinoziste," in *Spinoza: Puissance et ontologie*, ed. M. R. D'Allonnes and H. Rizk (Paris: Éditions Kimé, 1994), 163. In fact, I would go further than Matheron (and to some extent oppose him) and argue that the path on which Spinoza embarks in chapter 16 of the *TTP*, the equation of right and power, requires as a condition of its validity the absent concept of the multitude, a concept that I will thus regard not so much as absent as deferred from the *TTP*. Let me provisionally argue, then, that the constellation of problems surrounding the concept of the multitude, whether logically preceding it as its condition of possibility or necessarily following from it, cannot be grasped by following the apparent chronological order of Spinoza's texts and that the order of arguments is not identical to the order of the texts.

3   Étienne Balibar, "Spinoza the Anti-Orwell," in *Masses, Classes and Ideas* (London: Routledge, 1994).

4   Antonio Negri, *L'anomalie sauvage: Puissance et pouvoir chez Spinoza* (Paris: Presses Universitaires de France, 1981).

5   Matheron, "L'inignation et le *conatus* de l'état spinoziste," 163.

6   Benedict Spinoza, *Tractatus Theologico-Politicus*, trans. Samuel Shirley (New York: E. J. Brill, 1991), 237. Other Spinoza editions cited below include *Ethics*, trans. Samuel Shirley (Cambridge, MA: Hackett, 1992); *The Letters*, trans. Samuel Shirley (Cambridge, MA: Hackett, 1995); and *A Political Treatise*, trans. Samuel Shirley (Cambridge, MA: Hackett, 2002).

7   Spinoza, *Tractatus Theologico-Politicus*, 237.

8   Ibid., 250.

9   Negri, *L'anomalie sauvage*, 9.

10 Thomas Hobbes, *Man and Citizen*, ed. Bernard Gert (New York: Doubleday, 1972).

11 Étienne Balibar, "*Potentia multitudinis quae una veluti mente duciter*," in *Ethik, Recht und Politik bei Spinoza*, ed. M. Senn and M. Walther (Zurich: Schultheiss, 2001).

12 Matheron, *Individu et communauté chez Spinoza*; Antonio Negri, "Reliqua Desiderantur: Towards a Definition of the Concept of Democracy in the Final Spinoza," in *The New Spinoza*, ed. Warren Montag and Ted Stolze (Minneapolis: University of Minnesota Press, 1997); Lee C. Rice, "Individual and Community in Spinoza's Social Psychology," in *Spinoza: Issues and Directions*, ed. Edwin Curley and Pierre-François Moreau (Leiden: E. J. Brill, 1990); D. J. Den Uyl, *Power, State and Freedom: An Interpretation of Spinoza's Political Philosophy* (Assen: Van Gorcum, 1983).

13 Matheron, *Individu et communauté chez Spinoza* and "L'inignation et le *conatus* de l'état spinoziste."

14 Pierre-François Moreau, *Spinoza: L'éxperience et l'éternité* (Paris: Presses Universitaires de France, 1994).

15 Balibar, "*Potentia multitudinis quae una veluti mente duciter*," 135.

16 Louis Althusser, "On Feuerbach," in *The Humanist Controversy and Other Writings*, trans. G. M. Goshgarian (London: Verso, 2003).

17 Michel Foucault, *The Order of Things* (New York: Vintage, 1970).

18 Pierre-François Moreau, *Le récit utopique: Droit naturel et roman de l'état* (Paris: Presses Universitaires de France, 1982), 9.

19 Balibar, "*Potentia multitudinis quae una veluti mente duciter*," 5.

20 Spinoza, *Tractatus Theologico-Politicus*, 267.

21 Ibid.

22 François Zourabichvilli, *Spinoza: Une physique de la pensée* (Paris: Presses Universitaires de France, 2002).

23 Spinoza, *Tractatus Theologico-Politicus*, 267.

24 Negri, *The Savage Anomaly*.

25 Balibar, "*Potentia multitudinis quae una veluti mente duciter*," 135.

26 Matheron, "L'inignation et le *conatus* de l'état spinoziste."

27 Matheron, *Individu et communauté chez Spinoza*, 79–222.

28 Rice, "Individual and Community in Spinoza's Social Psychology."

29 Adam Smith, *The Theory of Moral Sentiments* (Oxford: Oxford University Press, 1976), 16.

30 Ibid., 12–130.

31 This raises the possibility of speaking, as Negri did in *The Savage Anomaly*, of a kind of

caesura separating parts 1 and 2 of the *Ethics* from the last three parts, even if my sense of what separates these "two foundations" is quite different from Negri's. I want to suggest in particular that the relation between the imagination as described in *Ethics* 2 and the affects discussed in *Ethics* 3 and 4 is marked by discontinuity and rupture. This is an area for future investigation.

32 Spinoza, *Letters*, 125.
33 Ibid., 126.
34 Ibid., 127.
35 Ibid., 125.

Malcolm Bull

The Social and the Political

The concept of the political presupposes the
concept of the social.

According to Carl Schmitt, the political "does
not describe its own substance, but only the
intensity of an association or dissociation of
human beings."[1] Association and dissociation
reach their lowest possible intensity at the point
when they become indistinguishable: the association of strangers for indeterminate ends. In
the political there can be no association of
strangers, only the association of friends and the
dissociation of enemies, and no indetermination
of ends, only the determination of death. At
its greatest intensity the political is total war.
But if there were always total war, the political
would not exist. As an intensification of association and dissociation, the political presupposes
the existence of association and dissociation at
something less than maximum intensity.

When intensity diminishes, "the state turns
into society": the will to fight the enemy becomes
a social or economic program, and a politically
united people divides into producers and con-
sumers.[2] In a total society, there would not only
be no more war, but also no more states, and
no social entities more political than "tenants

The *South Atlantic Quarterly* 104:4, Fall 2005.
Copyright © 2005 by Duke University Press.

in a tenement house, customers purchasing gas from the same utility company, or passengers travelling on the same bus."[3] Depoliticization reduces all associations to the level of interest groups, between whom there is limited potential for conflict. With only economic and technical questions to resolve, society functions automatically and things administer themselves.

The situation Schmitt envisages is recognizably that described by earlier sociologists as being characteristic of *Gesellschaft* rather than *Gemeinschaft*, organic rather than mechanical solidarity. Thanks to the division of labor, Émile Durkheim had noted, occupations coexist "without being forced into a position where they harm one another." Social differentiation is the "gentle dénouement" of the struggle for existence; "rivals are not obliged to eliminate one another completely, but can co-exist side by side."[4] The division between friend and enemy disappears, and both become cooperative strangers.

Schmitt acknowledges this process but argues that it can always be reversed: politics cannot be exterminated because any ethical or economic antagonism can intensify to the point at which it becomes political. Indeed, depoliticization—in the form of liberalism, the market economy, and technological rationalization—has created new forms of social tension which, in their turn, may reanimate political division and lead to new wars. Even the negation of the political "serves existing or newly emerging friend-and-enemy groupings and cannot escape the logic of the political."[5]

But although "the negation of the political . . . is inherent in every consistent individualism,"[6] the logic of the political does not extend all the way to the private individual. Schmitt emphasizes that the political aspect of the friend/enemy distinction emerges only in the public domain. The enemy is not a private adversary; he is *hostis*, not *inimicus*.[7] The social, it seems, constitutes a barrier between the political and the private individual. The political is not the intensification of the individual war of all against all, and, conversely, the deintensification of association and dissociation leads to the public sphere of virtual strangers, not to a private realm. The social may be the negation of the political, but it is also the condition that makes the political possible.

The implicit structure of Schmitt's argument emerges more clearly in the so-called *Langnamverein* address of 1932, where it is applied to the economic sphere. According to Schmitt, the old opposition between the state and the private entrepreneur was no longer adequate. Any account of the economy must now also include "an intermediate domain between the state and the singular individual." There are, accordingly, three domains: (1) the sphere of the state; (2) "the sphere of the free, individual entrepreneur, i.e. the *sphere of pure privacy*"; (3) "the intermediate *non-state, but still public sphere*."[8] The last of these is, Schmitt suggests, urgently in need of attention, for the state needs to distance itself from this intermediate sphere of "autonomous economic administration"—an act of separation that is in itself political.

Schmitt's articulation of the relationship between these three spheres is expressed slightly differently elsewhere, but it always carries echoes of Hegel's tripartite distinction between the family, civil society, and the state. Hannah Arendt, another theorist of the dichotomy between the social and the political, was also aware of this precedent and articulated the relationship in very similar terms. In the *Human Condition*, she argues that "the distinction between a private and a public sphere of life corresponds to the household and political realms . . . but the emergence of the social realm, which is neither private nor public, strictly speaking, is a relatively new phenomenon whose origin coincided with the emergence of the modern age."[9] Before then, the term *political economy* would have been an oxymoron, for whatever was economic was confined to the private sphere of the individual, but in the modern world the economic has entered the public realm and become a collective concern.[10]

Society, as Arendt later put it, is therefore the "curious, somewhat hybrid realm between the political and the private in which, since the beginning of the modern age, most men have spent the greater part of their lives." Like Schmitt, she sees the social as constituting a mediating space between the private and the political.[11] But although, in modernity, the social is presupposed by the political, it is not the sphere of politics itself. On the contrary, "what we traditionally call state and government gives place here to pure administration . . . [the] substitution of bureaucracy, the rule of nobody, for personal rulership."[12]

In Arendt, the social is always populous,[13] and as numbers increase, the intensity of the association and dissociation of human beings diminishes so much that eventually "the world between them has lost its power to gather them together, to relate and to separate them."[14] Instead of the difference of opinion, "society always demands that its members act as though they were members of one enormous family which had only one opinion and one interest."[15] The sheer weight of numbers helps to ensure conformity and unanimity. In contrast, the original public realm, the Greek *polis*, was sparsely populated, with enough space between individuals for them to maintain and define their identity against each other. It was reserved for individuality and "was permeated by a fiercely agonal spirit, where everybody had constantly to distinguish himself from all others."[16]

This public realm was free because it was insulated from economic necessity and nobody engaged in mere labor. According to Arendt, any genuinely political space has to exclude all those who work for a living and any form of public concern with welfare or the necessities of life. The political was always distinct from the everyday problems of the household; now in modern society it must distance itself from the social or economic issues that threaten to usurp the place of the political within the public realm. The social is cooperative, identity-destroying labor; the political is competitive, identity-disclosing action. The latter depends on the former but cannot exist unless distinguished from it.

Despite the recent interest in these thinkers and the appropriation of both to articulate the category of "the political," commentators have hesitated to bring Schmitt and Arendt into alignment, and even when they do, they insist that Arendt's concern with the political "bears little resemblance to Schmitt's conception of it."[17] It is certainly not identical, but Arendt and Schmitt nevertheless share a conception of the political that is in certain respects very similar, notably in its insistence that the political is the negation of the social. Both think of the social as an intermediate zone between the private and the political, a contamination of the private and public characterized by conformity rather than the contestation that, in modernity, threatens to undermine the political. The social is necessary to the political but should be minimized. Schmitt and Arendt are both powerfully motivated by a sense of the stifling ubiquity of the social, and for this reason they enjoin us to think politically—to escape from what, unbearably, is already there.

Contracts

If thinking politically is to be something other than escapist thought, its relationship to the social needs to be more fully articulated. Both Schmitt and Arendt suggest that the political represents the originary form of public life, yet they take the social as a given and offer the political as the alternative to it. The political therefore appears to enact a double movement: both the flight from the social and its point of origin. In the work of some contemporary theorists, this circularity is made explicit, and the political becomes, as Slavoj Žižek puts it, "the moment . . . when the very structuring principle of society, the fundamental form of the social pact, is called into question."[18] But if, as Schmitt and Arendt suggest, the social always precedes the political, where does that leave the originary pact itself?

The answer may depend on which type of contract is under consideration. As Arendt notes, in the seventeenth century there was a clear distinction between two kinds of contract: the mutual contract, which gives birth to society, and the social contract, which gives rise to government. The mutual contract contains *in nuce* the republican and federal principles, the social contract the absolute and national principles—the capacity "to overawe them all," as Thomas Hobbes had put it.[19] Both, however, are envisaged as contracts between isolated individuals in the state of nature, and no attempt is made to articulate the relation between them. How is government formed from a preexisting society, and how is society formed from within a government? Outside the fictional state of nature, human beings are always already socialized and governed to some degree, even as new societies and governments are formed within them. And if the political is specifically antisocial, in which type of contract does it find its realization and in which its antithesis?

Both Schmitt and Arendt are authors who raise more questions than they answer, and their texts do not easily yield a framework within which to address these issues. But a detour through another theorist of the political offers a model that can be applied to their work. One of the few writers to consider the political potential of both types of contract was John C. Calhoun. In his *Disquisition on Government*, Calhoun asks, "What is that constitution of our nature, which, while it impels man to associate with his kind, renders it impossible for society to exist without government?"[20] The answer, he suggests, is the imbalance between individual feelings and social feelings. Humans feel more strongly on their own account than they do for others, "hence, the tendency to a universal state of conflict, between individual and individual."[21]

However, before turning to the form of government required in such a state of conflict, Calhoun briefly considered the alternative:

> If reversed—if their feelings and affections were stronger for others than for themselves, or even as strong, the necessary result would seem to be that all individuality would be lost; and boundless and remediless disorder and confusion would ensue. For each, at the same moment, intensely participating in all the conflicting emotions of

those around him, would, of course, forget himself and all that concerned him immediately, in his officious intermeddling with the affairs of all others. . . . Such a state of things would, as far as we can see, lead to endless disorder and confusion, not less destructive to our race than a state of anarchy. It would, besides, be remediless—for government would be impossible; or, if it could by possibility exist, its object would be reversed. Selfishness would have to be encouraged, and benevolence discouraged. Individuals would have to be encouraged, by rewards, to become more selfish, and deterred, by punishments, from being too benevolent.[22]

Calhoun gives no explicit indication of how this inverted form of governance might work, but it is possible to reconstruct its features from a close reading of the *Disquisition* and Calhoun's other writings and political interventions.

Later in the *Disquisition*, Calhoun discusses the relative merits of government through concurrent and numerical majorities. His description of the workings of a concurrent majority, where a unanimous decision is always required, makes it sound rather like the world where social feelings predominate over individual. In such situations, "there will be diffused throughout the whole community kind feelings between its different portions; and, instead of antipathy, a rivalry amongst them to promote the interests of each other."[23] In the jury room, for example, "Under the influence of this *disposition to harmonize*, one after another falls into the same opinion, until unanimity is obtained."[24]

Similarly, in governments with a concurrent majority, "the prevailing desire would be, to promote the common interests of the whole; and, hence, the competition would be, not which should yield the least to promote the common good, but which should yield the most."[25] In contrast, government of the numerical majority divides the community into "two great hostile parties" whose mutual antagonism becomes so strong "as to absorb almost every feeling of our nature, both social and individual . . . [and] to destroy, almost entirely, all sympathy between them, and to substitute in its place the strongest aversion."[26]

Calhoun therefore contrasts governments of the concurrent and numerical majority in terms of whether social or individual feelings come to predominate:

When traced to its source, this difference will be found to originate in the fact, that, in governments of the concurrent majority, individual feelings are, from its organism, necessarily enlisted on the side of the social, and made to unite with them in promoting the interests of the whole, as the best way of promoting the special interests of each; while, in those of the numerical majority, the social are necessarily enlisted on the side of the individual, and made to contribute to the interest of parties, regardless of that of the whole.[27]

Where there are concurrent majorities, social feelings predominate; where there are numerical majorities, individual ones.

So, if concurrent majorities promote social feeling and numerical majorities individual feeling, what conclusions can be drawn on the question of which form of government is appropriate to a world where social rather than individual feelings are preponderant? The answer must be, for Calhoun, that just as concurrent majorities temper individual feelings, so numerical majorities would promote them: the tendency of the concurrent majority "is to unite the community, let its interests be ever so diversified or opposed; while that of the numerical is to divide it into two conflicting portions, let its interests be, naturally, ever so united and identified."[28]

Here we have the answer to the question of what sort of government would be suited to a world of social feelings. Just as Calhoun advocates government of the concurrent majority for a world in which individual feelings predominate, so, in a world where social feeling predominated and "selfishness would have to be encouraged, and benevolence discouraged," a divisive numerical majority would be required.

In practice, of course, matters are more complicated, which is why, for Calhoun, the formation of government has two distinct moments, the second the reverse of the first. In the nullification crisis of 1832, Calhoun had argued that the United States was "a union of States as distinct from that of individuals" and that whereas individuals might have ceded sovereignty to their state, the states themselves had not ceded sovereignty to the federal government. Later, in *A Discourse on the Constitution and Government of the United States*, he formalized the distinction between the two types of union as follows: "The government of States united in political union, in contradistinction to a government of individuals socially united; that is by what is usually called a social compact."[29] Rather than being united socially in the federal union, individual citizens are "politically connected through their respective States."[30]

Calhoun makes no reference to this distinction between social and political compacts in his thought experiment in the *Disquisition*, yet it is still possible to discern their outlines. Whereas the federal union was, at least in Calhoun's opinion, a political union governed by a concurrent majority, the states themselves were social compacts governed by a numerical majority. By implication, therefore, within each state social feelings predominate and so numerical majorities are needed, whereas between the states individual feelings predominate and so the best solution is a concurrent majority where each state has a veto. Here Calhoun talks not of social and political compacts but of government and constitution, positive and negative powers. Positive power is the power of acting derived from the formation of a government; negative power is "the power of preventing or arresting the action of government—be it called by what term it may—veto, interposition, nullification, check, or balance of power—which, in fact, forms the constitution."[31]

To his opponents, who did not make his distinction between social and political compacts, positive and negative powers, governments and constitutions, Calhoun's espousal of nullification had appeared not as formative of a second form of contract but, rather, as an attempt to dissolve the first, and so, in effect, to return the inhabitants of the United States to a state of nature where no one had to obey the law.[32] For Calhoun, however, the negative powers of the constitution are a long way from the state of nature. In his account, "*constitution* stands to *government* as *government* stands to *society*."[33] To this, he might perhaps have added: "and as society stands to the state of nature," for according to him, "man is so constituted as to make the social state necessary to his existence," just as government is necessary to society, and constitution to government.

Instead of thinking simply in terms of a single contract intervening between the sociopolitical state and the state of nature, Calhoun's theory allows for an alternating sequence of contracts, one where the balance shifts back and forth rather than one feeling being dominant throughout. Where social feelings predominate, there will be a form of social compact, based on the numerical majority, with a view toward establishing the positive power of acting in the interest of the whole. Where individual feelings predominate, there will be form of a political compact, based on the concurrent majority, so as to establish the negative power of arresting action in the interests of the individual. Because the social compact turns social feelings into individual ones, the next level, whether described as the federal union relative to states, or the constitution relative to government, must itself perform the opposite function and turn individual feelings back into social ones. The whole process would also work in the opposite direction: where the political compact transforms individual into social feelings, the next level would require a social compact to turn social feelings back into individual ones.

What Calhoun has unwittingly described is an entire sociopolitical economy of feeling, a machine that uses social and political compacts to generate positive and negative powers and transform social and individual feelings into one another. But rather than a closed circuit in which individual and social feelings are simply transformed back and forth, Calhoun offers a more nuanced account of the process: instead of returning to the same place, each sort of feeling may return at another level as the dynamic spirals outward.

And where does it all begin? Calhoun offers two seemingly inconsistent propositions on this point: first, that "our individual feelings are stronger than our social feelings," and, second, that humans always exist in the social state because the state of nature is an impossibility, and government is always preceded by society. But in a sense it does not matter, for the beauty of Calhoun's machine is that it can start anywhere. Calhoun's construction of a world in which social and individual feelings are transformed back and forth potentially offers a way of articulating the relationship between the social and the political in a fashion that does not presuppose the priority of either.

Revolutions

If we feed Schmitt and Arendt's accounts of the political into Calhoun's machine, the differences between Schmitt and Arendt emerge more clearly, and also the possibilities and limitations of any account of the political informed by their work. Arendt's distinction between the mutual and social contracts that produce, respectively, society and government clearly overlaps with Calhoun's articulation of the political and social compacts: for both, the (misleadingly named) social contract is the primary means of forming government; Arendt's mutual contract is recognizably what Calhoun thinks of as a political union, and its consequence, the impulse toward unanimity, characteristic of what Arendt calls the social. But how does each relate to the other within Arendt's texts?

Arendt's distinction between mutual and social contracts appears in *On Revolution*. For Arendt, there are two types of revolution, the political and the social, and the difference between them parallels that between the mutual and social contracts. Political revolution is exemplified by the American Revolution, whose protagonists were already "organized in self-governing bodies" and able to take for granted the material necessities of life.[34] They, like the citizens of the ancient Greek *polis*, focused not on the economic organization of society but on the question of the best form of government. The problem they posed was therefore "not social but political": how to maximize individual freedom of thought, expression, and action.[35] The solution came in the form of a constitution designed to ensure that the government was no more subject to the will of a majority than a building is subject to the will of its inhabitants.[36]

In contrast, the French Revolution was based on social feelings. With the men of the eighteenth century, the age-old indifference to the sufferings of others had finally disappeared. Among those who made the French Revolution, repugnance at seeing a fellow creature suffer became common, with the result that people began to lose their sense of individual separateness.[37] In this respect, compassion has the same effect as mass society, in that it "abolishes the distance, the worldly space between men where political matters, the whole realm of human affairs, are located." And because compassion diminishes the capacity of the world "to relate and to separate," it remains, "politically speaking, irrelevant and without consequence."[38]

In the American Revolution, compassion had played no role, so the founders were concerned only with balancing the interests of each actor within the political realm. But in the French Revolution, the objective was "to liberate the life process of society from the fetters of scarcity."[39] Driven by a different set of concerns, the French Revolution also took a different form. Compassion broke down the boundaries between people and so facilitated the formation of a single general will, a government of public opinion in which various diverse interests all converged upon a single purpose. In practice, Arendt argues, this was a form not of majority decision but of majority rule, where, after a decision had been taken, the majority "proceeds to liquidate politically, and in extreme cases physically, the opposing minority."[40] Social feeling had led to a revolution based on majority rule; this, in turn, was sustained by a terror that dissolved the very social feelings that lay behind the revolution and so set individuals at odds once more.

Arendt presses home the tragic ironies of the French Revolution, but although she does not make it explicit, a comparable paradox attends the American Revolution, one that is not fully articulated within her book on revolution but is arguably the motivating problem of her entire politi-cal philosophy.[41] The American Revolution, supposedly a mutual contract designed to prevent the tyranny of the majority and to take into account every political interest, in fact created a society in which individual differ-ences were eroded. In effect, the American Revolution had precisely the effect predicted by Calhoun's account of the political compact: it united diversified interests and so fostered the social conformism first noted by Tocqueville.[42] Arendt herself acknowledged the process: "The danger of conformism in this country—a danger almost as old as the republic—is that, because of the extraordinary heterogeneity of its population, social conformism tends to become an absolute and a substitute for national homogeneity."[43]

Arendt complained that Marx availed himself of the "reversibility of con-cepts . . . inherent in all strictly Hegelian categories of thought,"[44] but within her own account of revolution there is also a reversibility, perhaps even a circularity. Calhoun's model suggests how the change of direction occurs. Given that either individual or social feelings always predominate, contracts and revolutions alike serve to transform one into the other to remedy the excesses of each. So the social revolution is not just the expression of com-passion, but the remedy for it; political revolution is not just the expression of individualism but also its destroyer. Ironically, therefore, each form of revolution tends to create the circumstances that called for the other: the French Revolution created the need for a mutual compact or constitution that would reestablish social feeling; the American Revolution, the need for a divisive new social contract.

Beasts

It is possible to trace a similar dynamic in Schmitt's strange anti-Semitic text, *The Leviathan in the Political Theory of Thomas Hobbes*. According to Schmitt, Hobbes's choice of the seemingly inappropriate symbol of the Leviathan, the sea monster of ancient Hebrew mythology, must be seen in the context of medieval Jewish mystical speculation, in which Leviathan is killed and eaten. For Schmitt, this was indicative of the transhistorical role of the Jews as "the originators of the revolutionary state-destroying distinction between religion and politics."[45] But it also reflected a social situation in which various "indirect powers"—the church and the feudal estates—enjoyed relative autonomy thanks to the weakness of the state. It was against these destructive tendencies that Hobbes tried to use the Leviathan to restore the natural unity of religion and politics on which the state depended.

In Schmitt's account, Hobbes describes how "the terror of the state of nature drives anguished individuals to come together; their fear rises to an extreme; a spark of reason flashes, and suddenly there stands in front of them a new god." This creature is "much more than the sum total of all the participating particular wills," for "the state is something more than and different from a covenant concluded by individuals." On the other hand, he is also less than that, for "even though a consensus of all with all has been achieved, this agreement is only an anarchico-social, not a state covenant."[46] This disjunction means that the mortal god is also an artificial man, a machine as well as a divine animal. For all his awesome power, the sovereign-representative person is only the soul of the social machine, ultimately dependent on the collective will of those who created him.

According to Schmitt, the underlying tension between the two aspects of Leviathan found expression in Hobbes's willingness to allow for private dissent on the topic of the veracity of miracles. The sovereign would decide within the public sphere and could command the public allegiance of individuals, but nevertheless, the private man would still be free to believe or not believe in his heart. This one small concession to the freedom of the individual will was an implicit acknowledgment of the ambiguity of the original covenant, the crack that allowed Spinoza and subsequent Jewish philosophers to expand the private sphere of liberty into the public realm and so threaten the foundations of the state itself.

As a result, Schmitt argues, in the eighteenth century "the leviathan . . . was destroyed from within. The distinction of inner and outer became for the mortal god a sickness unto death." For "when the distinction between inner and outer is recognized, the superiority of the inner over the outer and thereby that of the private over the public is resolved."[47] The acknowledgment of the inner, private sphere "paved the way for new, more dangerous kinds and forms of indirect powers," based on the mutual association of those with shared private interests. Eventually, "the old adversaries, the 'indirect' powers of the church and of interest groups, reappeared in [the nineteenth] century as modern political parties, trade unions, social organizations, in a word as 'forces of society.'"[48] The result was just what the medieval Jewish mystics had predicted: "All the mythical forces embodied in the image of the leviathan now strike back at the state that Hobbes had symbolized."[49] The indirect powers join together to kill and eviscerate Leviathan, and society finally devours the state.

According to Schmitt, in Jewish mythology the land monster, Behemoth, was often cast as Leviathan's opponent, and this opposition was reflected in Hobbes's decision to title his account of the English Civil War *Behemoth*. Just as Leviathan symbolized the state, so his adversary Behemoth became the image for the civil disorder that destroys the state. Hence the ambiguity of Leviathan between state and anarchico-social covenants, mortal god and artificial man, could be conveyed in mythical terms as well. According to Schmitt: "State and revolution, leviathan and behemoth, are actually or potentially always present."[50]

Schmitt offers no persuasive textual evidence in favor of his reading of Hobbes, but there may be more to Schmitt's interpretation of Leviathan as the partial suppression of another beast representing the power and autonomy of the social than he states. Schmitt argues that the depiction of the commonwealth as a huge man can be traced to Plato, who in book 9 of the *Republic* describes an image of a man that contains within it a many-headed monster, a lion, and a man.[51] But there is another passage in the *Republic*, seemingly ignored by Schmitt (and other commentators on Hobbes), that is more relevant here. For in book 6, where Plato describes how the Sophists teach nothing except the opinions of the multitude and pass this off as wisdom, another great beast is invoked:

> It is as if a man were acquiring the knowledge of the humors and desires of a great strong beast which he had in his keeping, how it is to be approached and touched, and when and by what things it is made most savage or gentle, yes, and the several sounds it is wont to utter on the occasion of each, and again what sounds uttered by another make it tame or fierce, and after mastering this knowledge by living with the creature and by lapse of time should call it wisdom, and should construct thereof a system.[52]

Such a system would be based on nothing except the inarticulate reactions of the great beast—whatever pleased it would be good, whatever angered it would be wrong—yet the process of taming the monster would pass for a philosophy in itself.

This great beast has an afterlife quite distinct from that of Leviathan, for it clearly symbolizes not the state but, rather, the social aggregation of the multitude and the conformist pressure the multitude exerts on others.[53]

And it is primarily this passage in Plato's *Republic*, not the later one, that is reflected in Thomas Browne's *Religio Medici* (published nine years before Hobbes's *Leviathan*), where the author remarks that "the multitude, that numerous piece of monstrosity, which taken asunder seeme men, and the reasonable creatures of God; but confused together, make but one great beast, & a monstrosity more prodigious than Hydra." This great beast is, Browne suggests, the "great enemy of reason, vertue and religion."[54] Hobbes would have known both the passage in the *Republic* and also, probably, Browne's appropriation of it to create a monster out of the multitude. If anything, it is this beast that is subdued in *Leviathan*. The duality Schmitt recognized within the imagery of the beasts may have been more deeply inscribed than he admits: if the social is the dawn of the day when Leviathan is slaughtered and eaten, the political is the process through which that other Great Beast is tamed.

A World Turning Outside In

Schmitt and Arendt share a conception of the social as a zone between the private and the political formed by encroachment of the private on the public. For both, this state of affairs represents the primary characteristic of the societies in which they live, and the political is a way of exploring the forms of government appropriate not to a traditional state of nature but to a total society. Their tripartite division between private, social, and political therefore belies the essential dualism of their thought. For the political is not, as they sometimes claim, the route through which to reestablish the balance between private and public threatened by the social, so much as the negation of the social itself. For them, thinking politically is, of its very nature, a form of antisocial thought, a negation of the indifference we share with each other, a cessation of social in(ter)action, a welcome foretaste of social death.

Ironically, however, both Schmitt and Arendt also describe the political as the start of a process that leads back to the social. For Schmitt, the cycle goes as follows: indirect powers (society) prompt Hobbes's social contract, which in turn opens up the private sphere (not of economic necessity, as in Arendt, but of liberty of conscience) of individualism, which undermines the state and so creates the need for the political. For Schmitt, this flows from the essential ambiguity of the Leviathan—both organic and mechanistic, both state and anarcho-social covenant, both Leviathan and Behemoth—which already contains the principle of its own destruction. Arendt, in contrast, separates these two moments: for her the Leviathan is simply a social contract, one whose effects can and should be modified through the mutual compact or constitution.

The difference between Arendt and Schmitt therefore lies not in the direction of flow, but in the point at which they hope to arrest it. Schmitt hopes to stop the process at the very beginning, before individual feeling is privatized; Arendt, at the very end, before public contestation produces social conformity. Schmitt's concern is primarily with the re-creation of the political against the social; Arendt's, with the need to prevent the political from degenerating into the social. Together they mark the points between which the political might be located—not in either of the contracts themselves but rather in the space between the social contract and the political one, after government has transformed social feelings into individual ones, and before any constitution or mutual association has begun to change them back again.

Yet this interval, too, is only a stage on the route back to the social. As in Calhoun's thought experiment, every attempt to renounce the social seems to lead back inexorably toward it—not to the point of departure, but to an analogous situation which presupposes the political intervention that preceded it. The "forces of society" in the late medieval period and those of the nineteenth century are analogous, not equivalent, for the latter developed from and eventually devoured Hobbes's absolutist state; the disappearance of worldly space in eighteenth-century France and in twentieth-century America differs in that the latter was shaped by the American Revolution. In these accounts, the political does not primarily address itself to some previous political moment but both reacts to and forms the social—functioning, in effect, as the *via negativa* of the social, a detour in which the social returns to itself.

Of course, the process is structured in such a way that this description could easily be turned around. We can picture the social as the detour through which the political returns to itself, and this is precisely what those who argue for "the primacy of the political over the social" seek to do.[55] But this approach often relies on two presuppositions: first, that the political precedes the social and the moment of original institution of the social is irreducibly political; second, that the reemergence of the political will be a return to that originary point, with all its contingencies, rather than its recapitulation at another level. If, as has been argued above, it is possible to begin the cycle of the social and the political at any point and con-tinue it without returning to a place of origin, it is difficult to attach signifi-cant weight to the undecidability of a single foundational moment, for each recapitulation is liable to lead farther away from that moment rather than toward it.

Without an a priori commitment to the originary nature of the political, the question of the priority of the social or the political becomes contingent and historical. Which segment of the spiral you follow, then, depends on where you pick up the story. In the case of Arendt and Schmitt there can be little doubt that it is the social which is presupposed and to which the politi-cal returns. But their choice is not an arbitrary one. Despite the fact that its proponents dwell on its archaic or primal role, the political, in the sense that they define it, is exclusively modern in that the social to which the politi-cal responds is specifically that of capitalist modernity. Both the espousal of the political and the political itself appear to be heavily determined: you pick up the story where you discover yourself within it.

Anyone picking up the thread in the early years of the twenty-first century is liable to ask why there is no politics to match the scale and intensity of contemporary global social interaction. But the assumption that every social formation should sustain or generate a political dynamic of commensurate size and power is perhaps itself mistaken. If anything, the social and the political appear to stand in zero-sum relation. The greater the scope of the social, the more limited the sphere of the political. So as the social expands, it becomes "a field of force whose boundary conditions are political," while the political itself recedes to become the smooth edge of striated space.[56]

Notes

1 Carl Schmitt, *The Concept of the Political*, trans. George Schwab (Chicago: University of Chicago Press, 1996), 38.
2 Ibid., 72.
3 Ibid., 57.
4 Émile Durkheim, *The Division of Labor in Society*, trans. W. D. Halls (Basingstoke, UK: Macmillan, 1984), 213.
5 Schmitt, *Concept of the Political*, 79.
6 Ibid., 70.
7 Ibid., 28, 71.
8 Carl Schmitt, "Strong State and Sound Economy: An Address to Business Leaders," in *Carl Schmitt and Authoritarian Liberalism*, ed. Renato Cristi (Cardiff: University of Wales Press, 1998), 224–25; Schmitt's emphasis.
9 Hannah Arendt, *The Human Condition* (Chicago: University of Chicago Press, 1998), 28.

10 Ibid., 33.

11 "Each time we leave the protective four walls of our private homes and cross over the threshold into the public world, we enter first, not the political realm of equality, but the social sphere." Hannah Arendt, "Reflections on Little Rock," in *The Portable Hannah Arendt*, ed. Peter Baehr (New York: Pengion, 2000), 237.

12 Arendt, *Human Condition*, 45.

13 Ibid., 43.

14 Ibid., 52–53.

15 Ibid., 39.

16 Ibid., 41.

17 Emily Hauptman, "A Local History of the Political," *Political Theory* 32 (2004): 36.

18 Slavoj Žižek, *For They Know Not What They Do* (London: Verso, 1991), 193.

19 Hannah Arendt, *On Revolution* (London: Penguin, 1990), 169–71.

20 John C. Calhoun, *Works*, vol. 1 (New York: D. Appleton and Co., 1851–56), 1.

21 Ibid., 4.

22 Ibid., 5–6.

23 Ibid., 49.

24 Ibid., 66.

25 Ibid., 69.

26 Ibid., 47–48.

27 Ibid., 69–70.

28 Ibid., 47.

29 Ibid., 113.

30 If, as Daniel Webster (Calhoun's opponent in the nullification debate) had claimed, individual citizens had formed the "United States," then "the individuals of the several States, thus fused, as it were, into one general mass, would be united *socially*, and not *politically*" (ibid., 122).

31 Ibid., 35.

32 Webster complained that Calhoun's argument amounted to someone saying: "Such is my opinion, and my opinion shall be my law, and I will support it by my own strong hand. I denounce the law; I declare it unconstitutional; that is enough; it shall not be executed." Daniel Webster, "1833, Feb. 16. Webster's Reply to Calhoun," in *Constitutional Doctrines of Webster, Hayne, and Calhoun* (New York: A. Lovell and Co., 1896), 37.

33 Calhoun, *Works*, 1:6.

34 Arendt, *On Revolution*, 165.

35 Ibid., 68.

36 Ibid., 164.

37 "The magic of compassion was that it opened the heart of the sufferer to the sufferings of others, whereby it established and confirmed the 'natural' bond between men." Ibid., 81.

38 Ibid., 86.

39 Ibid., 64.

40 Ibid., 164.

41 See Hanna Fenichel Pitkin, *The Attack of the Blob: Hannah Arendt's Concept of the Social* (Chicago: University of Chicago Press, 1998).

42 "I know of no country where there is so little independence of mind and real freedom

of discussion as in America." Alexis de Tocqueville, *Democracy in America* (Ware, UK: Wordsworth, 1998), 103.

43 Arendt, "Little Rock," 238.

44 Arendt, *On Revolution*, 64.

45 Carl Schmitt, *The Leviathan in the State Theory of Thomas Hobbes: Meaning and Failure of a Political Symbol*, trans. George Schwab (Westport, CT: Greenwood, 1996), 10. See also Gopal Balakrishnan, *The Enemy: An Intellectual Portrait of Carl Schmitt* (London: Verso, 2000), 209–20.

46 Ibid., 31–33.

47 Ibid., 61.

48 Ibid., 73.

49 Ibid., 62.

50 Ibid., 35.

51 Plato, *Republic*, book 9, 588.

52 Plato, *Republic*, book 6, 493.

53 It is this image, for example, that lies behind Alexander Hamilton's reported remark to Thomas Jefferson: "Your people, sir, is a great beast." Quoted in David S. Muzzey, *An American History* (Boston: Ginn, 1911), 192. It also informs Arendt's observation that the "French concept of *le peuple* has carried, from its beginning, the connotation of a multi-headed monster, a mass that moves as one body and acts as though possessed by one will." Arendt, *On Revolution*, 94. In the work of Simone Weil, the Great Beast functions as a symbol of both the power of the social and, fused with the imagery of Christian apocalyptic, the eschatological adversary, the idolatrous Babylon. Simone Weil, "The Great Beast," in *Simone Weil: An Anthology* (London: Virago, 1986), 141–46.

54 Sir Thomas Browne, *The Major Works* (London: Penguin, 1977), 134.

55 Ernesto Laclau, *New Reflections on the Revolution of Our Time* (London: Verso, 1990), 33.

56 Cf. Willard Van Orman Quine, *From a Logical Point of View* (Cambridge, MA: Harvard University Press, 1980), 42; see also Malcolm Bull, "Smooth Politics," in *Empire's New Clothes: Reading Hardt and Negri*, ed. Paul Passavant and Jodi Dean (New York: Routledge, 2004), 217–30.

Fredric Jameson

Rousseau and Contradiction

The philosopher of the general will is not likely to be the favorite political thinker of an age of microgroups and new social movements, which, along with so many other political philosophizers nourished by the classics, he would have considered to be so many "factions." So within the history of the twentieth century he is most likely to have been characterized as totalitarian. But there are other Rousseaus, and indeed other Jean-Jacques: Sparta may have been totalitarian (in some rather different and unique way), but the simple and hardy pastoral villages of which Rousseau also dreamed are perhaps rather to be described as regressive; and as for the famous "state of nature" (so often wildly misconstrued), it is better to follow Claude Lévi-Strauss in considering it a contribution—the first and the most glorious!—to the scarcely even nascent discipline of anthropology.[1]

Meanwhile, Rousseau's self-portrait was so decisive in fixing an image of his subjectivity for all time—and like any image, it is only that, a construction—that we may well have some difficulty in taking seriously the thinking of an autodidact, a dreamer, a masturbator, a paranoid, and a pretentious imitator of antiquity. I want

The *South Atlantic Quarterly* 104:4, Fall 2005.
Copyright © 2005 by Duke University Press.

to argue that we can learn much that is useful about thinking and reasoning politically from Rousseau, without in any way having to endorse his ideas or opinions. Indeed, I see that as the purpose of any reconsideration of political philosophy: namely, to identify the form of genuine political thinking, whatever its content, in such a way that we can rigorously separate the political text from expressions of mere opinion or ideology. This is, to be sure, not a very satisfying approach for those—and I admire them—who feel that our duty and our vocation as intellectuals lies in the identification and denunciation of right-wing or even liberal positions. My own skepticism and pessimism are, however, so all-encompassing as to make me feel that such an approach has little chance of teaching us anything new or surprising.

So I will not unmask or denounce Rousseau today, although it is worth pointing out how uneasy his critics have always been, how ambiguous their judgments, how unsettled a place he continues to occupy in literary or philosophical history. He has been as embarrassing for the Marxists—was he not some kind of predecessor?—as for the fascists or the liberals: only Jacobin republicans have given him pride of place in their national pantheon. So perhaps the paranoid Jean-Jacques was right after all, and his greatest achievement was to have been loathed and attacked by all sides.

After that, it always comes as a shock to remember those slashing formulas by which Rousseau stunned the age and planted a dagger in its heart: "Man is born free, and everywhere he is in chains."[2] "The first man who, having enclosed a piece of ground, to whom it occurred to say, this is mine, and found people sufficiently simple to believe him, was the true founder of civil society."[3] These astonishing sentences, which only Rousseau could write, on the mode of declamation, are, it should be noted, temporal in their ambition: they aim to isolate, identify, and make dramatically visible not so much a fundamental Event as a fundamental change. That change can also be said to be the beginning of history, or, what is for Rousseau the same thing, the beginning of civilization: the beginning of something which, for him, and for Lévi-Strauss following him, had accidental causes and need never have happened in the first place. And indeed, we know today that it did take a very long time to happen: perhaps hundreds of thousands of years, compared to which our own history and civilization is a mere flash in the pan. Is a society without the state also a society without politics? In that case, it is the beginning of the political which is also at stake here; and I will not review the literature which, from the 1960s on, from Pierre Clastres to Michael Mann, has sought to solve the riddle and answer the question of the mechanisms whereby human beings were able to avoid state power for so long. In a way, Rousseau is less interested in solving the problem than in posing and articulating it: but we'll come to that distinction in a moment. And perhaps I should also add a historical observation—that the classical tradition, from Plato to More, from Locke to Fourier, always firmly identified the coming into being of so-called civilization with the coming into being of private property; but in the contemporary period, and not least in the modern Marxist tradition, civilization has been associated with power, and with state power at that, rather than with property and private ownership. It is, on my view, a momentous distinction, and ought to have its relevance in the definition for us today of the political.

I don't want to lose sight of Rousseau, however, and particularly of his texts, of his sentences, which must somehow for us today be inseparable from his thinking, and offer a more reliable object of study than those philosophical positions and ideas in which only idealists still believe. I would therefore want to say that the analysis of Rousseau's political thinking must somehow be inseparable from the analysis of his style: except for the palpable fact that with Rousseau we have to do, not with style—that modern, personal, idiosyncratic appropriation and production of language—but rather with rhetoric, and with the clumsy and grandiloquent imitation of ancient rhetoric at that. Who does not hear the oratorical accents of Rousseau's declamations, of his great rhetorical periods and perorations, of the grandiloquent egotism with which the speaker announces his intent to take a stand on all the great problems of the age? This eloquence is not personal; indeed, the only personal feature of this language is the awkwardness and self-consciousness of the classical imitation, while Rousseau's "ideas"— virtue, freedom, Sparta, self-sufficiency, physical hardiness, etc.—are the baggage the classical or rhetorical sentence carries within itself. Another generation or two, and all this will be swept away by Romanticism.

But now I need to say what is truly original, historically original, with Rousseau; and I suppose that in the history of ideas it bears the name of Enlightenment or Reason or one of those periodizing labels that have little enough to do with texts and a lot more with ideology and opinion in their most general sense, or with those peculiar fictive entities called "values." Thus Enlightenment has something negative to do with religion and superstition; Reason is another word for secularization; and so forth. What I have in mind is not Reason, however, but reasoning; and when we look at it more closely, we may find ourselves drawing closer to Rousseau's own opinion: namely, that he has little enough in common with the other *philosophes*.

Let's look at a specific passage: that climactic moment in the *Second Dis-*

course when he introduces the concept of *perfectibility*. It is an odd word for Rousseau to use; or rather it functions as something like camouflage, or a ruse, for his intellectual public who all presumably have a firm belief in human progress. But it is not the ideas—we already know, from the position of the *Second Discourse* itself, that Rousseau is far from believing in perfectibility in any conventional sense—that we need to analyze; it is rather his reasoning's shape and the sequence of ideas into which it is inserted that offer a more significant clue to everything unique and peculiar about Rousseau.

In a first mention, indeed, Rousseau endorses the commonplace view that it is perfectibility that distinguishes human beings from animals. At that point, we are astonished by a perverse and characteristic association of ideas, for in the next sentence Rousseau asks: "Why is man alone liable to become imbecile?"[4] He neither lists the positive achievements that would normally document the claim of perfectibility nor narrates the stages whereby "man" rises from an animal condition to an ever more perfected state. It is true that he will tell that story later on, but for a rather different, we may even say Lévi-Straussian, purpose; namely, to show that history and what we call civilization need never have taken place; that what we call perfectibility is the result of a series of accidents, that "perfectibility, the social virtues, and the other faculties which natural man had received in potentiality could never develop by themselves, that in order to do so they needed the fortuitous concatenation of several foreign causes which might never have arisen and without which he would eternally have remained in his primitive condition.[5] But I read this somewhat differently than Lévi-Strauss does (although the latter remains the appropriate reference) and will come back to this difference shortly.

For the moment, and returning to the initial passage already quoted, in which Rousseau associates man's "perfectibility" with his devolution into old age and senility, I want to observe that in his reflection on the matter, Rousseau characteristically isolates the form rather than the content of the idea of "perfectibility." He sets aside the positive valence of the latter, retaining only the formal identity of perfectibility with change or history. And this is all the more astonishing inasmuch as the ethical judgment, the eudaimonic framework in which notions of attraction and repulsion, pleasure and pain, good and bad, come into play—this framework will be the indispensable framework of the *Second Discourse* as a whole, which reaches the well-known conclusion that civilization and civil society are harmful states

which generate class inequalities. What then is this faculty of judgment sus-
pended in the passage that immediately concerns us, to the point where
not even the paradoxical effect of illustrating perfectibility with senility is
allowed to distract us? The fact is that Rousseau is not interested in what will
later on (in part 2) be his fundamental conclusion; he is not here interested
in judgment or content; rather, he is intent on observing the abstract form
of historical change itself. And it is at this point that I would wish to specify
Lévi-Strauss's interpretation more sharply, yet very much in his spirit. For
it seems to me that here Rousseau anticipates that great discovery which
remains associated with Lévi-Strauss's name and work, namely, the distinction between the synchronic and the diachronic. The diachronic—change
and history—is neither meaningful nor thinkable: it is the result of a series
of accidents. Only the synchronic—here the famous "state of nature"—is
thinkable and meaningful; only the synchronic has genuine content, while
the diachronic is an abstract sequence of events whose content or meaning
is variable and lacks necessity. Clearly enough, this is the point at which
it would be appropriate to raise the issue of narrative as such—the issue
of causalities, of telling the story of this sequence of meaningless events,
or indeed (in Lévi-Strauss's system) of transforming such a sequence into
a narrative myth, in which meaning is generated by borrowing terms and
oppositions from the synchronic as such.

But that is not my topic here, for I have only wanted to use this first
brief passage in order to demonstrate the way in which Rousseau is pre-
pared to follow his own thinking into the unthinkable. Let me now offer a
much larger and more dramatic illustration of this process, in which confidence in reasoning leads the thinker on fearlessly into a cul-de-sac. It is the
famous digression on the origin of language (not to be confused with Rousseau's later and equally unsuccessful attempt to confront this problem, in
a fragment henceforth rendered famous by Jacques Derrida's commentary
in *Grammatology*, but which exceeds the discussion in the *Second Discourse*
by raising the additional issues of writing, climate, music, and the like).

What the proportionally considerable digression in the *Second Discourse*
offers is the astonishing spectacle of a reasoning so self-punishing in the
demands it makes on itself that it renders the problem insoluble and in
effect incapacitates itself: "Let me be allowed briefly to consider the per-
plexities regarding the origin of Languages."[6] The digression is an enlargement of the discussion of the emergence of thinking and abstract ideas
among those "natural beings" who only know needs and passions and do not

as yet think any more than they speak. I summarize the various obstacles which Rousseau places in the way of the thinking the emergence of language: (1) why language should have been necessary in the first place; (2) how abstract meanings could ever have been communicated; (3) how the cry as such could have been domesticated and articulated in such a way as to serve the needs of everyday life; (4) how propositions and sentences could have emerged from that first form of language which was the individual word; (5) how general terms could have emerged from names of individual things; (6) a more concentrated summary of all of the above, involving the distinction between the intellect and the imagination (this moment will also be the point of departure for Lévi-Strauss's theory of *pensée sauvage*):

> Hence one has to state propositions, hence one has to speak in order to have general ideas: for as soon as the imagination stops, the mind can proceed only by means of discourse. If, then, the first Inventors could give names only to the ideas they already had, it follows that the first substantives could never have been anything but proper names. (150/148)[7]

At this point Rousseau breaks it off: "by means which I cannot conceive," "I pause after these first steps," "as for myself, frightened by the increasing difficulties, and convinced of the almost demonstrated impossibility that Languages could have arisen and been established by purely humans means, I leave to anyone who wishes to undertake it the discussion of this difficult problem"; and finally: "quoiqu'il en soit de ces origines"—"whatever may be the case regarding these origins" . . .

Rousseau has talked himself out of his own illustration; by the peculiar power of the reasoning proper to him, and which is at present our object of study, he has so effectively multiplied the problems involved in thinking the origin of languages that he has proven to his own satisfaction that they could not have come into being in the first place! It is no doubt a comic spectacle, akin to being too smart for your own good. But there is something salutary in the shock as well, and something temporally perverse and retroactive, with a kind of family likeness to Freud's *Nachträglichkeit*. The point is that the event to be modeled has already happened; we are in the process of foretelling the past, predicting what already exists behind us, as it were framing a guilty man. And the shock lies in the fact that the most airtight reasoning proves that it can never have happened in the first place. Thus, in the gap between our reasoning and the facts, a mystery suddenly emerges fully blown, which is the mystery of time and of historicity, the mystery of the Event itself, as a scandal and a stumbling block. The apparent discovery that we cannot think the diachronic does not abolish history, nor, as Lévi-Strauss believed, does it discredit historical thought: on the contrary, it establishes history for the first time in all its arresting freshness and unpredictability. The flight of the owl returns upon the world of daylight to confer a grisly clarity upon it, in which every leaf stands out without a shadow.

This is then an altogether remarkable outcome, which surely does not demonstrate the weakness of Rousseau's capacity for thought and his philosophical abilities so much as it exhibits their very power and his frightening resolve to follow his own reasoning wherever it leads him—a peculiar enough character trait to find in so inveterate a daydreamer and fantasist.

I see several ways of interpreting this peculiarity. One will predictably be the reading of Lévi-Strauss, on which we have already touched several times, and which again rehearses the opposition between the synchronic and the diachronic. But in the present context this opposition takes on unusual content. First of all, we confront the obvious fact that no one ever has accounted for the origins of language: this has to do at least in part with the absence of anthropological data (but it should be noted that Rousseau himself takes into account just such scientific lacunae: "Comparative Anatomy has as yet made too little progress," etc.);[8] and the linguistic paradox is given yet another twist by virtue of this very absence, which results from the necessary non-existence of writing in such an early period. But Lévi-Strauss's position is not merely an agonistic one: he affirms that language could never have come into being piecemeal, gradually, bit by bit (beginning with the cry and the gesture, and slowly passing into articulated sounds, and so forth). Rather, as a synchronic system, language had to appear all at once, complete and fully developed—a requirement that may well make the origins of language even more unthinkable than they were in Rousseau.

But we may also come at this from the vantage point of another reader of Rousseau, this time a follower from his own century, for whom the reading of Jean-Jacques was fully as decisive: Immanuel Kant. For was not at least one of Kant's great discoveries the conclusion that the human mind is constitutionally limited in what it can think and in its proper objects? And is this not one of the most dramatic lessons of Rousseau's procedures here—that when making the most rigorous demands on itself, the mind sometimes comes up short against the unthinkable? The conclusion Kant draws from this lesson, indeed, is the impossibility of thinking about origins (the first paralogism in the *Critique of Pure Reason*, or in other words "the antinomy of pure reason": "the world has a beginning in time," "the world has no beginning," etc.).[9] But as with language in Rousseau, this is not exactly a false problem: for clearly enough, like language, the world did have a beginning inasmuch as it exists. What is at stake is not that evident fact, but our capacity to think it in any adequate way.

Yet somehow both these readings (and Rousseau himself) tend to affirm the impossibility, if not of history, then at least of historical thinking. And this is very clearly the consequence Lévi-Strauss draws in his famous polemic with Sartre.[10] I want to suggest a somewhat different conclusion, which will affirm Rousseau's relationship to the then emergent dialectic and to dialectical thinking as such: for it seems to me that what his thinking arrives at, as its momentary terminus, is neither impossibility nor diachronic incoherence, nor is it the antinomy as such, but rather contradiction, the very motor power of the dialectic itself.

But let's now, in conclusion, try to see this at work in an eminently political text, namely *The Social Contract*. Here it is not so much a question of the origin of that bad thing civilization or civil society and its history, as of that second-best thing which is the social contract in its most vigorous and uncorrupted form, as it succeeds the so-called state of nature. The idea of the contract—that is to say, Rousseau's motivation in retheorizing it, since it is itself a very ancient idea—Rousseau's interest in the idea of the contract must be explored in several directions. One—and it is the great originality of this unique text—lies in the production of a new mental category: that of a relationship between the individual and the collective which is neither that of simple homology—the collectivity is simply the individual writ larger, it is a collective subject of some kind—nor that of an aggregate of individuals, a single individual multiplied in such a way that notions of majority, plurality, minority, and so on are ontologically relevant. Indeed, Rousseau wishes to establish something like a radical ontological difference between the individual and the collective whole, without the existence of any mediating groups or instances. Does he succeed in achieving this new category of thought, which would be, if it existed, distinct in form from oppositions like universal and particular or general and individual? The answer has never been clear or definitive, and the negative judgment, that the exclusion of factionalism and intermediate groups is simply totalitarian—an accusation powerfully reinforced by the Jacobin practice of Rousseau's idea—is as plausible as it is contradicted by the text.

For one of the other purposes of *The Social Contract* is to exclude the idea that a people can contract into slavery or voluntarily accept tyranny: the inalienability of freedom then gives content to and poses limits on the consequences of the contract as such, and inscribes the right to rebel in human nature.

But what interests us here, in the present context, is rather the slippage of the idea of the contract. It was designed to identify the deep structure of that social contract which replaced the state of nature—in such a way that disparities between the original contact and an increasingly corrupt modern society are underscored. Here, as always, there is a confusion and an interference between the political and the economic: is the degradation of the modern society the result of private property, as the *Second Discourse* affirms ("whoever first said, this is *mine*"), or is it, as the language of the *Social Contract* seems to imply, a matter of freedom and its loss? This second possibility would seem to be more a cultural or superstructural consequence, a waning of the consciousness of some original freedom, rather than, as with private property, the institution of new kinds of infrastructural constraints. Two rather different "revolutionary" solutions would then be implied by the alternative; but I want to focus on the fact that either seems to imply a solution, that is to say, that the idea of an original contract seems fatally to suggest the possibility of returning to it and of somehow rectifying the present fallen state of society.

In fact, in another part of his mind, Rousseau would seem to be convinced that a revival of the contract is possible only under very specific conditions which in modern times only rarely obtain. *The Project for a Constitution of Corsica*, the *Considerations on the Government of Poland*, and part 3 of the *Social Contract* underscore the unique historical opportunities of these two areas still relatively uncorrupted by "modern society," whose inhabitants still retain something of the vigor and independence of the simpler mountain tribes of ancient Switzerland, say. Indeed, the weakness of Corsica and Poland in the modern world are precisely their social strengths when it comes to a return to the virtues and strengths of an older Spartan state (to be sure, they are quite different weaknesses: in Corsica underdevelopment, in Poland feudal decentralization and Russian oppression). As for the so-called advanced nations of Western Europe, however, they are incorrigible, and no return to societal health or to the original contract is to be fantasized for them. We can already guess, from this pessimism, the presence of that mental operation we have already underscored: an attempt to fantasize, which is at every step interrupted and blocked by a kind of reality principle of the imagination itself, which combines its demands with an insistence on the difficulties of constructing the fantasy in the first place, and finally multiplies them to the point at which it talks itself out of the very possibility of conceiving an optimistic projection altogether.

We do not, however, have to deduce the operation of this characteristic process in Rousseau: we can observe it again in detail at one specific point, namely, that moment in the *Social Contract* when Rousseau describes the inauguration of the contract itself and the agency whereby it is first brought into being. I have already observed that Rousseau's formulations waver between base and superstructure, so to speak: between institutions and cultural habits, between the laws of the city and the practices and daily life of its inhabitants. At his weakest, he makes this hesitation, this alternation, visible as an inconsistency; at his strongest, he insists on the political necessity of uniting the two in a kind of cultural revolution. Meanwhile, and very much in the spirit of the Althusserian reading of the manifesto as a form,[11] he will not be content until he drives his imagination on to the very point of origin itself and confronts the necessity of grasping the agency responsible for the foundation of the new system. This agency is still an individual one, like Machiavelli's prince; and it lies in the past, as a historical act of foundation which is certainly exemplary and perhaps inimitable.

Everyone who has absorbed the atmosphere of neoclassical eighteenth-century political culture and has confronted the inescapable reference to Sparta in it will scarcely be surprised by the looming presence, in this discourse, of Lycurgus, the mythic founder. Plutarch's life then takes its place alongside Plato's *Republic* as one of the fundamental Utopian texts, something like the life of Utopus himself, whose inauguration of the perfect commonwealth is, in More, shrouded in mystery, not least because, like Lycurgus himself, he then seems to have programmed himself out of the system, if not out of history and legend.[12] Meanwhile, Heidegger assures us that the founding of a state is, along with the work of art, the philosophical concept, and the ominously named "essential sacrifice," one of the fundamental places of truth and of the disclosure of being.[13]

Rousseau observes all this with characteristic and we may even say remorseless lucidity. But given his method, as we have just outlined it, he arrives at a somewhat different perspective on the conclusion. We may translate this method into contemporary terms as follows: Rousseau's reasoning is the reconstruction of history in thought. It is neither a historiographic narrative nor a historical representation exactly: something we can verify by comparing that first part of the *Discourse on Inequality*, of which we have already spoken, with the second, in which he attempts to recuperate his losses and paper over the extraordinary train of reasoning of the first with a far more conventional historical story of the stages of the emergence of civil society and class injustice. Rather, it seems to me more appropriate to compare Rousseau's procedure—the reconstruction of historical development by way of presuppositions and preconditions—with what Althusser called "the concrete-in-thought," a nonrepresentational mode which often has surprises in store for us.

Let's follow the process in the case of Rousseau's "reconstruction" of Plutarch's Lycurgus. We are warned of the looming thunderclouds of paradox and antinomy by the opening sentence, which posits the need, in the founder, of "une intelligence supérieure, qui vit toutes les passions des hommes et qui n'en éprouvât aucune."[14] Rousseau is very clear that the transformation of human nature itself, as he says, means the end of the individual and the creation, in his place, of the group itself. Meanwhile, this rare and unusual process requires a very distinctive kind of agency: the lawgiver cannot impose his new constitution either by force or by rank or position. A strict differentiation must be established between conventional rules and their offices and this one: "Si celui qui commande aux hommes ne doit pas commander aux lois, celui qui commande aux lois ne doit pas commander aux hommes."[15] (It would have been worth pausing here to note the emergence in Rousseau of that trope of the dialectical chiasmus which is omnipresent in Marx and which is indeed the sign and symptom of a whole new mode of thinking.)

At any rate, it is clear that the lawgiver, the founder of the state, cannot himself be an individual exactly: it is the inverse and the logical concomitant of the social contract: the people as a whole must function as something more and other than a collection of individuals, while the individual who sets the contract in place must stand outside that collection, and in no way constitute a part of the whole of which he is the godlike cause. Thus, just as the collectivity of the social contract requires a new conceptual category, different in kind from either that of the individual or that of the multiple, so also the founder must be conceptualized in a new way: "Ainsi [concludes Rousseau] l'on trouve à la fois dans l'ouvrage de la legislation deux choses qui semblent incompatibles: une enterprise au-dessus de la force humaine, et pour l'exécuter, une autorité qui n'est rien."[16] Were we to con-

tinue our juxtaposition of Rousseau with the thinking of modern structuralism, we would be inclined to feel that Rousseau has here discovered the
essentials of what Lévi-Strauss calls a myth, namely, a figure which unites
incompatible semes or signifying traits. I would thus conclude that Rousseau has (as with the invention of language) proven that Sparta never was
founded (and, indeed, could never have existed in the first place). But now I
want to draw a further conclusion from this conclusion: that what Rousseau
has discovered here (if he has not indeed invented it) is what will shortly,
in the emergent dialectical tradition, be called a contradiction. Indeed, the
greatness of Rousseau lies precisely in this, to drive his thought on until it
reaches that ultimate limit which is the contradiction, what is incompatible
and ultimately unthinkable. That this has something to do with his fantasy-
production and his inclination toward daydreaming I have already hinted;
and perhaps I can theorize that connection by evoking the reality-principle
within fantasy itself, and the rigorousness with which a certain daydreaming makes demands on itself and attempts to secure the conditions of possibility of its own fantasies and daydreams. At any rate it is that peculiar
rigor which we find here and which impels Rousseau toward the implacable
undoing of his own fantasies in contradiction as such.

Meanwhile, this is no ordinary contradiction, insofar as it has as its object
history and temporality: here, indeed, is the revolutionary vicious circle
which the mystery of the founder and the contradictory myth of Lycurgus
contains within itself:

> Pour qu'un peuple naissant pût gouter les saines maximes de la poli-
> tique et suivre les regles fondamentales de la raison d'état, il fau-
> drait que l'effect pût devenir la cause, que l'espirit social qui doit
> être l'ouvrage de l'institution présidat à l'institution même, et que les
> hommes fussent avant les loix ce quils doivent devenir par elles.[17]

It is an astonishing conclusion, in no way vitiated by the feeble Enlightenment appeal to persuasion and reason by which Rousseau attempts to cut
his Gordian knot and solve his unresolvable problems.

So Rousseau was not only the impossible founder of structuralism; he
was the equally impossible founder of the dialectic itself. He was not only
the discoverer of the tension between synchrony and diachrony; he also
stumbled upon that necessity of the dialectic which is rooted in the historicity of language itself. (I have often, to this effect, quoted the extraordinary footnote in the *Emile* on the relationship between words and modes of

production.)[18] But it would be enough to return to the *Second Discourse* to observe the same dialectical lucidity at work in his frequent identifications of anachronism in the language of his philosophical opponents. What can the word *misery* mean, when applied to the state of nature? he responds to Hobbes;[19] "explain to me what the word *oppression* means" in such a state, he adds;[20] and finally, how could the words *power* and *reputation* have any significance for those people you call "savages"?[21] This is the other face of the opposition between the synchronic and the diachronic; it reflects the secret historicity of this apparently historical and antihistorical opposition—the history revealed by the inapplicability of the elements of our own synchronicity, our own historical system, to a radically different one.

So it is that Rousseau discovers revolution as the unthinkable gap between two systems, the untheorizable break between two distinct synchronicities: perhaps it would be enough to evoke a contemporary rediscovery of that mystery, such as Antonio Negri's notion of constituent power,[22] to glimpse again the positive energies that begin to emanate from this seemingly negative and self-defeating act of thought. I believe that political thinking is to be surprised here, as it were in its moment of emergence, and by that very method of the implacable reduction to conditions of possibility which was Rousseau's own historical invention.

Notes

1   Claude Lévi-Strauss, *Tristes tropiques* (Paris: Plon, 1955), 421.
2   Jean-Jacques Rousseau, "Du contrat social" (the so-called *Social Contract*), in *Oeuvres complètes*, vol. 3 (Paris: Gallimard, 1964), 351. All translations from this work are mine.
3   Jean-Jacques Rousseau, "Sur l'origine de l'inégalité" (the so-called *Second Discourse*), in ibid., 164. English translations from this text are from Rousseau, *The Discourses and Other Political Writings*, ed./trans. Victor Gourevitch (New York: Cambridge University Press, 1997), 164.
4   Ibid., 142 (French, *Oeuvres complètes*, 3:142).
5   Ibid., 162 (French, *Oeuvres complètes*, 3:165).
6   Ibid., 145 (French, *Oeuvres complètes*, 3:146).
7   Ibid., 148 (French, *Oeuvres complètes*, 3:150).
8   Ibid., 134 (French, *Oeuvres complètes*, 3:134).
9   Immanuel Kant, *Critique of Pure Reason* (New York: Cambridge University Press, 1997), 470–71.
10 Claude Lévi-Strauss, *La Pensée sauvage* (Paris: Plon, 1962), 336.
11 Louis Althusser, "Machiavel et nous," in *Ecrits philosophiques et politiques*, vol. 2 (Paris: Stock, 1995).
12 Plutarch, "Lycurgus," in *Lives of the Noble Grecians and Romans* (New York: Random House, n.d.), 49–74.

13   Martin Heidegger, "Origin of the Work of Art," in *Philosophies of Art and Beauty*, ed.
      A. Hofstadter and R. Kuhns (New York: Random House, 1964), 685.

14   "A superior intelligence, capable of contemplating all human passions without feeling
      any of them" ("Du contrat social," 381).

15   "If he who has authority over men should have no authority over the law, he who has
      authority over the law should not have authority over men" (ibid., 382).

16   "We thus find two seemingly incompatible things in the work of legislation: an enter-
      prise beyond all human powers, and, for its execution, an authority which is nothing"
      (ibid., 383).

17   "In order for an emergent people to enjoy the healthy maxims of politics and to follow
      the fundamental rules of the state's reason [the untranslatable *raison d'état*], it would be
      necessary for the effect to become the cause, and for the social spirit which was to have
      resulted from this institutionalization to have presided over the founding of the institu-
      tion itself, in other words, for men to have been before law what they were to become by
      virtue of its existence" (ibid., 383).

18   Jean-Jacques Rousseau, "Emile," in *Oeuvres complètes*, vol. 4 (Paris: Gallimard, 1969), 345
      note: "J'ai fait cent fois réfléxion en écrivant qu'il est impossible dans un long ouvrage de
      donner toujours les mêmes sens aux mêmes mots. Il n'y a point de langue assez riche
      pour fournir autant de termes, de tours et de phrases que nos idées peuvent avoir de modi-
      fications. La méthode de définir tous les termes et de substituer sans cesse la definition
      à la place du défini est belle mais impraticable, car comment éviter le cercle? Les defini-
      tions pourroient être bonnes si l'on n'employoit pas des mots pour les faire. Malgré cela,
      je suis persuadé qu'on peut être clair, même dans la pauvreté de nôtre langue; non pas
      en donnant toujours les mêmes acceptations aux mêmes mots, mais en faisant en sorte,
      autant de fois qu'on employe chaque mot, que l'acceptation qu'on lui donne soit suffisa-
      ment determinée par les idées qui s'y rapportent, et que chaque période où ce mot se
      trouve lui serve, pour ainsi dire, de definition. Tantôt je dis que les enfans sont incapables
      de raisonnement, et tantôt je les fais raisoner avec assez de finesse; je ne crois pas en
      cela me contredire dans mes idées, mais je ne puis disconvenir que je ne me contredise
      souvent dans mes expressions."

19   Rousseau, *Second Discourse*, in *The Discourses and Other Political Writings*, 150 (French,
      Oeuvres complètes, 3:152).

20   Ibid., 158 (French, *Oeuvres complètes*, 3:161).

21   Ibid., 187 (French, *Oeuvres complètes*, 3:193).

22   Antonio Negri, *Insurgencies* (Minneapolis: University of Minnesota Press, 1999).

Stathis Kouvélakis

The Marxian Critique of Citizenship:
For a Rereading of *On the Jewish Question*

Marx's *On the Jewish Question* (*Zur Judenfrage*) is one of those texts that perfectly illustrate Hegel's famous adage that "what is well known is, precisely because it is well known, generally unknown."[1] There are at least two reasons for *On the Jewish Question*'s paradoxical popularity: first, it has fed an overabundant and (with rare exceptions) confused debate on Marx's supposed "anti-Semitism" and second, as if to accent this "heretical" quality, it has been passed down to posterity as announcing all "Marxist totalitarianisms," due to its radical critique of "the rights of man."

In what follows, I will not undertake a detailed exegesis of this text, which is short but particularly dense and rich. More particularly, I deliberately will leave aside all that pertains to the political and religious *stricto sensu* (including the Marxian vision or, rather, category of Judaism as it appears in this text)[2] and will content myself with a few remarks on the second aspect: the Marxian critique of "the rights of man and of the citizen." This aspect is particularly scandalous today, after the end of "totalitarianisms," that is, after the defeat of the twentieth-century revolutions. In this conjuncture, the vocabulary

The *South Atlantic Quarterly* 104:4, Fall 2005.

and the juridico-political category of "citizenship" and, with the latter, political liberalism (in its multiple and often competing versions, whether from "the Right" or "the Left"), seem to form the final horizon of politics. For we must not avoid the question; there is indeed in Marx a radical critique of citizenship defined as a specific moment that dictates the equality and freedom of individuals as bearers of rights and rightful subjects. The emancipation promised by the project of communist revolution as Marx conceives it cannot be expressed in the language of citizenship, of right or rights. Socialism or communism cannot be categorized as and cannot result from an accumulation of rights or from an extension of citizenship, even if the latter is posed as "social citizenship."

So, given the judgment of our day, should we resolve ourselves to cast aside the critique formulated by the socialist and communist tradition, and especially by Marx, of citizenship and of right? The cause I will plead here is that Marx has a right to have his case reexamined before he is definitively condemned. It seems to me that his radical critique of citizenship, his effort to think modern politics—and particularly that modern politics par excellence, *revolutionary* politics—outside the figures of right, should be taken seriously, especially today, before it is consigned to the oubliette of history.

I will begin by specifying that, in the text in question, Marx does not aim to treat systematically the question of citizenship or of the rights of man but to respond to Bruno Bauer, and particularly to his work *Die Judenfrage*.[3] Here Bauer continues, with customary ultraradical phraseology, his battle against the German-Christian state of his time in terms that, according to Marx, remain in fact theological, internal to the very state Bauer claims to combat. Bauer thus misses the content of both "political emancipation," as delivered by the Revolution of 1789, and "human emancipation," which, Marx concludes in the two texts included in the *Deutsch-Französische Jahrbücher*,[4] had become the horizon of a *new* revolution. Marx thus undertakes to clarify the contents of this distinction, particularly with the goal of dissipating Bauer's illusions with respect to what is meant by the advent of the modern political state, which, for Bauer, promises the liberation of all religious consciousness. To this end, Marx turns to the most advanced or "pure" case of the liberal democratic state, of which the United States is a model. Marx shows that, despite its rupture with the Old Regime, the modern state retains something of the former's transcendence, in an of course secularized form. He also demonstrates that this transcendence is expressed in a juridical universalism, which is abstract and truncated, blind to its own presuppositions and impotent to resolve the questions it poses. The critique of the figure of the citizen, and the necessity of its "overtaking" or "abolition" (*Aufhebung*) in the perspective of the new revolution, condenses the ensemble of Marx's argument, which we will approach from a threefold point of view: the anthropological foundation of the utterances (*énoncés*) of citizenship, the "abstract" character of their form, and the status of right circumscribed herein.

The Anthropological Presupposition of the Rights of Man

According to Marx's well-known dictum, the rights of man, insofar as they are *distinguished* from the rights of the citizen, are those of the "*member of civil society*, i.e., the rights of egotistic man, of man separated from other men and from the community."[5] Marx thus examines the four "natural and imprescriptible" rights as they are articulated in "the most radical" version of the Declaration of the Rights of Man and of the Citizen, that of 1793, to wit equality, liberty, security, and property. He shows that all come back to property,[6] of which they serve as metaphors and whose free enjoyment they aim, in turn, to guarantee. "Natural" rights are conceived on the model of the individual-monad, ideally self-sufficient and motivated by the unlimited desire to satisfy personal needs, what C. B. MacPherson designates as "possessive [or proprietary] individualism."

Often considered to be a moral critique, due to its denunciation (quite banal for the time) of the "egotism" of bourgeois society, Marx's argument rests on the following: that this anthropological figure of man-as-property-owner results from an exclusion, from a primordial separation (from the point of view of a "synchronic" analysis of bourgeois society, for the rest of the text will strive precisely to reconstitute its genesis) between man and his "generic essence" (*Gattungswesen*), that is, man considered in constitutive multiplicity of his relations with other men and with social activities. This concept, which has clear Feuerbachian overtones, Marx takes up only to transform it (to "Hegelianize" or "historicize" it, let's say, to make a long story short) in an essentially *reactive* sense. The "generic essence" must be understood above all as a *critical machine* directed against the abstract universalism of rights, which it shows is unable to determine the conditions, and substantial content, of freedom. Indeed, it is the illusion of an "original," and of course final, "independence"[7] of man-as-property-owner (via "natural rights," whose "conservation" the political association of citi-

zens is called on to guarantee), that is targeted here, to the extent it pro-
hibits us from considering the effective conditions of production of a common liberty: "This individual liberty and its application form the basis of
civil society. It makes every man see in other men not the *realisation* of his
own freedom, but the *barrier* to it."[8] This "generic life" is thus in no way
"natural";[9] on the contrary, it is "egotistic man" in bourgeois society who
retrogrades to the rank of "*natural* object," precisely in the sense that, separated from social mediation, he is nothing more than the "*passive* result
of the dissolved society, . . . an object of *immediate certainty*."[10] Here we
can glimpse, but only in intaglio, the meaning of the emancipation of this
atomized individual of bourgeois society who, by reuniting with his generic
essence, makes possible the social "recognition" and "organisation" of his
"social force" in his "particular work," in his "particular situation," to borrow
the formulations of Marx's text.[11] In this framework, it should be stressed,
the "abstract citizen" is not purely and simply eliminated; he is reabsorbed
into the real individual man; he ceases to exist as transcendental double, as
reality separated from social as well as individual life, which is henceforth
reconstructed in the immanence of its mediations.

Reticent to make more explicit the determinations of this "generic life"
that succeeds bourgeois society, therein faithful to his fundamentally anti-
utopian stance, Marx is more committed to showing how the very text of
the Declaration is haunted by the hidden face of the abstract universalism
that it proclaims. What is excluded in the constitutive moment of bourgeois
society, "generic life," will return, but in "alienated" form (in inverted projection, imaginarily mastering its creators), in the "idealism" of the community of citizens, which will renew the originary separation in the form
of a multiplicity of "concrete" exclusions. In *On the Jewish Question*, Marx
goes no further. But he says enough for us to decipher the functioning of
the utterances of abstract universalism. For if the "man" of the Declaration of the Rights of Man and of the Citizen is the property owner, it follows that the unpropertied person is revealed to be, logically, a bit less of
a "man." To put it another way, if all men are born and remain free and
equal before the law, if the citizen can only be that particular man, the question of citizenship, and of access to it, becomes: Who, or rather what, is
a man? Is an unpropertied person a "man," in the full sense of the term?
Is a woman a "man"? Is a slave or a colonized person a "man"? We know
that the founding fathers of liberalism, in impressive unanimity, answered
these questions in the negative.[12] Locke subsumes the black slave under

the category of merchandise, next to the horse. He considers the laboring class, and all those who find themselves excluded (even if only temporarily, as in the case of a salaried worker engaged in a contractual relationship) from the ownership of themselves as well as from the possibility of accumulating goods, to be incapable of living a rational life and, naturally, of having access to active citizenship.[13] We know that early on, the figures of the slave and of the proletarian were linked, that one rubbed off on the other, especially in the representation of the proletariat as a race distinct from that of the masters, a vision that was extraordinarily popular during the entire nineteenth century. Even Emmanuel Sieyès, author of the most famous political text of the French Revolution, speaks of "the majority of men" as "work machines" and "bipedal instruments."[14] Benjamin Constant, one of the favorite authors of today's sycophants of neoliberalism, compared unpropertied people, the "immense majority," as he stressed, to minors, who will "always be deprived of leisure, an indispensable condition for the acquisition of enlightenment."[15] Alongside the proletarians, slaves, and other representatives of a subaltern humanity, women must not be forgotten. Their "natural" equality (as members of a same "human kind") immediately confronts the insurmountable sexual "difference," identified as a "difference" of "rationality" (at least from the point of view of its practical exercise) that legitimates their exclusion from citizenship and their relegation to the "domestic" or "private" space.[16]

I will stop here an enumeration that could quickly grow tiresome: it is clear that the abstract universalism of rights rests on an anthropological figure that defines the subjects of these rights and that this figure functions according to a "principle of hidden exclusion," to borrow the words of André Tosel.[17] The *égaliberté* that exists in principle among "men" in no way prevents there being an internal hierarchization of their humanity, provided that no obstacle of "nature," that is, of birth,[18] forbids a priori the passage from one degree to another, as, for example, Kant has demonstrated.[19]

Of course, one could counter that it is precisely through the reiteration of these abstract universalist utterances that the exclusions in question "gradually" have been overcome, even if only partially, and that the effectivity characteristic of these utterances, inseparable in this sense from the internal tension that results from their specifically "abstract" character,[20] has been deployed. Of course, but we must recall that this has been anything but a linear process, that long and arduous struggles have been required, and that, as a result (as we will see later), the "reiteration" of "abstract" utterances must itself be seen more as their *transformation* than as their sheer repetition. To speak only of suffrage and electability, the postrevolutionary period, which in France followed the Declaration of the Rights of Man and the emergence of citizenship, saw not an enlargement but, on the contrary, a significant *restriction* of the right to vote,[21] both for unpropertied people (local or general assemblies of the "Estates," especially the Third, had been elected by nearly universal male suffrage) and for women (some women, especially among the nobility, had had the right to seats in these assemblies), since the Constituent Assembly quickly installed a system of suffrage that was strictly masculine and based on a franchise restricted to property-holders. The domination of proprietary liberalism (excepting the brief interlude of the Jacobin Republic) was not a simple, more or less residual or *arrière-garde* "resistance" but the unleashing of a formidable movement of "disemancipation"[22] through the imposition of the figures of "passive citizenship" on unpropertied people and women and the frenetic pursuit of colonial and slaveholding barbarism.

As for the struggles that managed to bring down at least a few of the exclusions and separations under discussion, they only succeeded when they took aim at their anthropological blind spot and at their constitutive abstraction: by revealing as "political," and even as politics' contents par excellence, those "simple component parts" of civil life whose "political character" the "political revolution" had abolished, making them into simple "social" differences.[23] In this way, these struggles have also revealed the abstract universal for what it is, a barely veiled *particularism*, contaminated by the very "particular" that it excludes from its field, and which, in turn, is shown to be the true "universal." The more that the universal perseveres in its abstraction, the more it is revealed to be the particularism of white, male, colonizing property owners,[24] while the intrusion of "particularisms," or of "corporatisms" (of proletarians, of colonized peoples, of women), is shown to bear effective universality.[25]

Citizenship and the Political State as Abstractions

No doubt carried away by the brilliance of Marx's formulations, commentators have been very loquacious in general about the text's religious metaphors, especially when Marx poses the truth of the schism imposed by political emancipation between, on the one hand, a civil-bourgeois society devoted to the pursuit of particular interests and, on the other, a state that guarantees égaliberté to all citizens, whatever their position within the said civil-bourgeois society. And yet, contrary to the mystification conveyed by the state, which claims that the citizen is the truth of the man, the reverse is true, according to Marx: "This *man*, the member of civil society, is thus the basis, the precondition, of the *political* state."[26] This amounts to saying, turned around, that the citizen, the ideality proclaimed by the Declaration, is the projection of profane man, devoted to the materialism of bourgeois society, who thenceforth appears as the natural man. Society reproduces the Heaven/Earth duality that characterizes Christianity (the bearer, and even "inventor" of universalism, thanks to the figure of Paul). Politics, the kind defined by the abstraction of the citizen, is then revealed to be the true religion, the secularized transcendence, of modern society.

But this is not what is essential. Instead, what this notion of abstraction highlights above all is that the "political revolution"—the very one that constitutes, "by *one and the same act*," the political state and the atomized individuals who are qualified as citizens of right—"resolves" "civil life into its component parts, without *revolutionising* these components themselves or subjecting them to criticism."[27] And this is true because, as Marx continues, these elements are the "*basis of its existence*," but a basis that it, precisely, abstracts to constitute the political state.[28] That state is thus incapable of acting on the socioeconomic presuppositions that appear to it thenceforth as a natural reality, as a "precondition not requiring further substantiation."[29] The state claims to dominate, and even transcend, this reality even though the state is in fact dominated by it and condemned to reproduce its constitutive separations.

This, according to Marx, is in any case the solution to the "enigma of the Terror," that is, the limits of the Jacobin-Robespierrian effort to resolve the antagonism of bourgeois society (which, let us not forget, was considered the model to follow by the great majority of revolutionary currents of his era and even after, especially those inspired by Gracchus Babeuf). It is precisely because the objectives of the Jacobin leadership went beyond abstraction and simply juridical equality that they collided, in the most exacerbated fashion, with the limits of a politics cut off from its conditions, mobilizing all its energy in an effort to act on these conditions from a position of irreducible *exteriority*.[30] Out of the Jacobin failure, reconsidered in its full amplitude, to carry the movement for political emancipation beyond itself arises then the need for a new emancipatory horizon, without which society will regress into ineffective, historically obsolete forms of universality.

This is why what is habitually designated as "the expansion of citizen-ship," as "the political emancipation" of those who have been excluded (or at least a significant portion thereof: we are still waiting for civil rights to be extended to that part of the proletariat designated, or rather "reified," as "immigrants") does not mean a simple broadening of "rights" but a pro-found transformation of the relations between the political and the non-political, the "private" and the "public."[31] The access of working-class people (men only at first) to suffrage is indissociable from the (very partial) pro-cess of "decommodification" of their status as "force of labor," of recognition of the workplace as a "political" place (or at least as a legitimate place for the collective organization of working-class people), and even of a kind of "socialization" of state institutions themselves (through the certainly quite bureaucratized forms of "neocorporatist" management linked to the forma-tion of the "welfare state"). Women's right to vote is similarly inseparable from a profound transformation of the "space of the family," and from a rec-ognition (again, partial) of its public/political character, especially through women's entry into the realm of production, the assumption by the state of a number of functions connected to the sphere of reproduction (schools, child-care centers, elder care, etc.) or the right to contraception. In short, if there has been an "extension" of citizenship, this has been as a very con-dition of its "disabstractification," of the extension of the sphere of politics itself, of the reexamination, under the effect of struggles by classes and dominated groups, under the effect of the separations of civil-bourgeois society. It becomes possible, in any case, to better understand why, accord-ing to Marx, this process of politicization, if it crosses a decisive threshold and challenges anew the very presuppositions of bourgeois society (the rela-tions of property and production, to use Marxian language that postdates this text), must undertake to surpass the "merely" political state, and the abstraction of the citizen with it, especially as the foundational moment of right.

The Critique of Right

The preceding critiques could be considered as "soluble" in the internal dia-lectics of the founding utterances of citizenship, if they did not lead, and in return even suppose, a critique of their very *form*, as founding utterances of right (and, in a sense, of law). Right only exists, from Marx's point of view, in the act that constitutes the abstract political state and civil bourgeois society, the latter decomposed into independent individuals, freed from the traditional, personal bonds of the feudal era. Right thus only exists after the schism that it expresses, or translates, just as religion expressed and translated the old unity that connected the diverse spheres of activity of the feudal world. This translation, we should specify, operates in a "language"—to borrow a key term from the analysis of right in *The German Ideology*[32]—that assumes itself as foundational and arises in denial of the schism to which it nonetheless owes its existence. This amounts to saying that right, and its declaration, did not come first (contrary to their own pretensions). They are the effect of a process that dissolves a directly political social form and makes possible "by *one and the same act*" the existence of unbound individuals, as well as their recognition by the political state as legitimate legal subjects, a recognition inscribed in the rights of man and of the citizen.[33]

The problem Marx poses is therefore not that the rights of man and the citizen are formal but that *they are rights*, to borrow the trenchant formulation of Bertrand Binoche.[34] As such they are absolutely *real*: I can very well be both a believer and a citizen, just as the modern state can very well eliminate the restricted franchise, thereby removing all directly political significance from property, effectively guaranteeing the right to vote to those who do not own property, and yet leave intact even the most concentrated ownership of property, since property is now "merely" a civil difference. Or, to give a more contemporary example, I can very well be a black South African, with the right to vote in postapartheid South Africa (a right won at the cost of blood), and live in the same township as before and work under the orders of the same white boss. It remains to be seen, of course, how South African capital, in the long term, can manage and assure the reproduction of a force of labor freed from under the "iron heel" of apartheid.

An obvious objection nevertheless arises here: If the "rights" of man and of the citizen are real rights, and if the "extension" of citizenship has "enriched" men and citizens with a whole series of "social rights," has not Marx's objection as to the insurmountable limits of right been invalidated "practically" by the historical evolution (which we can even admit is, at least largely, due to the effects of his critique)? And, in this case, rather than abandoning the reference to the rights of man, would it not be more appropriate to seize it in order to redefine the content of those rights? Several remarks are necessary on this point. We should remember first of all that, in this text, Marx speaks of the rights of man only in the sense that they differ from the rights of the citizen, of the foundational core of the "natural" and "unconditional rights" of man, structured, still according to Marx, around the right to property. Now, it must be acknowledged that, whatever the reworkings and "enrichments" of the founding declaration, manifest in the numerous rewritings and revisions that succeeded it, the primacy of the right to property was never questioned. Quite the contrary, it is the property right that accounts (at the level of positive right) for the discrepancies, hierarchies, and asymmetries henceforth inscribed in the order of "rights." Rather than being linear extensions of the notion of "right," the different "social" rights, because they cannot, precisely, be legally defined in the mode of the property right and its corollaries (as so many individual rights that can be opposed to a specific "debtor"), but only as "claims on the collectivity," opposable to everyone and no one in particular (if not public power, that is, the state), turn out to depend on political determinations and thus cannot claim the same legal status as other rights. This is why they can be drastically limited, even eliminated, according to circumstances (such as the current neoliberal counterreform), in a completely "legal" fashion compatible with existing juridical and constitutional order. For purposes of comparison, consider the decision to seize an owner's property without compensation, which entails a radical overturning of juridical order, a break with legality, and the shift to an "exceptional" political logic that openly determines the legal norms. An asymmetry internal to "rights" is revealed here, partially covered over again by the homogenizing effects of juridical language, which allows liberal theoreticians to establish a hierarchy that only grants "rights-claims" a secondary place (or even no place at all, as in the work of Friedrich Hayek) to "freedom rights," even while it can be easily seen that the former will degenerate into pure formalities without the support of the latter (to be checked in the work of the inventor of the distinction of these two forms of rights, Isaiah Berlin in *On Liberty*).

The extreme case, from this point of view, is obviously that of the "right to work," the demand for which, during the 1848 revolution in France, made the limits of right readily apparent. For, at the outset, any attempt to define this right makes its incompatibility with bourgeois society's relations of property and exchange clearly perceptible. This is why, according to Marx, "behind this right" lay the "revolutionary demands of the Paris proletariat,"[35] demands that could not be reduced to the language of right and of rights. Later proclaimed in texts such as the United Nations' 1948 Universal Declaration of Human Rights, the "right to work" has only been translated concretely (and fragilely at that, as we can see today) as the "right to employment,"[36] that is, de facto (including in the sense of positive right), as the

right to compensation in case of job loss.[37] This "right," even in such a limited form, is in danger of rapidly becoming a mere memory, including in
countries with strong traditions of the "welfare state."

It is therefore not a question of abandoning the field of right (struggles
in the realm of right and for rights are constitutive dimensions of class
struggle) but of determining its limits. We must see that the struggles of
dominated peoples, even when they are expressed in terms of right and
rights, *exceed* right; they speak, in the final analysis, of something else.
"Political emancipation" differs from "human emancipation," to use the
terms of *On the Jewish Question* (Marx would soon speak only of "*the emancipation of the proletariat*")[38] to the extent that human emancipation requires
not realizing right, or denouncing it, but breaking with the foundational
claims that are simply the fictive reverse of its function of legitimating a
state power separated from society.

The point of view of "human emancipation" thinks from the *internal*
limits of political emancipation, that is, from its own failure. Political emancipation is, for Marx, a "big step forward"; it is not the final "*form* of human
emancipation," but it remains "the final form of human emancipation
within the hitherto existing world order," the "partial emancipation" that
"leaves the pillars of the house intact."[39] Its failure thus seems retrospectively necessary, in the new perspective of emancipation that attacks both
the pillars and the roof of the existing order. To put this another way, political
emancipation is no more an illusion than it is a strictly functional mechanism of bourgeois domination;[40] it is simply—if I may say so!—weighted
down[41] by an internal, structural limit that prevents it from answering the
question to which it leads (by its very "failing"), that of the advent of concrete
universality.

Beyond Citizenship: Revolution

This internal limit, in my view, has also made it impossible to account for
the historic process of access to "political emancipation" as an "extension" of
citizenship; instead, this process appears as a subversion of the very notion.
In a way, the "emphatic" return of citizenship that we are witnessing attests
to the crisis that the process is undergoing, or rather, it shows that this crisis
is taking a new form. The movement (to continue using this terminology)
of the "extension" and "concretization" of citizenship, in the framework of
compromises imposed by class struggles,[42] was followed by an era of "cold"
counterrevolution, a profound movement of disemancipation put forward

by neoliberalism. The exclusion of the dominated classes from the public sphere (indissociable from the destruction of the social conquests of the previous period), and even from the exercise of their right to vote (witness the collapse of the turnout in the main European countries and these nations' underlying alignment with the U.S. model), that is, the de facto reestablishment of the restricted franchise and of passive citizenship, represents a decisive dimension of this. We thus have proof, if proof were needed, of the unstable and (spatially and temporally) limited character of compromises currently—that is, *retrospectively*—interpreted (and often idealized) as "social citizenship."

If this is true, the current proliferation of the "citizen" discourse, which contrasts sharply with its relative effacement in a preceding period nonetheless marked by the "advances" of "citizenship" (essentially expressed, we should say, by the discourses of socialism and of the anticolonial revolution), far from being a paradox, must be seen as a symptom (albeit ambiguous) of disemancipation. Sometimes a protest against certain of disemancipation's effects (in the name of "qualitative" or "social" dimensions incorporated into the definition of "citizenship"), sometimes a justification of that process's overall logic (in the name of a return to the virtues of abstract universalism), the figure of the "citizen" celebrated everywhere today accelerates the disemancipating process on the discursive plane by excluding the only critique that radically calls its presuppositions into question, that is, the socialist and communist critique.

Perhaps we can now better understand the reach of the Marxian critique of citizenship. For one can restate "égaliberté" and "citizenship" as often as one likes, but one will never thereby obtain the "transformation of the relations of production," "seizure of power," "abolition of wage labor, of the market, and of classes," or the "withering away of the state." Naturally, one might judge that, from the very point of view of an emancipating project, these objectives are quite outdated, even dangerous or at least harmful; but to do this, it seems to me that one first has to discuss them seriously, confronting their radical nature and making sure that abandoning them will not entail a serious weakening of the project. Just as it would be illusory to believe that Marx's theory can avoid confrontation with the defeats of the past century, it is essential that we understand the meaning of the resistances that his theory continues, and will continue, to inspire.

Translated by Alex Martin

Notes

1　Hegel's preface to *The Phenomenology of Spirit*.
2　On this point, I refer the reader to the excellent synthesis of G. Bensusan, "Question juive," in *Dictionnaire critique du marxisme*, ed. G. Labica and G. Bensusan, new ed. (Paris, 2003).
3　Thus the title Marx gave his text was *Zur Judenfrage*: "On [or "About"] the Jewish Question," and not simply "The Jewish Question," as it is often translated erroneously.
4　That is, in addition to *On the Jewish Question*, the introduction to the *Contribution to the Critique of Hegel's Philosophy of Right*. It would also be appropriate to include in this list Marx's letters to Arnold Ruge.
5　Karl Marx, *On the Jewish Question* (hereafter *JQ*), in *Karl Marx, Frederick Engels: Collected Works*, vol. 3 (New York: International Publishers, 1975), 162. Unless otherwise stated, emphasis in all quotes is in the original. For the original German, see *Marx Engels Werke*, vol. 1 (hereafter *MEW* 1), 363–64.
6　This primacy of property has repercussions at the level of positive right, which accords to the right of property guarantees unknown to others, and especially "social" rights (we will return to this).
7　*JQ* 164, *MEW* 1:366.
8　*JQ* 163, 1:365. Even Rousseau (as Marx emphasizes later in *On the Jewish Question*), despite his conception of a "civil liberty" that entails not the loss of "natural liberty" but rather the production of a new freedom based on the entire alienation of the individual forces of all those who found the political association, remains a prisoner of this model of liberty-independence.
9　This suspicion nonetheless remains that this "essence" itself functions on the mode of a nature, of an original given altered by the atomism of bourgeois society, which "human emancipation" serves to reestablish. These ambiguities led Marx later (in the sixth thesis on Feuerbach) to repudiate explicitly the concept of "species" and of "generic essence" as "internal, mute universality binding the numerous individuals in a natural fashion" (from *Karl Marx: Les thèses sur Feuerbach*, ed. G. Labica [Paris: Presses Universitaires de France, 1897], 22).
10　*JQ* 167, *MEW* 1:369.
11　"Only when the real, individual man re-absorbs in himself the abstract citizen, and as an individual human being has become a *species-being* [*Gattungswesen geworden ist*] in his everyday life, in his particular work, and in his particular situation, only when man has recognised and organised his '*forces propres*' as *social* forces, and consequently no longer separates social power from himself in the shape of *political* power, only then will human emancipation have been accomplished." *JQ* 168, *MEW* 1:365.
12　On this question, see D. Losurdo, "Marx: La tradition libérale et le concept universel de l'homme," *Actuel Marx*, no. 5 (1989): 17–31; and Losurdo, "La construction du concept universel de l'homme: De la tradition libérale à la Révolution française," in *La philosophie et la Révolution française*, ed. B. Bourgeois and J. d'Hondt (Paris: Vrin, 1993), 49–58.
13　Cf. C. B. MacPherson, *The Political Theory of Possessive Individualism: Hobbes to Locke* (Oxford: Oxford University Press, 1964). On the political (and foundational) implications of Lockean anthropology, see Neal Wood, *The Politics of Locke's Philosophy: A Social*

Study of "An Essay Concerning Human Understanding" (Berkeley: University of California Press, 1983).

14 Quoted in R. Zapperi, introduction to E. Sieyès, *Qu'est-ce que le Tiers Etat?* (Geneva: Droz, 1970), 46. Sieyès even envisaged, in absolute seriousness, the perfection, through successive crossings, of a new "race" of "anthropomorphic monkeys" destined to be "slaves," alongside the race of "negroes," serving as "auxiliary instruments of labor," and of a "race" of "chiefs of production," composed exclusively of "whites" (ibid., 11).

15 B. Constant, *Principes de politique* (Paris: Hachette, 1997), 179.

16 Cf. G. Fraisse, *Muse de la Raison: Démocratie et exclusion des femmes en France* (Paris: Gallimard, 1995). Fraisse correctly emphasizes that "it can be said that equality is true in theory and false in practice, but the procedure is in fact more perverse, because theory itself bears inequality, the possibility of subordinating women" (286); she concludes that "the Declaration of the Rights of Man is not contradictory with exclusion" (330).

17 A. Tosel, *Démocratie et liberalismes* (Paris: Kimé, 1995), 20–26. This principle is "hidden" not because the utterances of the exclusion remain implicit (on the contrary, we have seen that they are clearly affirmed) but because they are situated *at another level* of the discourse, one that is more "empirical," or "concrete," leaving formally intact the primary utterance that was supposed to "subsume" them from the heights of its impassive universality. Thus the fragmented, proliferating, and finally instable character of this particular type of utterance.

18 Like the relationships of filiation in feudal society, the exclusion of women and the "racization" of proletarians show that the "naturalization" of relationships of domination is displaced and reformulated in the terms of anthropological difference.

19 See esp. "Sur le lieu commun: Il se peut que ce soit juste en théorie, mais, en pratique, cela ne vaut point," in E. Kant, *Oeuvres philosophiques*, vol. 3 (Paris: Gallimard, 1986), cf. esp. 275–78, an eloquent plea for the exclusion from citizenship of women, minors, and all those who sell their force of labor (*operaii*).

20 See, e.g., E. Laclau's argument in *Emancipation(s)* (London: Verso, 1996).

21 Cf. D. Losurdo, *Démocratie ou bonapartisme* (Paris: Temps des Cerises, 2003), 25–27; and, for women, Fraisse, *Muse de la Raison*, 275–76.

22 Losurdo, *Démocratie ou bonapartisme*.

23 "The political revolution thereby abolished [*hob ... auf*] the *political character of civil society* [*bürgerliche Gesellschaft*]. It broke up civil society into its simple component parts; on the one hand, the individuals; on the other hand, the *material* and *spiritual elements* constituting the content of the life and civil position of these individuals." *JQ* 166, *MEW* 1:368.

24 E.g., like the abstract universal of "republican laicity" that today is wielded against "communitarian particularisms," and which reveals itself to be the true particularism, one that affirms a "national" identity, openly exclusive since it is built on the massive repression of the colonial fact and of the racial discrimination experienced daily by entire sectors of French society.

25 J. Rancière suggestively renders this dialectic of the universal by defining the political as an "institution on behalf of those with no share" [*institution de la part des sans part*], whose irruption reveals the contingency of any social order (the management, the counting, of which defines the "police" for Rancière) that affirms itself as the all, the singular universal that is born, in the polemical mode, of the fundamental wrong, the exclusion of

the "uncounted." Cf. Rancière, *La mésentente* (Paris: Galilée, 1995). No doubt, but on the condition that we not oppose (as Rancière does) symbolic exclusion and social determinations—or, in other words, "politics" and "police"—in order to illuminate the "politicity" of the "police" itself.

26 *JQ* 167, *MEW* 1:369.

27 Ibid.

28 "Far from eliminating these artificial differences [the political state] only exists through their presuppositions"; *JQ* 153, *MEW* 1:354.

29 *JQ* 167, *MEW* 1:369.

30 Cf. *JQ* 156, *MEW* 1:357.

31 It also entails a transformation of the "rights" in question, as we will return to later.

32 K. Marx and F. Engels, *The German Ideology*, in *Karl Marx, Frederick Engels: Collected Works*, vol. 5 (New York: International Publishers, 1975), 320.

33 "The *establishment of the political state* and the dissolution of civil society into independent *individuals*—whose relations with one another depend on *law*, just as the relations of men in the system of estates and guilds depended on *privilege*—is accomplished by *one and the same act.*" *JQ* 167, *MEW* 1:369.

34 B. Binoche, *Critiques des droits de l'homme* (Paris: Presses Universitaires de France, 1989), 111.

35 Cf. K. Marx, *The Class Struggles in France, 1848–1850*, in *Karl Marx, Frederick Engels: Collected Works*, vol. 10 (New York: International Publishers, 1975), 77–78. "Behind the right to work stands power over capital; behind the power over capital, the appropriation of the means of production, their subordination to the associated working class and, therefore, the elimination of wage labor, of capital and of their mutual relations. Behind the '*right to work*' stood the June insurrection" (78).

36 Contrary to what is often claimed, it is under this formulation that the right to work figures in the preamble to the French constitution of 1946, confirmed in 1958, where it appears, furthermore, not as an unconditional right but as counterweight to the "duty" to work.

37 Cf. J.-J. Goblot, *Le droit au travail: Passé, présent, avenir* (Paris: Syllepse, 2003).

38 E.g., in *Class Struggles in France*: "The secret of the revolution of the nineteenth century" is "*the emancipation of the proletariat*" (10:57).

39 *JQ* 155, *MEW* 1:356 (my emphasis); Marx, introduction to *Critique de la philosophie de droit de Hegel*, trans. E. Kouvélakis (Paris: Ellipses, 2000), 16, 18, *MEW* 1:388, 389.

40 This is S. Petrucciani's objection in his stimulating study "Marx et la critique de l'égalité politique," *Actuel Marx*, no. 8 (1990): 67–86.

41 Behind the original past participle *grevée* lies a pun on the noun *grève* (strike). *Trans.*

42 We should stress the extent to which these compromises were indebted to October 1917, including from the strict point of view of "political emancipation": Soviet Russia was the first nation to recognize simultaneously the political rights of those who do not own property, of women, and of oppressed nationalities.

Anne F. Garréta

Autonomy and Its Discontent

"Thinking Politically" announced itself as a quest. Participants (in the colloquium, in this special issue, in the quest) would embark in search of the lost political. Barring the miraculous encounter of a *petite madeleine* or a stumble on the disjointed pavement of some Hotel de Guermantes courtyard (and even those epiphanies have to be recognized, interpreted, and seized to yield a glimpse of their Grail), this endeavor faces a number of obstacles, enumerated in the successive restatements of the initial project, and not unlike those faced by the Proustian hero: piercing through the obfuscations of ideology, weeding out the counterfeit discourses, stripping away the corruptions or the inessentialities affecting the genuinely political, rescuing it from obsolescence, and restoring its proper figure and place.

But the model invoked for "Thinking Politically" is not Marcel Proust and *In Search of Lost Time*, but "the inaugural attempt of Carl Schmitt to establish the autonomy of the political as such."[1] However, invoking such a model can't fail to open up the rather disagreeable possibility that "all genuine political theory and text might necessarily be reactionary ones."[2]

The *South Atlantic Quarterly* 104:4, Fall 2005.

It is difficult, moreover, to escape the irony entailed by the Schmittian precedent: his restitution of "autonomy" to the political is but a move to reestablish heteronomy in the form of the theologico-political. Thus the need, in a subsequent restatement of the project's purpose, for the following rejoinder: "It will be crucial to identify and eliminate all traces of ethical, theological or civic-republican value theory."[3]

Stripped of these possible groundings, where could the political be located? Is there any ground left, once one has disposed of the ethical and the theological and the civic and the republican?

Is "Thinking Politically," as both a discourse and a quest, doomed to reiterate the predicament of modernity and locate *ab initio* all possible answers to its master move within the horizon modernity itself circumscribed? If, for fear of reactionary stains, we exclude as possible grounds for a renewal of the political what modernity has itself already excluded, how are we to answer its challenge?

Isn't in effect the impulse behind the avowed project of thinking politically ("the anxiety that a whole tradition is in danger of being erased by the logic of the market")[4] an old anxiety, an anxiety as old as modernity?

I

A similar anxiety, accompanied by the recognition of its historicity, lies indeed at the root of Carl Schmitt's attempted salvage of the political: "Nothing is more modern than the battle against the political."[5] Liberal thought is the force that has strived to empty the political of any meaning, relevance, authority. Schmitt intends a radical critique of liberalism and liberalism's essential instrument in achieving the neutralization of the political: autonomy.[6]

Autonomy affects the modern worldview at two levels. First, culture (defined as "the totality of human thought and action") is divided into individual provinces, each answering only to its own sovereign logic: thus the autonomy of aesthetics, of morality, of science, of the economy, and so on. Second, culture itself as a whole is autonomous, rather than heteronomous: it is a "sovereign creation," a "pure product" of the human spirit,[7] rather than a realm ordered and ordained by an absolute, transcendental exteriority. Ironically, the political itself ends up being denied the autonomy liberally granted all other spheres: "The political [is] robbed of all independence and subordinated to the norms and orders of Morals, Law and Economics" (72).

Carl Schmitt's *Concept of the Political* was decisively radicalized and clarified by the intervention, between its first edition (1927) and its second (1932), of the critical reading of his piece by Leo Strauss. This reading took the form of the 1932 "Notes on C. Schmitt's Concept of the Political,"[8] which Schmitt himself helped get published in the *Archiv für sozial Wissenschaft*.

As Heinreinch Meier's study of Strauss's critique and Schmitt's subsequent modifications of his tract demonstrate, the thrust of Strauss's influence was to lead Schmitt's critique of liberalism beyond the horizon of liberalism within which his first formulations kept him defensively enclosed.[9] Strauss radicalizes or helps radicalize Schmitt. For example, this would be the strategic interpretation of the following Straussian consideration: "In certain passages [Schmitt] expresses himself in such a way that a superficial reader could get the impression [that] after liberalism has brought the autonomy of the aesthetics, of morals, of science, of the economy into recognition, [he] now seeks for his part to bring the autonomy of the political into recognition, in opposition to liberalism but nonetheless in continuation of liberal aspirations for autonomy" (N8).

In truth, there is no such thing as the autonomy of the political in a consistent critique of liberalism: autonomy is already the mark of liberalism's grip. Strauss deciphers and brings to the fore what Schmitt implies by his identification of the true political distinction with the distinction between friend and foe. This "concrete opposition" synonymous with the potential for war, for "dire emergency" (which opens the field for the famous state of exception), implies that "the political is fundamental, and not a relatively independent domain. The political is the authoritative" (N9).

The political is not therefore another of these autonomous provinces of culture parceled out by liberalism: it stands outside, beneath, and above. Even more radically, it can be described as *ubiquitous*. Being a pure potential of opposition without a domain or a matter of its own, it can spring up everywhere. It is ever present—if not in actuality, at least in potentiality.

We need not remain bonded to Schmitt's own (catholic) representation of the political: spectacularly sacrificial, embodied exclusively in the form of the State, and unified by a singular *agon*. For, considered in this light, and thus identified, other or new figurations and locations of the political might remain unrecognizable. However, if we distinguish the political from its specific Schmittian incarnation and ponder its defining characteristics, it appears that the apparent evanescence or invisibility of the political to those who seek it might be a function not of its loss or obsolescence but of its very ubiquity.

And we might discern distinct figurations or investments of a ubiquitous political. One, apocalyptic, would be represented in Giorgio Agamben's development of the Schmittian problematics in the enigmatic figure of *Homo sacer*.[10] Another would be figured in the late Foucauldian analysis of power as a diffuse, pervasive, capillary force: modern power is ubiquitous, and so is resistance to it.

II

Schmitt and Strauss's convergence is remarkable in their discontent with autonomy. The roots of that discontent are seriousness incarnate: "Politics and the state are the only guarantee against the world's becoming a world of entertainment; what the opponents of the political want is ultimately tantamount to the establishment of a world of entertainment, a world of amusement, a world without *seriousness*" (N27). For Schmitt this loss of seriousness would be, ultimately (and that is the theological ground of his concept of the political), the loss of the sense of original sin, of the enmity between the arch friend and foe, Christ and Antichrist.[11] On the pacified globe of ultimate bourgeois triumph, an unpolitical world would still know "oppositions and contrasts," "competitions and intrigues" of all kinds, but "no ground on which it could be demanded of men that they *sacrifice* their lives" (N11). We would have economic competition, we would have Olympic games, World Series, Yankees and Marlins, even the fateful enmity of Yankees and Red Sox, the folkloric curse of the Cubs, intrigues and plots, but it would all have devolved into spectator sports and soap operas. There would remain only differences that make no difference.

Economization, aesthetization, and the spirit of technicity are, for Schmitt, the three most debased forms of this veiling of the political. On this battlefield of modernity, Marx stands as the "true cleric of economic thought,"[12] remaining, in Schmitt's view, within the orbit of liberal mentality, characterized by the turn to the economic, "the mass faith of anti-religious, this-worldly activism" (55–56). The ultimate globalization of liberal autonomy, and its attendant pacification, would be attained at the cost of the meaning of human life—a meaning, for Schmitt, to be found in the theological; a meaning, for Strauss, synonymous with the "right life" (i.e., the urgency, for the few chosen souls privy to the esoteric teachings of philosophy, of the classical question of philosophy: what is right?).

For Schmitt, then, the opposite of entertainment is *the real possibility of physical killing*. The neutralization of politics and the triumph of autonomy spell the end of sacrifice, the end of seriousness, the reign of pure play, in which nothing is of consequence any longer. In this world of liberal entertainment you might of course still choose to kill yourself or risk getting killed, of your own private choice, in the private pursuit of whatever pleases you. But this will be no sacrifice.

III

The Schmittian and Straussian radical critique of culture and its autonomy resonates uncannily with the discontent of some of their French contemporaries at the time, authors by now as canonical as Georges Bataille and his associates of both *Acéphale* and the Collège de sociologie.[13]

As we started in search of the lost political, three elements seemed to ground the project of "Thinking Politically": the problematic status of the semantics of decision, commitment, and denunciation; the surmised link between a current development of theory by way of an exclusion of the political as such; and the question of knowing at what point we might reach the political dimension of aesthetics or art.

The problematics of commitment (or *engagement*), of Sartrian fame, entails a liberal presupposition. In Straussian terms, *engagement* is a critique or an attempted turn to the political which remains caught *within* the horizon of autonomy. To posit that the subject can choose whether or not to be committed supposes that abstention or neutrality is a possibility. A subject considering a possible political *engagement* is already installed comfortably (but maybe not without a certain discontent) on the side of autonomy. In a heteronomous space, no one is ever granted the leisure to contemplate the options of *engagement* or *désengagement*: the only out is, at best, exile or banishment. Commitment describes, in reality, the passage from the private sphere to the public sphere; as such, it only registers the already established scission between the two spheres.

In the sphere of aesthetics or literature, autonomy entails that a certain use of language is shielded from certain legal consequences, for it is in the legal terms of censorship, of "free" speech and its institutional limits, that the question presents itself publicly.[14] The long historical process which, starting in the seventeenth century, dissolved in Europe the grip of heteronomy (a dissolution achieved as the condition to bringing civil, religious wars to an end) and secured for writers a political immunity (if not a civil immunity) is also what left them feeling robbed of agency (though, of course, "political agency" is a description already embedded in the logic of autonomy). The more sovereignty seemed to accrue to literary authority in the process of autonomization, the more it came to feel its practice acutely threatened with irrelevance and, ultimately, total consumption or dissolution into the forms of entertainment. This paradoxical status, keenly felt by writers in the modern era, amounts to both a freeing and a neutralization of the act of writing.

The discontent with autonomy and its seeming inescapability is crucially registered and deployed in a text such as Michel Leiris's preface to *Manhood*. Dreaming of catharsis, dreaming of writing that would be an act, of writing that would endanger the subject, he can locate his attempt on no other ground than the confession of the subject's private sexual peculiarities, and ends up locating its language in the unrecognized matrix of a *rhétorique désoeuvrée*, of speech laboring under the shield and curse of public irrelevance. Tauromachia is willed to figure the ideal arena of a practice of writing that would be an act (i.e., a sacrificial ritual). But the "real possibility of physical killing" it is meant to signify will never materialize: Leiris dreams of reintroducing into literature (which has degenerated into mere dance, by contrast with serious bullfight) not even a bull's horn, but, mournfully, the mere *shadow* of a bull's horn.[15]

One could adduce other evidence of this loss of implication of the writing subject in his discourse. For example, the striking turn of the form of the literary essay in the French twentieth-century tradition toward the fictional, toward an obliqueness of its enunciation, an indirection or (but the result is the same) a compensatory veering of the polemical discourse toward the posture of the lyrical subject.[16] The obliqueness or indirection of the enunciation might function (and in Maurice Blanchot it certainly does) as an attempt at securing a denial of imputability. It might also function (in someone like Roland Barthes) as a deliberate attempt at politeness, a manner of civilizing discourse, suspending its possible violence. Mourning heteronomy or phobically avoiding the locus of its repressed violence might well be the two sides of the same neurosis of autonomy, and paradoxical symptoms of the discontent it generates.

IV

Theory itself, in its ordering of discourses and their modes, conspires in this exclusion or waving off of the political. Fiction in some of its current theorizations (from John Searle to Gerard Genette to Jean-Marie Shaeffer)[17] is negatively defined as a (pragmatically) "nonserious" mode of assertion.

Schaeffer, for example, develops what could be called a perfectly liberal doctrine of the status of fiction as "playful pretense," a doctrine geared at clearing away the last remaining fears of mimetic confusion. This type of theory, playing Aristotle against Plato,[18] formalizes and enshrines the absence of traction (on the world and on beliefs) of fiction, conceptualized as "playful pretense," as pure "as if," cognitively useful simulation, and crucial technique in the humanization of social relationships.

Between factual discourse and fictional discourse stands a stable categorical barrier that insulates them: a barrier established and guaranteed by the formal pretense, or presence (even if sometimes implicit), of a reading pact signaling the pragmatic status of the discourse. Contractuality undersigns — is it surprising? — the liberal literary pact. Immersion in a realm of fiction does not — we should rest assured — lead to quixotic self-delusion. The theory postulates the existence of a "natural" inhibiting factor that "prevents imaginative simulations from contaminating the cognitive representations controlling our actions and grasp of reality."[19] But representations thus insulated from simulations yield, strangely enough, a practice of no practical consequences: a form of pure entertainment promoting subjective dispositions unlikely to ever be dispositive.

Is it any wonder that those formal theories of the status of fictional discourse encounter their moment of dire crisis around such cases as that of the Benjamin Wilkomirski text/hoax?[20] Or as soon as language is involved with what Agamben, radicalizing the Schmittian decision, identifies as the true figure of the state of exception, the death camp? The return of the political takes the form of a haunting, threatening a collapse of all those painfully (rather than playfully) erected categorical boundaries.

V

But truly, and even without invoking the extremes of modern terror, how could the theoretical grounding of modern poetics in the Aristotelian paradigm guarantee a thorough neutralization of the activity of mimesis? Can we so easily split the *Poetics* from the *Rhetoric* or the *Politics* or the *Nichomachean Ethics*? Can we so easily overlook the evidently political function of cultural forms such as ancient Greek theater?

A general, nonspecific characterization of what theatrical *mimesis* does used to go like this: it works a purgation of the passions.[21] If we remember correctly, Aristotle is very specific when it comes to the passions in question: the point is "to accomplish through pity and fear the catharsis of such passions." Why pity and fear, may I ask, and not greed, lust . . . ?

Pity and fear are rather peculiar passions, it seems. One could construe them as the political passions par excellence. Fear drives the Hobbesian logic of the flight from the state of nature into the civil and political state. Rousseau grants pity a most singular status in the description of his own version of state of nature: it is, in his *Discourse on the Origin of Inequality*, the sole faculty of natural man (besides the entirely negative capability that is perfectibility), and the faculty above all others which ensures that Rousseau's state of nature will differ from Hobbes's picture of *Homo homini lupus*. For natural pity has this most remarkable effect, in Rousseau's construct, of producing an identification of self with the other. Fear and pity could then be regarded, in a Schmittian sense, as the two essentially political passions: the root of the identification of the other as foe, the root of the identification with the other as friend.

Now, what would their catharsis signify? A purgation, whereby our excesses of fear and pity are drained off by the application of a small spectacular supplement? Or a purification, a moral purification that would direct our passions toward their proper moral objects? The point here is not to solve the philological enigma but to reengage the political significance of the Aristotelian model.

Indulging in overbroad generalizations, we could ask whether—unlike the Greeks, who had tragedies, and modern Westerners, who had novels—we are now bereft of cultural forms through which to exercise our most decisive passions. The relevant object of our quest then is not so much to recognize *at what point* might we reach the political dimension of aesthetics or art, but *under what new forms* we might today encounter mimesis: what are the new mimetic *technai*, and what process of subjectivation might they drive?

A Schmittian view locates the political in the real possibility of physical killing. The political happens where this possibility is shaped and instantiated or figured and held in reserve. The most significant recent cultural development, then, could well be the rise of a new cultural form: the video (or computer) game.

In 2003, for the first time, more hours were spent in the United States in front of video games than TV. Video games are, in fictional and potential ways, the visual, aesthetic, and mimetic forms of the life-and-death decision in our culture. Of course, they are what narratologists would call nonserious activities, playful entertainment, fictions, simulations no one should confuse with reality. But what are we to make of the use to which they are put? Since 2003, the U.S. military has been using actual, specially developed video games as recruitment tools (and not simply advertising clips mimicking the aesthetics of video games themselves). *America's Army* (and the soon to be released *Overmatch*) offer in the form of training and combat simulations an entry into *the real possibility of physical killing*. Naturally, many of the technologies that drive the development of ever more sophisticated games were initially funded for strategic purposes (war games, combat training and simulation, etc.). We may have learned from Jean Baudrillard as early as the first Gulf War and its high-tech images of precision, laser-guided, infrared video documented precision bombings, that all wars were now vaporized into a virtual war, that the border between the real and its spectacular simulation had been vaporized.

The ironic twist today is that *le spectacle* is spectacle no more. It is a ubiquitous practice. Entertainment is a weapon of mass subjectivation. Mimesis, in its full (vs. narratologically cabined) sense, returns with a political vengeance. The simulations (*techne* wedded to *muthos* wedded to mimesis) of video games are luring and producing the new subjects of the new wars, and their bodies (literally and figuratively): virtual communities trained in the new technaï of eminently political passions, recruited and bonded through the Internet.

It may be time to take pure play and its imaginary autonomy seriously, since they threaten to turn virtually ubiquitous.

Notes

I wish to thank Erin Post, my research assistant at Duke in the fall of 2003, for her help in researching the sources for this contribution.

1   I am quoting here from Fredric Jameson's second statement of the conference problematics for "Thinking Politically."
2   Ibid.
3   Ibid., third statement.
4   Ibid.
5   Carl Schmitt, *Political Theology: Four Chapters on the Concept of Sovereignty*, trans. George Schwab (Cambridge, MA: MIT Press, 1985), 25.
6   Obviously, Schmitt's polemical setup of the antithesis between autonomy and heteronomy does not allow for the existence of possible tensions within the liberal tradition.

The heirs to the Enlightenment are all, indistinctly, his opponents. But the thrust of his polemics registers differently depending on whether one directs it at Kant's construction of the autonomy of Reason (Reason prescribes itself its own rules of operation), at the classical liberal distinction expounded by Benjamin Constant of negative and positive freedom (and its concomitant promotion of the private sphere), or at the more subtle shadings of the relationship between the spheres of culture, mores, and institutions delineated by Alexis de Tocqueville in the second volume of his *Democracy in America*. Tocqueville's project is an explicit attempt to salvage the dignity and the authority of the political in the modern (i.e., democratic) era.

7   Carl Schmitt, *The Concept of the Political*, trans./intro./notes by George Schwab, with comments on Schmitt's essay by Leo Strauss (New Brunswick, NJ: Rutgers University Press, 1976), 71. Subsequent citations to Schmitt's text are given parenthetically by page number in the text.

8   Included in ibid.

9   Heinrich Meier, *Carl Schmitt and Leo Strauss: The Hidden Dialogue*, trans. J. Harvey Lomax (Chicago: University of Chicago Press, 1995); this volume includes Strauss's notes on Schmitt's *Concept of the Political* and three letters from Strauss to Schmitt. Subsequent citations to Strauss's contribution are given parenthetically in the text, by section number preceded by the letter N.

10 See Giorgio Agamben, *Homo Sacer, I, Le pouvoir souverain et la vie nue*, trans. Marilène Raiola (Paris: Editions du Seuil, 1997); *Ce qui reste d'Auschwitz: L'archive et le témoin*, trans. Pierre Alferi (Paris: Éd. Payot & Rivages, 1999); *L'Etat d'exception*, trans. Joël Gayraud (Paris: Editions du Seuil, 2003). The latest volume states nothing less than that the Schmittian state of exception is now the rule, or norm, of our existence.

11 In medieval theology, the devil is called nothing other than the Adversary, the Foe.

12 Carl Schmitt, *Donoso Cortés in gesamteuropäischer Interpretation: Vier Aufsätze* (Köln: Greven, 1950), 74.

13 See the anthology edited by Denis Hollier, *The College of Sociology* (1937–39), trans. Betsy Wing (Minneapolis: University of Minnesota Press, 1988). An examination of the links between these two traditions of discontent with modernity should look into the contacts between Alexandre Kojève (a key influence on Bataille, Michel Leiris, and others of the same generation) and Carl Schmitt as well as Leo Strauss. See Kojève, *La notion de l'autorité* (Paris: Gallimard, 2004), and Leo Strauss, *On Tyranny*, rev./exp. ed., ed. Victor Gourevitch and Michael S. Roth (New York: Free Press, 1991), which includes the Strauss-Kojève correspondence.

14 The current theoretical articulation of this question takes the form of a critical theory of (1) speech acts and performativity and (2) the status of fictional speech acts, the logic of the "as if." On the former, see Judith Butler, *Excitable Speech: A Politics of the Performative* (New York: Routledge, 1997); on the latter, see Thomas G. Pavel, *Fictional Worlds* (Cambridge, MA: Harvard University Press, 1986); Gérard Genette, *Fiction et diction* (Paris: Editions du Seuil, 1991); Jean-Marie Schaeffer, *Pourquoi la fiction* (Paris: Editions du Seuil, 1999).

15 Michel Leiris, *Manhood: A Journey from Childhood into the Fierce Order of Virility*, trans. Richard Howard (New York: Grossman, 1963). The gendered logic of this fantasy is inescapable: tauromachia stands as the antidote and antithesis to literature, equated with "des grâces de ballerine" (an emphatically feminine figure). The liberal neutralization of lit-

erature registers with the modern (male) subject as a neutering, a threat to the writing subject's virility. Manhood would be regained (imaginarily) through the subject's (imaginary) exposure to death in the spectacular arena of bullfighting. The *épreuve* of castration figures the threshold of sovereignty.

16 See the PhD thesis of Marielle Macé, "L'Essai littéraire en France au XXème siècle" (Paris: Université Paris IV), and its critical summary at www.litterature20.paris4.sorbonne.fr/positions.php#Mariellemace.

17 See Genette, *Fiction et diction*, and Schaeffer, *Pourquoi la fiction*.

18 And a rather lame or depoliticized version of Aristotle at that. For a critical view, see Catherine Perret, "La fiction ou l'image de personne," *Littérature* 123 (September 2001): 86–100. My analysis is heavily indebted to her reading of Aristotle.

19 Schaeffer, *Pourquoi la fiction*, 175.

20 See ibid.

21 That's how the French classical age translated, construed, and repeated the Aristotelian catharsis. Further analysis should be devoted to evaluate the pertinence of this historical nexus of theatrical representation and institution of autonomy: a crucial case in point would be the example of Corneille and the Querelle du Cid. On this, see Hélène Merlin-Kajman, *L'Excentricité académique: Littérature, institution, société* (Paris: Belles Lettres, 2001).

Teresa M. Vilarós

A Big Idea: The Cold War, Ultracolonialism,
and the *Estado Dirigido*

> Tienen su período los Imperios. El que más duró, más
> cerca está de su fin.
> —Diego de Saavedra Fajardo, *Empresas*, OC 612

On January 16, 1991, just after the United
Nations deadline for Iraq to pull its military
forces out of Kuwait had passed, President
George Herbert Walker Bush addressed the U.S.
Congress to declare his administration's determination to launch an attack against Saddam
Hussein. Bush presented the Gulf War as a
necessary step to guarantee world peace, and in
the series of presidential speeches given in the
wake of the war he made the first mentions of an
idea for a new world order. "This is an historic
moment," the president said: "We have in this
past year made great progress in ending the long
era of conflict and Cold War. We have before us
the opportunity to forge for ourselves and for
future generations a new world order."[1]

Although the war was going to be led and
carried out mostly by the United States, the
president strongly emphasized his continuing
support of the UN, and he repeatedly reassured
the world that even after the successful outcome
of the Gulf War and the achievement of global

The *South Atlantic Quarterly* 104:4, Fall 2005.
Copyright © 2005 by Duke University Press.

peace, the UN's role as an international arbiter was going to be kept in place: "When we are successful, and we will be," Bush Sr. explained, "we have a real chance at this new world order, an order in which a credible United Nations can use its peace-keeping role to fulfill the promise and vision of the UN's founders."[2]

Because the first references to a new world order maintained an agreement with a Schmittian friend/enemy structure inherent to the whole period of Eurocentric constitutional order, at one level a real change in the order of the political seemed not to be at stake. However, while the January speech did not propose an alternative to the current forms of sovereignty, the overall public interventions made by the United States in the wake of the Gulf War can in fact be conceptualized as the confirmation of a change in the order of the political. True, the change was not processed as a substitution per se, but it was present nevertheless. And, delivered as a form of translation or passing of sorts from one order to the next, the State of the Union address given in February of the same year clearly and openly placed the United States as the central player of the new world order:

> Mr. President, Mr. Speaker, members of the United States Congress. I come to this house of the people to speak to you and all Americans, certain that we stand at a defining hour. Halfway around the world, we are engaged in a great struggle in the skies and on the seas and sands. We know why we're there. We are Americans: part of something larger than ourselves. For two centuries, we've done the hard work of freedom. And tonight, we lead the world in facing down a threat to decency and humanity. What is at stake is more than one small country; it is a big idea: a new world order.[3]

The 1991 presidential speech series linked the emerging world order to an American "big idea," as President Bush expressively termed it, implicitly addressing a change between two modes of global order. In the wake of the fall of the Soviet Union and the consequent end of the Cold War, the Gulf War activated a displacement of the *nomos* of the earth similar to the way Carl Schmitt conceptualized it:[4] a displacement that was finally and effectively taking the globe from the former Eurocentric *nomos* of industrial and colonial manifestation, still evident today, to a U.S.-centered, postindustrial order of imperial and ultracolonial qualification.[5] It is true that in 1991 the unleashing of the Gulf War had sought and received a clearance from the United Nations. But it is also true that despite the references to the United

Nations—a nod of recognition to the former "old" order the new one was about to supplant—and despite the public presentation of that war as one still being fought under a friend/enemy paradigm, the United States was unequivocally assuming global leadership in an exceptional situation of war that was quickly dismantling the notions of exceptionality, of friend and of enemy, and, ultimately, of the colonial performance and postcolonial effects of Eurocentric hegemony.

The war, the president said, was fought not to determine the fate of a "small country" (Kuwait or Iraq) but to open a clearing for a "new world order" of peace at a moment when the capitalism-versus-communism context of the Cold War period (1950–91) had just vanished. The Cold War—a complex friend/enemy order that had functioned not only as a de facto guarantor of global peace but as the major form of deterrence for global nuclear destruction—had suddenly disappeared, leaving a void in the order of the political. And because the end of the Cold War also meant the end of the deterrent to an all too real possibility of global nuclear destruction, the collapse of the USSR opened a void in the order of peace that pointed to the possibility of absolute U.S. sovereignty.[6]

It was in the face of that opening that the United States arrogated to itself the leading role as mediator for global peace: "We've learned the hard lessons of history," explained the president. "The victory over Iraq was not waged as 'a war to end all wars.' Even the new world order cannot guarantee an era of perpetual peace. But enduring peace must be our mission."[7] In Bush's perspective the Gulf War was a necessary move in order to activate a worldwide strategic plan. It acted out that "big idea" to which the president had referred: the vision of a new world order of peace under the watch of the United States. But how should that order of peace alluded to by President Bush be interpreted within the context of a displacement, of a paradigmatic translation from the old Eurocentric order to the new one the United States was orchestrating? Into what kind of political, or postpolitical, zone of peace was the world entering? With the Cold War formation gone as a deterrent for nuclear war, what kind of social contracts and juridical constitutions needed to be kept in place? Or should they be rethought anew?

Was the 1991 Gulf War, a virtual/real war that still has not ended, a first move in a kind of a post–friend-versus-enemy state of affairs surfacing after the end of the Cold War? Was the 1991 big idea a novel rotation of the United States toward the occupation of a new center of gravity of capitalist globalization, toward a kind of macromanaged corporate sovereignty, as the president implied in a March 1991 address, intent on implanting a new order of global peace?[8] Or was that big idea not a new idea after all, but just the latest turn of events in a series of displacements that had its point of origin in 1945? Was the world in 1991 just witnessing the last moment of an already weakened industrialization, the moment when the techno-economic state of modern industrialization was closely gravitating toward its latest incarnation—toward its own new "central ambit," as Schmitt would have it?[9] Toward a new center of gravity informed by biotechnical/economic, informational, nuclear, and virtual technologies? Toward a form of corporate empire that, centered in the United States, was in fact starting to move away from its own former constitutional model? And if so, was there going to be or had there already been a transitional period that would take us or had already taken us from one mode of the state, and/or one mode of the political, to the next? And, again, if so, what kind of transitional time zone would that be? Or could 1991 perhaps be read as an evental time, as a fissural moment?

The period of about fifteen years comprising the fall of the Berlin Wall in 1989, the final collapse of the Soviet Union in 1991, the al-Qaeda attack on the World Trade Center in 2001, and the second Iraqi war of 2003 is usually conceptualized as a transitional time, an accelerated time of interregnum, of flows of postmodern biopolitical crossings. But mostly it was the period between 1989 and 1991, described by Giorgio Agamben as a time of "political indistinction," the one perceived as marking the final acceleration of an economic and political order that was firmly and assuredly moving its center of gravity away from Europe and toward the United States. Culminating with three major and related historical milestones—the final collapse of communism in Russia, the subsequent end of the Cold War, and the Gulf War—1991 could perhaps be thought of as eventual time if we think of the event, in Alain Badiou's sense, as the thing "that prompts the coming of 'something else' than the situation, than opinions, than institutionalized knowledge; that that is a risky supplement, that that is unforeseeable, already gone when just appeared."[10]

If a displacement of the center of gravity from Europe to the United States was effectively at work in the Schmittian sense, if the world in 1991 was experiencing the moment of the coming of "a something else," then that year (and not 2001, or 2003) could be thought of as the year of the event, provided that the "something else" the event was referring to was something other than the situation. But because the idea for a new order in the wake of the 1991 Gulf War always refers to a displacement and not to a rupture from one order (Europe-centered) to the next (U.S.-centered), they appear to confirm not an event but a situation. It would not seem accurate, therefore, to take 1991 as an eventual time, since America's big idea would not be offering something completely new, something completely other. What was affirmed, on the contrary, was a metonymic change of biopolitical order, so to speak, a seamless transfer of the political forms and parlance of the Eurocentric order of primary industrial technologies to the U.S.-centered, postindustrial paradigm of secondary ones.

As a fluid continuum of what was, at the deep core, a transfer of bio-political circulation, the United States seemed then to be offering "more of the same," intent upon maintaining the political formations and structures of the modern constitutional state sitting at the base of the former Euro-centric order.[11] But in order to maintain movement in the biopolitical flows formerly activated by industrial modernization, when entering the post–Cold War period of political indistinction, the new order needed to overcome at least partially the formations of the political inherent to the period of the second modernity and of the constitutional state, a process identified by Agamben in 1995 as follows:

> Only because at the end of the twentieth century biological life and its needs had become the politically decisive factor is it possible to understand the otherwise incomprehensible rapidity with which twentieth-century parliamentary democracies were able to turn into totalitarian states, and with which this century's totalitarian states were able to be converted almost without interruption into parliamentary democracies. In both cases these transformations were produced in a context in which for quite some time politics had already turned into biopolitics, and in which the only real question to be decided was which form of organization would be best suited to the task of assuring care, control, and use of bare life. Once their fundamental referent becomes bare life, traditional political distinctions (such as those between Right and Left, liberalism and totalitarianism, private and public) lose their clarity and intelligibility and enter into a zone of indistinction.[12]

Agamben was clearly attuned to the transfer of biopolitical flows taking place after 1989. But because for him the possibility of a biopolitical formation is contained within the juridical frame of the period of second modernity—that is, within the conceptualization of the secular, constitutional state and of the figure of the modern citizen—the current weakening of the modern political constitutional system would contradict the massive bio-political reactivation evident after the end of the Cold War. Agamben does not explain why the time zone of political indistinction brought by the end of the Cold War, the time of debilitation of previous forms of the political coming to the fore *after* the Cold War, actually reinforces and strengthens the flows of the biopolitical. A reconceptualization of the Cold-War period, therefore, seems to be in place, since the Cold War was not a deterrent for the biopolitical. On the contrary, it provided the necessary ground for the successful transfer of biopolitical flows. And although it was perceived as a fierce, highly charged political battlefield between the two nuclear super-powers, the Cold War period was in fact already performing in postpolitical, post–friend-versus-enemy ways. Functioning as the transitional time zone needed for capital to turn into biocapital, the Cold War paved the way for the expansive installment of new forms of imperial administration that were leaning toward ultracolonialism.

Ultracolonialism, as the postindustrial form of imperial colonization per-taining to the U.S.-centered era, is somewhat akin to the colonial struc-ture imposed by the Spanish Empire in the sixteenth and seventeenth cen-turies. This proposition is confirmed in Spain with a look at the dictatorial regime of Generalísimo Francisco Franco between 1950 and 1975, when after the onset of the Cold War, Spain emerged as a partial ultracolonial site of the United States—that is, as a postmodern and postindustrial sub-imperial formation sustained and protected by the United States. During the Cold War period, Francoist Spain performed as one of the first transi-tional zones for capitalist biopolitical transfer in the Western world. The Francoist regime—a nonsynchronic theological and imperial state form with a nonconstitutional foundation nestled amid the Western constitu-tional states—demonstrated uncannily enough that the economic postin-dustrial flows of the biopolitical actually circulate better within the frame of nonconstitutional, nonsecular imperial state forms than within a politi-cal body informed by constitutional industrialization.[13] From the United States' perspective, Franco's defeat of communism in 1939 and his immedi-ate refusal to implement a constitutional state with representative political parties, in addition to Spain's political and economic isolation from the rest of Europe after World War II, made the nation highly desirable at the onset of the Cold War.[14] Spain offered the United States a prime geopolitical site officially voided of communism, with the added advantage of being a state with no political parties.[15] Consequently, Franco's nonparty state, Franco's "neutral" and highly depoliticized state, quickly embraced capitalism as its central economic system, turning into one of the first Western examples of partial ultracolonization when in 1953, pressured by the United States, the UN welcomed Spain as a new member.[16]

As a geopolitical ally of the United States, the Francoist regime contradicted the logic of the modern European order that according to Schmitt took the states through a series of linear passages from a particular ambit or central sphere to its next.[17] Schmitt explains that the different states of Europe acquired their strength from what in each different historical period had constituted a central spiritual or cultural sphere, displaying over time a series of "central ambits" that historically moved from the theological, to the secular, then to the economic, and, finally, to the techno-economic.[18] But Francoist Spain, a confessional Nationalist-Catholic state of imperial legacy with no political party representation and very precarious industrialization, did not completely follow the Schmittian logic of consequent displacements of central spheres. Going against the grain, Franco's regime seamlessly moved Spain from an almost premodern configuration (in the sense of the second modernity) straight into the age of globalized corporate capitalism. After 1950, that is, after the beginning of the Korean War and the onset of the Cold War, Franco skipped secularism and merged Spain's theologico-political imperial structure, her fundamentalist nationalist-Catholic core, with a very particular techno-economic one: that of capitalism turning into biocapitalism at the very beginning of its third stage of development.[19]

In 1953 Spain became one of the first examples of the process of global ultracolonization to come, almost a U.S. *estado dirigido*. Thanks to the signing of the bilateral pacts between Spain and the United States in 1953 and 1957, and despite periods of high friction between the two nations, the partial ultracolonizing of Spain set in motion a process pointing to a globalized, United States–centered, postconstitutional, and corporate model of state administration.[20] And it was only when Spain became a geopolitical strategic formation of the United States in the Cold War period that, after the economic accommodation of the 1950s, the Francoist regime was able to catapult Spain's economy from abysmal poverty to a peak of development in an astonishingly short period of time. During the 1960s, a decade known as the "década del desarrollo," the Franco regime explicitly merged its theological state-system with globalized capitalism, helped by a Catholic governmental cadre of technocrats mostly led by Opus Dei members. A

Catholic techno-economic system voided of communism suddenly became the political reason of the Francoist state, and with that unique merger, the regime engaged further in a process of depoliticization that already foreshadowed contemporary postpolitical state-forms.[21]

Spain's "neutral," precariously industrial, totalitarian, nonmodern, nonconstitutional, and confessional state proved to be a good laboratory for U.S. neo-imperial and ultracolonial forms of world governance. Right after 1950, once the Cold War had begun, Spain became a prime geopolitical and economic site, the first real territory for advanced forms of *Pax Americana* marking the postindustrial age of globalized capitalism. From 1950 to 1975, and most evidently from the early 1960s through the 1973 oil crisis, the Francoist regime turned Spain into the ultimate postpolitical, postindustrial site from whence to procure the adjustment and transfer of the biopolitical inherent to the Eurocentric order of constitutional and colonial modernization to new forms of biopolitical circulation.[22]

We should ask, therefore, whether our current biopolitical formations and their manifestations—the emerging figure of the nonsubject of the political, the time zone of the vanishing of the friend/enemy paradigm, the time of the nonpartisan, of the posthuman, and so on[23]—is engaging in a process perhaps similar to the one activated right after the beginning of the Cold War by the totalitarian regime of Francisco Franco in Spain, which organized the last nonconstitutional, confessional state in the Western world. It is perhaps time to ponder whether the U.S. big idea of 1991 was in fact already there in 1950 in an embryonic form, when America chose Spain as a military nuclear warehouse and airbase, a strategic military site of high priority, in order to access the fringes of the USSR by flying not over Europe but over the Mediterranean.[24]

When Franco aligned Spain as a satellite of the United States, Spain became the first active "directed" state of the nuclear times, and a mirror of what was coming: a U.S.-inspired macrocorporate world state that, aiming to establish an imperial administration comprising a series of *estados dirigidos*, would come to use the former constitutional parlance of the Eurocentric order only as an empty shell. As the last mutation formation of the Spanish Empire, as its simulacrum, the Francoist state became the ultimate postindustrial state, a sort of postpolitical formation within the global macrocapitalist corporate state emerging after the Cold War. And as a voided state of the nuclear times, as an *estado dirigido*, Spain engaged with gusto in the production and consumption not of goods, or not of goods alone, but of life itself—the most valuable commodity—under the entrepreneurial leadership of Manuel Fraga Iribarne, the Spanish minister of information and tourism between 1963 and 1969. Fraga astutely engineered Spain's rapid ascendance into corporate capitalism through the hugely successful implementation of a state-sponsored mass tourist industry that was deeply dependent on the U.S. military nuclear geopolitical strategy.[25] Spain's new mass tourist industry was an industry (or, better, postindustry) that, ingrained within a new economic formation, produced its corresponding figures of the biopolitical: the mass tourist and the mass tourist provider, both of them corresponding to the *Pax Americana* and American Way of Life imaginaries touted since the 1950s.

Spain's successful development of mass tourism functioned as a postindustrial model of economic and social life aiming at subject depoliticization. It is true that the 1960s were a highly charged, intensively politicized time of civil rights struggles within and outside the hegemonic belt of dominance; the black subaltern population's fight in the United States is one of the best-known examples. But in Europe, the 1960s' booming tourism development was a first act in an early performance intent on a weakening of the political. An early variation of that big idea Bush Sr. was trying to sell to the world in his 1991 speeches, the Francoist Spain of the 1960s emerged as a partial rehearsal of the voiding of the state, a foreshadowing of the corporate biostate to come.[26]

The Cold War period already incorporated the zone of political indistinction Agamben was referring to in 1995. Seen through the prism of the Francoist state, the turbulent global politics of the mid- to late 1960s appear as a last convulsion, the last breath expelled by the emaciated, already passing body of the industrialized state and its correlating figures, that of the proletarian and the socialist militant. A spectral global biostate was rapidly developing, busy in Spain turning proletarians into naked tourists, and in Paris turning socialist militants into naked activists. This new biostate preburied socialism in the aftermath of May 1968, then finally disposed of it in 1991.[27]

Because the opening of an unobstructed passage for the transfer of biopolitical flows from the modern to the postmodern was already made possible with the Francoist state, Agamben's zone of political indistinction needs to be taken further back than the fall of the Soviet Union. Further back even than the almost twenty years of the Spanish political transition, a process that took the state without rupture from a nonconstitutional, nationalist-imperial, and Catholic fundamentalist mode to a constitutional and representative democracy that in fact consolidated the corporate bio-capitalist mode in a neoliberal format.[28] Further back also than Francisco Franco's cyborg-death in 1975, as Michel Foucault has it,[29] and further back than 1974, the year the Salazar dictatorship fell in Portugal and the victory of the so-called Socialist Revolution took place, inaugurating a political transition close to the Spanish one. And even further back then to 1973, when the socialist regime of Salvador Allende in Chile was aborted in that other sinister 9/11, and Chile became another *estado dirigido* similar to the old Francoist one under the totalitarian and biopolitical administration of Augusto Pinochet. Mostly the time zone of political indistinction should be pulled back to the end of World War II: to 1945 and the event of the nuclear, to the onset of the Cold War and the corresponding consolidation of the Francoist regime by the United States.

The massive move of paradigmatic displacement (with its corresponding biopolitical circulation), the transfer from the former Eurocentric order of the earth to the emerging U.S.-centered one, the change in the order of the political to which the 1991 presidential speech series refers is a process that starts moving at the end of World War II, continues its course during the period of the Cold War with the help of Franco's Spain as a partial ultracolonial site, and finally lands at the end of the second millennium in the form of our current postpolitical, biocapitalist configuration, often described as a global corporate state.[30]

The Cold War of 1950–91 was, as Schmitt perceived in 1963, a new mode of waging war,[31] not, or not only, a confrontation between two modalities of the modern industrialized state: the capitalist state of democratic form on one side, and the communist state on the other. Instead, the Cold War period is a struggle between two modes of biopolitical circulation as they relate to two forms of the state that are anchored in two different paradigms: one linked to a USSR still tied to modern industrialization, the other linked to a United States emerging as a bioimperial force willing to carry on the transformation of the industrial constitution-based state into one correlative with the current postindustrial scene of secondary technology. From 1950 on, an emerging U.S.-centered postindustrial formation evolved into a factual corporate global state with new biopolitical modes, means, and ends: a biopolitical state not specifically intent on the control, punishment, and discipline of life characteristic of the period of industrial modernization or of primary technology but intent instead, as Foucault notes, on the production of life inherent to the postindustrial era of secondary technologies;[32] an emerging mode of state formation that apparently wants to move away from the Hobbesian social contract at the basis of the constitutional state formations of the second period of modernity;[33] a state formation correspondent with our contemporary postindustrial age, which, seemingly unwilling to move its center of gravity away from the techno-economic, lapses into the biotechnical.[34]

The Cold War encrypts itself as an ever-evolving techno-nuclear-biotechnological mode of deterrence of total war—that is, as the biotechnical mode of preservation of the human. But because the Cold War is also the system that makes possible the total destruction of the human, it paradoxically becomes the enabling system for the conception and implementation of new forms of production and consumption of life. Simultaneously preserving human life and threatening to destroy it, the Cold War stimulates an ongoing economic and technological process mode that cannot think, produce, consume, and invest in anything but human life. It emerges as a solely homogenous biotechnological process-organism, a state apparatus encrypted within the horizon of a pure, solely economic state, that, as President Bush Sr. explicitly said in 1991, cannot offer a Kantian peace: only a neutral, truly bio-techno-economic macromanaged peace intent on producing, consuming, and discharging life.

Because the Cold War provided fertile ground for the production and consumption of life, it is therefore not a coincidence that it was during its apex in 1960s Spain when the mass tourist figure appeared on the global stage. This figure emerged as the product of the shifting flows of a globalized financial capital truly at ease within the habitus procured by the last European confessional form of state-empire, one favoring a hierarchic, organic, a-representative mode of state. A form of life that effectively eroded the figure of the proletarian Western subject, the highly depoliticized mass tourist figure of 1960s Spain hints at the figure of the disposable subject of postindustrial times, occupying a transitional role in the biopolitical paradigm of the postindustrial era as an early and subtle *tropos* for depoliticization and desubjectivation.[35] A prototype figure-formation of the Cold War, the Spanish mass tourist figure becomes in the Europe of the 1960s the encrypted, administered life of a Cold War triggered by the event of the nuclear.

The year 1945 prestaged the possibility of total human destruction and triggered a U.S.-centered ultracolonial order. Perhaps 1945, therefore, when

746 Teresa M. Vilarós

the world shifted from a Eurocentric *nomos* to a U.S-centered one, could be thought of as a time of the event. But since in Badiou's conceptualization the event would never announce a situation,[36] unless the Cold War were itself something other than a situation, the event of the nuclear in 1945 would have brought the coming of something other than the Cold War. What the nuclear age would have "made come," in Badiou's terminology, was the Cold War as the possibility of the times of imperial administration of the biopolitical. It would allude not to the situation of the Cold War but to a state of things rapidly shifting away from the social contract and its forms: a state of things, but not a situation, that would preannounce the ultracolonial order of empire as a series of voided states, a proliferation of *estados dirigidos* aiming at the administration of human life. The event of 1945 would allude to a massive macromanagement of human life that would not necessarily refer to state sovereignty anymore, to its institutions or its constitutions, but would instead refer to absolute sovereignty.

Absolute sovereignty seemed to be at the core of the 1991 series of speeches by President Bush. In establishing the need for a macromanage-ment of global peace and freedom as the ultimate goal of the Gulf War, the president was attempting to give the world a sense of assurance of political stability precisely at the moment when, while announcing the coming of a new mode of global sovereignty that envisioned the United States as its leader, the age of the political as we knew it was coming to an end:

> Tonight I come to this House to speak about the world—the world after war.... It's time to turn away from the temptation to protect unneeded weapons systems and obsolete bases. It's time to put an end to micro-management of foreign and security assistance programs, microman-agement that humiliates our friends and allies and hamstrings our diplomacy. It's time to rise above the parochial and the pork barrel, to do what is necessary, what's right and what will enable this nation to play the leadership role required of us.[37]

Already present in Francoist Spain during the Cold War as a possibility, the new, U.S.-centered order, the "big idea," was to depart from the former political order and embrace a postpolitical formation defined by the presi-dent as a kind of global macromanagement. Leaving behind the Leviathan, this new state-form would be willing to enter a post-Hobbesian state ready to dispose of the political modes and structures brought up by the former Eurocentric order of the times of industrialization, as they were increasingly being considered inefficient political micromanagement. A big idea embedded into the postindustrial paradigm of secondary technologies, it would finally emerge in 1991 as the macrocorporate bio-techno-economic state of the nuclear age: an ultracolonial age of *estados dirigidos*.

Notes

1 President George Herbert Walker Bush, "Attack on Iraq" speech, Washington, DC, January 16, 1991, available at www.famousquotes.me.uk/speeches/Georges_Bush, accessed December 15, 2004.
2 Ibid.
3 President George Herbert Walker Bush, "We Are the Nation That Can Shape the Future" speech (State of the Union Address), Washington DC, February 1991, available at www .famousquotes.me.uk/speeches/Georges_Bush, accessed December 15, 2004.
4 See Carl Schmitt, *The Nomos of the Earth in the International Law of the Jus Publicum Europaeum*, trans. G. L. Ulmen (New York: Telos, 2003).
5 I propose the term *ultracolonial* for the postindustrial form of colonization pertaining to a United States–centered era. While the initial mode of ultracolonial political intervention can be traced back to President Monroe's doctrine on the rights of intervention, with its follow-up on the political notion of *estado dirigido*, I am currently developing the notion of ultracoloniality, reading both concepts in relation to the Jesuit notion of a politics of *intención dirigida* in the seventeenth century. See Baltasar Gracián's *El político* (Madrid: Anaya, 1961) and Carl Schmitt's *The Nomos of the Earth* for further information on Gracián's *intención dirigida* and Monroe's doctrine on the political rights of foreign intervention.
6 At the end of World War II, and with the reality of the nuclear destruction of Hiroshima and Nagasaki in view, absolute sovereignty was briefly in reach for the United States as the only world power with access to and control over the production and military use of nuclear weapons. However, and if sovereignty is understood in the classical Schmittian proposition of power of decision over the means in a state of exception, absolute sovereignty could not be an option for the United States in 1945, since its sole control of nuclear capability did not last long.
7 President George Herbert Walker Bush, "New World Order" speech, March 6, 1991, available at www.al-bab.com/arab/docs/pal/pal10.htm, accessed December 15, 2004.
8 See a pertinent excerpt from ibid. at the end of this essay.
9 In 1929 Schmitt gave a lecture in Barcelona on neutrality and depoliticization, "La época de la neutralidad," where he developed his idea of the centers of gravity, or "central ambits." The lecture was first published in the second German edition of *The Concept of the Political* (Munich, 1931). See Schmitt, *The Concept of the Political*, trans. George Schwab (Chicago: University of Chicago Press, 1996); and (same essay but revised title) "La era de las neutralizaciones y de las despolitizaciones," in *El concepto de lo político*, trans. Rafael Agapito, 107–22 (Madrid: Alianza, 1991).
10 Alain Badiou, *Abregé de métapolitique* (Paris: Seuil, 1998), 91. In the French original, "ça qui fait advenir 'autre chose' que la situation, que les opinions, que les savoirs institués; qui est un supplément hasardeux, imprévisible, évanou aussitôt qu'apparu."

11   Interestingly enough, "More of the Same" was a slogan used in 2004 by the Republican
      supporters of George Bush Jr. in the election that gave him his second mandate.

12   Giorgio Agamben, *Means without Ends: Notes on Politics* (Minneapolis: University of Min-
      nesota Press, 2000), 122.

13   The peculiar Francoist state, with no political parties and no constitution, was neverthe-
      less recognized as a state after 1945, maintaining through 1975 a useful status of "neu-
      trality" and therefore of depoliticization, thanks to its U.S.-protected political isolation
      from Western Europe. As José María Roca has explained, Franco could establish the Span-
      ish state without drafting a constitutional democratic base, "acogiéndose a los discutibles
      postulados del positivismo jurídico que identifican los términos Estado y Derecho, en vir-
      tud de los cuales cualquier Estado -de hecho-, con independencia de sus características y
      de cuáles hayan sido sus orígenes, es, como conjunto de normas jurídicas, considerado
      un Estado de Derecho. El general Francisco Franco estimaba que el Estado surgido de la
      victoria de la alianza de las fuerzas políticas conservadoras en la guerra civil constituía un
      Estado de derecho, y las llamadas Leyes Fundamentales, lo que con gran reserva podría-
      mos denominar el sustrato legal de su Régimen, compendiaban una peculiar forma de
      Constitución; una Constitución abierta y en evolución, como le gustaba definirlas a él
      mismo."("Fuentes de legitimidad del estado franquista," comunicación presentada en
      el IV Encuentro de Investigadores del Franquismo, organizado por la Fundació d'Estudis
      i Iniciatives Sociolaborals y el Departamento de Historia Contemporánea de la Universi-
      dad de Valencia, celebrado en esta ciudad entre los días 17 y 19 de noviembre de 1999,
      available online at www.inisoc.org/fuentes.htm, accessed February 20, 2005).

14   During the first years of his military regime, from 1939 to 1945, Francisco Franco de-
      clared a state of neutrality for Spain during the Second World War, but his sympathies
      for Nazi Germany and Fascist Italy were openly displayed. After 1950, Franco explained
      to the international audience that his pro-Axis tendencies only supported Spain's high-
      est mission: to stop communism in Europe. His articulation of Spain's civil war as a
      "crusade" movement ("la Cruzada del Movimiento Nacional") that dispelled the evil of
      communism, *and* as a precursor in the international liberal fight against communism,
      is highly relevant for the idea that after 1950 Franco saw no ideological or spiritual frac-
      ture in merging Spain's fundamentalist Catholic state with a capitalism that was already
      functioning in postindustrial ways. See Franco's *Discursos y mensajes del Jefe del Estado:
      Edición cronológica*, vol. 1 (Madrid: Dirección General de Información, 1955), and *Textos de
      doctrina política: Palabras y escritos de 1945 a 1950* (Madrid: Publicaciones españolas, 1951).

15   "España es una precursora en esta universal contienda ideológica que conmueve dra-
      máticamente los cimientos de toda la civilización." Francisco Franco, "Mensaje de fin de
      año (31 de diciembre de 1950)," in *Discursos y mensajes*, 8.

16   The bilateral pacts of 1953 and 1957 signed by President Eisenhower and Franco kept
      the United States–Spain alliance strong during the whole period of the Cold War despite
      some tensions. See Angel Viñas's *En las garras del águila: Los pactos con Estados Unidos de
      Francisco Franco a Felipe González (1945–1995)* (Barcelona: Crítica, 2003) for a detailed
      account of the political relations between the United States and Spain.

17   Carl Schmitt, "La época de las neutralidades," 114.

18   Ibid.

19   For a follow-up on the cultural turns of capitalism at its third stage of development, see

Fredric Jameson's "Culture and Finance Capital," in *The Cultural Turn: Selected Writings on the Postmodern* (London: Verso, 1998).

20   See Stanley Payne's *Fascism in Spain, 1923–1977* (Madison: University of Wisconsin Press, 1999) and *Franco: El perfil de la historia*, trans. Carlos Carnaci (Madrid: Espasa Calpe, 1993) for an accurate account on the history of Francoism, the 1960s Spanish economic boom, and the role the Opus Dei played in the economic recovery. See also Paul Preston, *Franco: A Biography (*London: HarperCollins, 1994). For a history of the Opus Dei, see Michael Walsh, *Opus Dei: An Investigation into the Powerful, Secretive Society within the Catholic Church* (San Francisco: Harper, 1989).

21   Although Franco died on November 22, 1975, the Francoist state lasted until 1978, when Spain signed a democratic constitution and finally discarded its theological sphere. The period of political transition in Spain is historically known as "La transición." For a historical account, see (among many others) Javier Tusell, *Franco y los católicos: La política interior española entre 1945 y 1957* (Madrid: Alianza, 1984). For a cultural account see my *El mono del desencanto: Una crítica cultural de la transición española.* (Madrid: Siglo XXI, 1998); see also Cristina Moreiras-Menor, *Cultura herida: Literatura y cine en la España democrática* (Madrid: Libertarias, 2002).

22   See Xavier Casals, *El fascismo: Entre el legado de franco y la modernidad de Le Pen* (Barcelona: Destino, 1998), for a better understanding of the role played by the so-called neofascisms in the postindustrial age.

23   I owe to Alberto Moreiras the concept of what he has termed "the nonsubject of the political," "the nonpartisan," and "the posthuman." See his articles "Children of the Light," *The Bible and Critical Theory* 1.1 (2004), available online at http://publications.epress.monash .edu/loi/bc (accessed May 27, 2005); "Preemptive Manhunt: A New Partisanship," *positions* 13.1 (special issue, "Against Preemptive War," ed. Tani Barlow et al.) (forthcoming, May 2005); and "A Post-Theology of Praxis: Donoso Cortés and the Political," lecture delivered at the "Thinking Politically" conference, Duke University, October 24, 2004.

24   For the nuclear implications of the development of mass tourism in Spain see my essay "The Lightness of Terror: Palomares, 1966," *Journal of Spanish Cultural Studies* 5.2 (2004). For a detailed account of the 1966 nuclear accident in Palomares see Isabel Alvarez de Toledo's memoir *Palomares (Memoria)* (Madrid: UNED, 2001); Randall Maydew, *America's Lost H-Bomb: Palomares, Spain, 1966* (Manhattan, KS: Sunflower, 1997); and Rafael Lorente, *La bomba de Palmares, ayer y hoy* (Madrid: Libertarias, 1985).

25   See Tatjana Pavlovich, "The Mobile Nation," *Journal of Spanish Cultural Studies* 5.2 (2004), and my article "The Lightness of Terror" for more on Spain's mass culture in the 1960s.

26   Francoist Spain in the 1960s became the most provocative, neutral site of massive depoliticization in the Western world, luring down the Northern European proletarian masses who, following the European economic recovery after the implementation of the Marshall Plan in the early 1950s, were ready for an endless, cheap fun of fiesta, sun, beaches, toros, and sangría. See my essay "Banalidad y biopolítica," in *Desacuerdos* (Barcelona: MACBA, 2005), for more information on the dynamics of Spanish biotourism in the 1960s.

27   For an account of the events of May 1968 from a Spanish perspective, see Gabriel Albiac's *Mayo del 68* (Madrid: Temas de Hoy, 1993). Appropriately, Albiac starts the narration in the Père Lachaise Cimetière in Paris.

28   In 1976, in a process that in Spain was once again prestaging the 1989–91 collapse of communism, the three main communist and socialist national parties in Spain (PCE, PSUC, and PSOE) became the first in Europe to willingly sever their respective Leninist and Marxist denominations.

29   See chapter 11 of Foucault's *"Society Must Be Defended": Lectures at the Collège de France, 1975–1976* (New York: Picador, 2003), a posthumously published collection of lectures.

30   The pulsing kernel of the postindustrial paradigm to which the postpolitical corporate state of today adheres can be traced back to the United States' imperial will, which first surfaced with the 1898 Spanish-American War, then went latent in the first half of the twentieth century. It was with the 1898 war that for the first time America's nascent imperial desire was acted out, with the United States trying to control strategically located territory (the Philippines, Puerto Rico, and Cuba) that had been made vulnerable by years of colonial rapacity as protectorates of the Spanish Empire. However, it was not until the massively deadly secular imperial collusions of the first half of the twentieth century — and not until the United States was directly attacked by the Japanese Empire — that America finally made its move as the leading allied force during World War II.

31   Schmitt, prologue to *El concepto de lo político*, 48.

32   The importance Foucault gave to the paradigm of secondary technologies can best be followed in his *"Society Must Be Defended."*

33   As first conceived by Thomas Hobbes in *De Cive* (The Citizen) and in *Leviathan*, the social contract is the basis for the constitutional state formations (from republicanism to fascism) of the modern era, which is quickly passing away.

34   Carl Schmitt suggests in his reading of Hobbes's *Leviathan* that the state form of the seventeenth century that took hold in the European continent can already be considered "the first product of the technical era, the first political mechanism of grand style"; and that "in Hobbes's state there are already implicit not only the sociological and historical pre-suppositions of the next techno-industrial era, but is itself typical and even prototypical work of the new technological era" (my translation, from the Spanish version of Schmitt's *El Leviatán en la teoría del estado de Tomás Hobbes* [Buenos Aires: Struhart, 1990], 33. To my knowledge, there is no English translation of Schmitt's text, one of his most disturbing due to his anti-Semitic remarks).

35   The mass tourism of the 1960s — the descent into Spain of large numbers of low-class, blue-collar workers from Europe's Marshall Plan–benefiting, war-recovered northern areas — happily marches South, toward the massively cheap and disposable infrastructure of consumption provided by the Francoist state. Born a potentially disposable life formation, the tanned and naked mass tourist cavorting on the beaches of Benidorm, Costa del Sol, or Lloret de Mar, the postindustrial disposable habitat built in the 1960s, is an already weakened form of the figure of the proletarian subject. See MVRDV, *Costa ibérica: Hacia la ciudad del ocio*, ed. Winny Maas (Barcelona: Actar, 1998).

36   Badiou, in *Abregé de métapolitique*, conceives of the event as one of three main dimensions of the process of truth upon which Evil would depend in order to exist, the other two dimensions of the process being "Fidelity" (91) and "Truth" proper (92). In the French original, "La verité proprement dite, qui est ce multiple interne a la situation que construit, peu a peu, la fidelité; qui est ce que la fidelité regroup et construit" (91).

37   President Bush, "New World Order" speech.

Bruno Bosteels

The Speculative Left

> Communism is for us not a *state of affairs* which is to be established, an *ideal* to which reality [will] have to adjust itself. We call communism the *real* movement which abolishes the present state of things.
> —Karl Marx and Friedrich Engels, *The German Ideology*, ed./trans. C. J. Arthur

Communism without Marxism?

A friend of mine once provocatively described Alain Badiou as a philosopher who is first and foremost a communist before being, or perhaps even without being, a Marxist. A passage from *Of an Obscure Disaster: On the End of the Truth of State*, which is Badiou's take on the collapse of the Soviet Union, might seem to confirm this bold assessment. Thus, in an otherwise unsurprising rebuttal against all nostalgic and/or posthistorical judgments regarding the "death" of communism, Badiou all of a sudden affirms the invariant and seemingly eternal nature of a certain communist subjectivity:

> From Spartacus to Mao (not the Mao of the State, who also exists, but the rebellious extreme, complicated Mao), from the Greek

The *South Atlantic Quarterly* 104:4, Fall 2005.

democratic insurrections to the worldwide decade 1966–1976, it is and
has been, in this sense, a question of communism. It will always be a
question of communism, even if the word, soiled, is replaced by some
other designation of the concept that it covers, the philosophical and
thus eternal concept of rebellious subjectivity.[1]

Badiou's affirmation of an invariant form of communism in need of an
audacious resurrection would seem to put him in the company of a small
but significant number of radical thinkers in the late 1980s and early 1990s
who likewise seek to salvage a certain communist notion from the simultaneous collapse of so-called totalitarianism and of the revolutionary project
that the various state regimes of "really existing socialism" had long ceased
to stand for. "The project: to rescue 'communism' from its own disrepute,"
Félix Guattari and Antonio Negri write in the opening lines of *Communists
Like Us*, before explaining what they mean by such an operation: "We need
to save the glorious dream of communism from Jacobin mystifications and
Stalinist nightmares alike; let's give it back this power of articulation: an
alliance, between the liberation of work and the liberation of subjectivity."[2]
Guattari and Negri even seem to anticipate Badiou's very own style when
they juxtapose the dream of "communism" with a notion of "democracy"
that similarly would have to be saved from its disrepute:

> At this juncture the word "democracy" begs redefinition. The word
> "communism" has clearly been defaced, but the word democracy itself
> has been trashed and mutilated. From the Greek *polis* to the popular
> uprisings of the Renaissance and Reformation, from the proletarian
> rebellions that coexisted with the great liberal revolutions, democracy
> has always been synonymous with the legitimation of power through
> the people.[3]

Like democracy when properly understood, communism would name this
invariant process whereby the people constitute themselves as people or,
conversely, people constitute themselves as the people in a movement of
immanent self-legitimation.

We can also find a defense of communism in an otherwise very different
philosophical tradition, one more indebted to Jacques Derrida and Martin
Heidegger than to Gilles Deleuze or Benedict Spinoza. "*Communism*, without doubt, is the archaic name of a thinking which is still entirely to come,"
Jean-Luc Nancy thus suggests in *The Compearance*: "When it will have come,

it will not carry this name—in fact, it will not be 'thought' in the sense that this is understood. It will be a *thing*. And this thing, perhaps, is already here and does not let us go. But perhaps it is here in a manner that we are unable to recognize."[4] Earlier, in *The Inoperative Community*, Nancy had already ventured out into the vast expanses of this unpredictable future: "The community of the interrupted myth, that is, the community that in a sense is without community, or communism without community, is our destination. In other words, it is that toward which we are called, or remitted, as to our ownmost future."[5] In this case, to be sure, the future of communism will not be given over to the pure self-immanence of the people as people; instead, it belongs to the core of all future politics, according to the temporality of what is yet to come, to be marked by the radical finitude of each and every community. Communism, in other words, not as the exposure of sheer immanence but as the tracing of a groundless being-in-common, torn away from the nightmarish dreams of immanence and transcendence alike, and incommensurate to all known attributes and properties, whether of substance or of the subject. Nancy concludes:

> We have no model, no matrices for this tracing or for this writing. I even think that the unprecedented and the unheard-of can no longer come about. But perhaps it is precisely when all signs are missing that the unheard-of becomes again not only possible but, in a sense, certain. Here the historicity of our history comes in, as does the future-to-come of the suspended meaning of the old word "communism."[6]

Despite the shift from absolute immanence to radical finitude, in this orientation too we are witnessing a project to salvage an idea or practice of communism from the agonizing history of its own defacement. In a long footnote Nancy even goes on to cite Badiou himself as someone who would be "better placed" to speak of the "paleonymy" (in Derrida's sense) that would affect the word and concept of "communism." Nancy quotes the following words from Badiou's *Theory of the Subject*:

> The word "communism" has contracted some mould, that's for sure. But the roses and the gladioluses, the hairdresses, the sirens and the consoles, were also eaten by moths in that fin-de-siècle poetry which was given the name of "symbolism" and which all in all was a catastrophe. Let us try to be no more communist in the sense of Brezhnev or Marchais than Mallarmé was a symbolist in the manner of Vielé-

Griffin. If symbolism has held up so gloriously well with the swans and the stars, let us see if we can do as much with the revolution and communism. It is because we take the exact measure of their power, and thus of their sharing, that words may be innocent.[7]

If we were to continue along the lines of this shared genealogy, to which we could no doubt add several other proper names, we might indeed have to conclude that Badiou participates in a wider trend to salvage communism, as an unheard-of type of rebellious subjectivity or an unprecedented form of being-in-common, both from its actual fate in the collapsed socialist states and perhaps even from its place throughout the history of Marxism. Nothing could be more misleading, however, than the premise behind this genealogy—namely, that communism may be understood apart from Marxism—just as, conversely, few tasks could be more urgent than specifying the exact relations between communism and Marxism in Badiou's view.

For Badiou, there emerges a speculative type of leftism whenever communism is disjoined, and nowadays supposedly set free, from the historicity intrinsic to the various stages of Marxism. The critique of speculative leftism in this sense is actually a constant throughout Badiou's work. At the same time, though, a common objection among readers of this work holds that Badiou himself, by sovereignly divorcing the theoretical fidelity to an event from any concrete genealogical inscription of the event, over the years increasingly would have painted himself into a similar corner as a dogmatic, absolutist, or even downright mystical thinker. According to this objection, Badiou himself would be yet another example of "left-wing communism" as the "infantile disorder" of Marxism, to use Lenin's well-known words, even if we might have to turn these words around today, following the example set not so long ago by Gabriel and Daniel Cohn-Bendit, in terms of Marxism as the "senile disorder" of an eternally youthful and invariant "leftism."[8] Once we grasp the logic behind Badiou's critique of speculative leftism, however, we will also be better equipped to address this objection, according to which he himself, if not earlier then ever more clearly so in recent years, falls prey to precisely such a leftist temptation of wanting to be a communist without also being a Marxist.

The Communist Invariants

> In what historical conditions does the universal ideo-
> logical resistance of the exploited take the form of
> a radical vindication, which bears on the very exis-
> tence of class contradictions and of the state, and
> which envisions the process of their annihilation? Key
> question of universal ideological history: who then is
> communist?
> —Alain Badiou and François Balmès, *De l'idéologie*

The first task consists in refining our understanding of the invariant nature
of communist subjectivity briefly recapitulated in *Of an Obscure Disaster*.
Badiou originally proposed the idea of invariant communism, or of communist invariants, nearly thirty years ago in his Maoist booklet *Of Ideology*,
written in collaboration with the Lacanian psychoanalyst François Balmès.
Based in large part on *The Peasant War in Germany* by Friedrich Engels, particularly as seen through the intriguing case of Thomas Münzer, Badiou
and Balmès propose that all mass revolutionary uprisings throughout history aspire to realize a limited set of communist principles: "Our hypothesis holds that all the great mass revolts of the successive exploited classes
(slaves, peasants, proletarians) find their ideological expression in egalitarian, anti-property and anti-state formulations that outline the basic features
for a communist program."[9] Such spontaneous rebellion of the exploited
masses typically leads to a war of insurrection, in which communism comes
to define a general ideological position against the state: "The elements of
this general positioning of the insurgent producers are what we call the
communist invariants: ideological invariants of communist type that are constantly regenerated in the process of unification of the great popular revolts
of all times."[10] We thus can begin to understand at least superficially why
the later Badiou, when faced with the many purported "deaths" of Marxism, would want to retrieve this invariant communism as an eternal form
of rebellious subjectivity.

We should not forget, though, that the communist invariants are the work
of the masses in a broad sense. There is as yet no specific class determination to the logic of revolt in which slaves, plebeians, serfs, peasants, or
workers rise up against the powers that be: "The communist invariants
have no defined class character: they synthesize the universal aspiration
of the exploited to topple every principle of exploitation and oppression.
They emerge on the terrain of the contradiction between masses and the

state."[11] In this broad-based resistance against the state apparatuses lies the unlimited power and energy of the masses; in fact, the authors see no other reason why communists should have infinite confidence in the people as such. Badiou and Balmès, however, also argue that this massive ideological communism remains deficient without the historical means for its realization. As a rule, they even posit a certain counterfinality at the root of history. That is to say, most often the spontaneous revolt of the masses is appropriated and diverted by those historical forces that are in the process of becoming dominant precisely as an unintended effect of the revolt itself. This is the argument, so frequently used for the sake of a reactionary disavowal, about how history always seems to proceed behind the back of the masses. Engels himself is forced to admit at the end of his study that the princes were the only ones to profit from the Peasant War. Similarly, the Jacobins are often said merely to have paved the road for the bourgeoisie, just as the rebellious spirit of the students and workers who took to the streets in the late 1960s, unbeknownst to themselves, would have worked to the benefit of the newly emergent technocrats.

Within any ideological struggle, we can thus distinguish a minimum of three factors. First, we find the relatively *old form* of the revolt, that is, the ideology of the old dominant classes, as when the religious ideology of Protestantism is used heretically to organize the peasants in Münzer's Germany. Second, we have the *unchanged content* of the communist program, that is, the immediate popular substance of all great revolts, from Spartacus to Mao. Finally, true *historical novelty* is the work no longer of the masses in general but of that specific fraction or class which, under the given circumstances, is able to take hold of the moment for its own long-term benefit: "Ideology, seized as a conflictual process, always puts into play a triple determination: two class determinations (old and new, counterrevolutionary and revolutionary), and one mass determination (the communist invariants)."[12] The real key in the discussion over the historicity of communism, as opposed to its spontaneous eternity, lies in this difficult dialectic of masses and classes, in which both get caught at cross-purposes in the uneven struggle between the old and the new.

With the revolt of the proletariat, however, there supposedly would come an end to the rule of historical counterfinality. Instead of seeing their egalitarian demands co-opted and drained for the benefit of the newly emergent dominant classes, the workers who after the massive revolts of 1848 in Europe organize themselves as proletariat would be the first historical force actually to take control of the basic communist program: "With the proletariat, ideological resistance becomes not only the *repetition* of the invariant but also the mastery of its *realization*."[13] This unique moment of course coincides with the birth of Marxism. The latter in fact is nothing but the accumulation of the knowledge conveyed by the millenarian ideological struggle around the communist invariants—including many of the failed revolts from past centuries, whose broken and repressed memory is never entirely lost but rather haunts the present as its uncanny and shadowy double: "Marxism-Leninism is that which avers that the proletariat, heir to a secular ideological struggle surrounding the communist program, is also the realizer of this heritage. Marxism-Leninism not only accumulates the ideological resistance but also transforms it into knowledge and project."[14] Marxism and communism thus rely on each other in a paradoxical history of eternity—that is, the historical unfolding of an eternal revolt. Let us say: Marxism without communism is empty, but communism without Marxism is blind.

Only under the direction of the proletariat would the complete dialectic of masses, classes, and the state become adequate to its historical task. As for the materialist question regarding the specific conditions that make this adequation possible, suffice it to say that it is capitalism itself that first brings into existence and then organizes the proletarian revolutionary capacity. The proletariat is even said to acquire an unprecedented logical and epistemological capacity. Perhaps, then, we are not so far removed after all from the central idea in Georg Lukács's *History and Class Consciousness*. "The proletariat is the producer of the first logic of the revolution," Badiou and Balmès solemnly claim: "In this sense, the proletarian ideology, in its concrete form of Marxism-Leninism, stops being the resistance displayed on the basis of the radical but historically utopian critique of class society in general, so as to become the revolutionary knowledge of this society and, consequently, the organizing principle of its effective destruction."[15] This also means that, in the absence of an organized accumulation of critique, the spontaneous and immediate antagonism of masses against the state runs the risk of quickly being reversed. As Badiou and Balmès warn while reflecting back upon May 1968 in France: "This purely ideological radicality inevitably changes over into its opposite: once the mass festivals of democracy and discourse are over, things make place for the modernist restoration of order among workers and bosses."[16] The regeneration of the invariant communist program, in other words, is a powerful but insufficient weapon: "We say that, left to its own devices, abandoned to the unilateral exaltation of libertarian tendencies, this regeneration does not outlive the movement itself of which it is the reflection, and it ineluctably reverses into capitulation, into ideological servilism."[17] Unless of course it is to remain an ideal that will be always yet to come, communism names the real movement that abolishes the present state of injustice only when it is historically tied to the various stages of Marxism.

Marxist Politics

> We must conceive of Marxism as the accumulated wisdom of popular revolutions, the reason they engender, and the fixation and precision of their target.
> —Alain Badiou, *Théorie de la contradiction*

We might also ask somewhat bluntly: What do Badiou's critics mean when they deplore the fact that he would not (or would insufficiently) be a Marxist? "Marxism" in this context seems to stand alternatively for a philosophy, a science of history, or, above all, a critique of political economy. Badiou would not be able to give us an up-to-date critique of global capitalism, or of the new world order. No matter how sophisticated they may well turn out to be in their own right, though, such readings nonetheless fail to grasp the strictly political significance of Marxism. Paul Sandevince, in the brochure *What Is a Marxist Politics?* published by the Maoist organization in which both he and Badiou were active until the early 1980s, sums up this significance with his usual concision: "Marxism is not a doctrine, whether philosophical or economical. Marxism is the politics of the proletariat in its actuality," and later: "Marxism is the politics of communism."[18] "Science of history?" Badiou also wonders in disbelief about the nature of Marxism in his *Theory of the Subject,* only to serve up a firm rebuttal of his own: "*Marxism is the discourse through which the proletariat supports itself as subject.*"[19] Though Marxism is no less unable than any other form of knowledge to make a totality out of the constitutive dispersion of history, it nevertheless cannot be grasped outside the framework of periodized referentiality in which communism becomes part of a real historical movement.

There are two perspectives, or two directions, from which we might read the problem of historical referentiality which alone organizes the communist invariants and thereby gives structure to the body of accumulated knowledge that is Marxism. If we start mainly from within this corpus itself, the question becomes one of periodizing the systematizations to which the substance of mass revolts, under the guidance of the proletariat, becomes subject in the writings of Marx, Engels, Lenin, Mao, and so on. Rather than concentrating on the discovery of a new, structural type of causality in *Capital* or even, for that matter, on the *Grundrisse* as the dynamic center of Marxian thought, Badiou and his friends thus always favor the more historical and interventionist writings, such as Engels's *The Peasant Revolt in Germany*, Lenin's *What Is To Be Done?* or Mao's *Problems of Strategy in China's Revolutionary War*, in addition to the all-too-obvious choice of *The Communist Manifesto*. Marxism, Leninism, and Maoism are thus tied to the principal episodes in an otherwise orthodox periodization of revolutionary activity:

> The great stages of Marxism are punctuated by the proletarian revolutions and, precisely, the great Marxists are those who have directed and synthesized the findings of the theory, ideology, and politics of the proletariat in the light of these same revolutions: Marx and Engels for the Paris Commune, Lenin and Stalin for the October Revolution, Mao Zedong for the Cultural Revolution.[20]

Much of Badiou's *Theory of the Subject* and several of his recent investigations and talks that will be taken up in *Logics of Worlds* deal extensively with this periodization, most notably through a new appraisal of the rapport between history and politics in the Paris Commune and the Great Proletarian Cultural Revolution. These texts actually form a strong component of historical materialism that is necessarily contained within the materialist dialectic according to Badiou.

This first historical perspective does not pretend foolishly to ignore the crisis that affects every piece of knowledge associated with Marxism. To the contrary, as Badiou declares in a seminar from *Theory of the Subject*, dated as early as November 7, 1977, at the height of fame and media-coverage of the New Philosophers:

> Yes, let's admit it without beating around the bushes: Marxism is in crisis and atomized. Past the élan and creative scission of the sixties, past the national liberation struggles and the cultural revolution, we inherit, in times of crisis and the threat of war, a fragmentary and narrow disposition of thought and action, caught in a labyrinth of ruins and survivals.[21]

However, this unabashed admission of the sense of an ending does not foreclose the possibility, and perhaps even the obligation, to give Marxism a new beginning. "To defend Marxism today means to defend a weakness," Badiou may well state in the same seminar from *Theory of the Subject*, but then he adds: "We have to *do* Marxism."[22] For Badiou and his friends, this means first and foremost to take cognizance not so much of the solutions as of the problems left unsolved during the last revolutionary sequence from the twentieth century, the one marked by the name of Mao Zedong. As we can read in another brochure from their Maoist organization, published several years after the death of the Chairman:

> Today, a Marxist is someone who, in the framework of an organized politics, makes an effort to resolve on his or her own the PROBLEMS left hanging by the initial Maoism, the Maoism of Mao Zedong, the Maoism that is contemporary to the Cultural Revolution. Except for this, there is no other Marxism.[23]

One thus necessarily must remain a Marxist even, or especially, when it comes to understanding the unresolved problems of Marxism: "We must study contemporary history and practice historical materialism with regard to Marxism itself."[24] There is no need for a post-Marxism.

Another perspective from which to read the problem of historical referentiality would move in the opposite direction, starting from the emancipatory events of the past two centuries themselves and studying when and where they rely for support on the discourse of Marxism. Once again following the arguments of his friend Sandevince, Badiou outlines three such moments or referents in *Can Politics Be Thought?* which contains his contributions to the early 1980s seminar at the Center for the Philosophical Study of the Political, organized by Nancy and Philippe Lacoue-Labarthe in Paris. These three moments correspond to the workers' movement, the victorious formation of socialist state regimes, and the national liberation struggles. The sense of an ending is no less painfully obvious from this perspective, to be sure, than from the first one. Indeed, nothing seems to be left standing in terms of Marxism's capacity to lay claims upon history after the collapse of the Soviet Union, after the revealed capacity for military expansion of liberated countries such as Vietnam, and especially after the appearance of workers' movements such as Solidarity in Poland that are openly anti-Marxist:

> The great historical mass pulsations no longer refer to Marxism since—at least—the end of the Cultural Revolution: Look at Poland, or

at Iran. Because of this we see an expatriation of politics. Its historical territoriality is no longer transitive to it. The age of auto-referentiality is closed. Politics no longer has a historical homeland.[25]

However, from this point of view, too, there is space for a possible re-composition, even a second birth, of Marxism. Badiou proposes in particular not just to repeat but to reinvent Marx's founding gesture in *The Communist Manifesto*, which consists in listening to the social hysterias of the 1840s only to answer them with the hypothesis of a hitherto nonexistent political capacity. "If Marxism today is indefensible, it is because we have to start it," Badiou claims: "We must redo the *Manifesto*."[26] Even in Marxism's irredeemable loss of referents, more emphasis should fall on the question of referentiality than on the melancholic experience of loss. This also means that one should be the subject, rather than the cynical object, of the crisis and destruction of Marxism. "What does it mean to be a Marxist today?" Badiou asks before venturing an answer of his own: "To stand for Marxism means to occupy a place that is destroyed and, thus, uninhabitable. I posit that there exists a Marxist subjectivity that inhabits the uninhabitable."[27] In the end, the important point remains that, without the consistency of a previously invisible political subjectivity, without the hypothesis of an unwarranted capacity of nondomination, or without the ability to give organizational form to the wager of an invariant communism, there is not a breath of life to be found in the whole doctrinal body of Marxism.

Critique of Pure Leftism

> It is never "the masses," nor the "movement" that as a whole carry the principle of engenderment of the new, but that which in them divides itself from the old.
> —Alain Badiou, *Théorie de la contradiction*

Where do we stand today with regard to the dialectics between masses, classes, and the state, between the people and the proletariat, or between the dispersed elements of an invariant and generic communism and the organized forms of knowledge concentrated in the writings of Marxism?

Everything would seem to indicate that, in an era marked by the end of referentiality, all that is left in the eyes of our most radical contemporary thinkers is the unlimited and spontaneous affirmative energy of pure communism, purged of all its historically compromising and/or saturated ties to the parties, groups, organizations, or state regimes that once invoked the now infamous names of Marx, Lenin, or Mao. The Yanan-Philosophy Group in Badiou's Maoist organization even charges that all revisionist tendencies in French thought—not only among the so-called New Philosophers but also among Deleuzeans, Althusserians, and Lacanians—can be said to presuppose categorical oppositions that seek to stamp out any possible diagonal term—whether class, party, or organization—between the masses and the state:

> The political essence of these "philosophies" is captured in the following principle, a principle of bitter resentment against the entire history of the twentieth century: "In order for the revolt of the masses against the state to be good, it is necessary to reject the class direction of the proletariat, to stamp out Marxism, to hate the very idea of the class party."[28]

Today, I would risk to add that we find a similar principle at work not only in Antonio Negri and Michael Hardt's argument over multitude and empire but also among other thinkers who are still variously influenced by the opposition emblematized in Pierre Clastres's *Society Against the State*, starting from the relation of exteriority between war machine and state apparatus, as posited by Deleuze and Guattari in their *Nomadology*, all the way to the very recent repetition of a similar scheme in Miguel Abensour's *Democracy Against the State*. In all these cases, leftism involves a reified external opposition, one as radical as it is politically inoperative, along the lines of the spontaneous and unmediated antagonism between masses and the state discussed by Badiou and Balmès. This is communism without Marxism, as if all that is left were nothing but the communist invariants outside their determination in terms of a specific historical class, fraction, party, or other, guided by the knowledge referred to in Marxism.

Badiou, however, has always argued against the leftist operation that radically unties the dialectical knot between masses, classes, and state, or between communism and Marxism. We can actually find a number of variations on this theme, a detailed overview of which would produce some sort of critique of pure leftist reason.

1. There is first of all the philosophical variation which opposes *place* and *force*, or *structure* and *tendency*, as discussed in *Theory of Contradiction* and *Of Ideology*. On this view, leftism ignores the fact that every force is necessarily determined by a system of assigned places in which it finds its space.

This structural element inherent in every tendency is neglected in favor of a viewpoint of pure, unlimited, and affirmative becoming, as in many a "movementist" tendency fostered by May 1968: "If, indeed, one neglects the structural element, one takes the tendency for an accomplished state of affairs."[29] Everything thereby fuses into the being of pure becoming.

2. In the moral variation, we have the familiar dualism of *freedom* and *necessity*, or of *autonomy* and *determinism*, which Badiou attributes to the hidden Kantianism of the authors of *Anti-Oedipus*. "Deleuze and Guattari don't hide this much: return to Kant, here's what they came up with to exorcise the Hegelian ghost," Badiou charges: "The old freedom of autonomy, hastily repainted in the colours of what the youth in revolt legitimately demands: some spit on the bourgeois family."[30] Moreover, Badiou finds that this moral dualism also underlies the oppositions between *subject-groups* and *subjugated groups* as well as between the *molecular* and the *molar*.

3. In the political variation, we find the dualisms of *plebes* and *state*, or of *students* and *cops*, especially during and after May 1968. These too receive a harsh critique. "There is not only the law of Capital, or only the cops. To miss this point means not to see the unity of the order of assigned places, its consistency. It means falling back into objectivism, the inverted ransom of which consists by the way in making the state into the only subject, whence the antirepressive logorrhea," Badiou warns in *Theory of the Subject*. "It is the idea that the world knows only the necessary rightist backlash and the powerless suicidal leftism."[31] Critics of the necessarily repressive or totalitarian nature of the state can then pontificate endlessly about the virtues of the masses, or of civil society, without even for a moment taking their eyes off the fascinating omnipotence of the state's coercive and hegemonic machinery.

4. Finally, we also obtain a psychoanalytical variation on the same theme in terms of the dualism of *tuchè* and *automaton* that roughly corresponds to the encounter with the real and the automatism of the reality principle. In *Can Politics Be Thought?* Badiou not only draws on this Aristotelian conceptual dyad by way of Lacan but also applies it to the rather more deconstructively inspired arguments of Nancy and Lacoue-Labarthe regarding the retreat of the political: "The thought of the essence of the political as retreat slips into the distance, which is almost nil and which our time makes into its misfortune, between fortune and repetition, between *tuchè* and *automaton*."[32] In this case, the anticipation of the transcendental conditions of possibility of an unforeseeable event or encounter with the real, which are also

always its conditions of impossibility, is substituted for the actual interruption of the automatism of capital.

Given this ongoing critique of the speculative Left in all its variations, to what extent can we say that Badiou himself is capable of resisting the leftist temptation? Have not most of his critics, including Slavoj Žižek, Peter Hallward, Françoise Proust, Stathis Kouvélakis, and Daniel Bensaïd, suggested in one way or another that Badiou is actually one of the most formidably dogmatic leftists of our time? In the exemplary words of Bensaïd:

> The absolute incompatibility between truth and opinion, between philosopher and sophist, between event and history, leads to a practical impasse. The refusal to work within the equivocal contradiction and tension which bind them together ultimately leads to a pure voluntarism, which oscillates between a broadly leftist form of politics and its philosophical circumvention. In either case, the combination of theoretical elitism and practical moralism can indicate a haughty withdrawal from the public domain, sandwiched between the philosopher's evental truth and the masses' subaltern resistance to the world's misery.[33]

This hard judgment, however, cannot absorb a single element in the long-standing critique of leftism that we find throughout Badiou's writings. Even *Being and Event*, a book which the sheer power of mathematical abstraction at every turn of the page almost seems to push in the direction of dogmatism, seeks to avoid the traps of a relation of pure exteriority between its two founding terms. As a matter of fact, it is precisely at the heart of this book that we find an acute definition of the speculative Left as the temptation to turn the notion of a political intervention, for example, into the blind voluntaristic or miraculous event of an ultra-one, or an absolute beginning, utterly cut off from the structure of the situation at hand. "We can call *speculative leftism* every thinking of being supported by the theme of an absolute beginning. Speculative leftism imagines that the intervention is authorized only by itself, and breaks with the situation with no other support than its own negative will," Badiou writes. "Speculative leftism is fascinated by the ultra-one of the event, and thinks it is possible in its name to deny all immanence to the structured regime of the count-for-one."[34] Badiou's own philosophy, in my view at least, does not pretend to save the purity of the event by haughtily withdrawing from all immanence and situatedness. The point is to study the consequences of an event within the situation, not to elevate the event into a wholly other dimension beyond being.

More important, however, I wonder why all those critics mentioned above, in their implicit or explicit quest for a more historically or dialectically grounded mediation between being and event, cannot find a meeting place somewhere in between, whereby they might find an accomplice rather than an adversary in Badiou. I admit that such a renewed understanding of the common project to think an emancipatory politics would entail a radical overhaul of some of our most deeply ingrained intellectual habits—such as the habit of polemicizing among fractions within the Left, always positioning oneself relative to other speakers in terms of a neither/nor response, rather than in the inclusive terms of a both/and stance, or the habit of preferring the self-destructive radicalism of an ever more vigilant deconstruction over and above the making of a common front. Without in turn wishing to speculate about this, in these times of global political reaction few tasks seem to me more urgent than actively and historically to reconstruct the positive elements, beyond the polemics, that many of these thinkers share in their common rejection of speculative leftism.

Notes

1   Alain Badiou, *D'un désastre obscur: Sur la fin de la vérité d'Etat* (La Tour d'Aigues: L'Aube, 1998), 14; in English, "Philosophy and the 'Death of Communism,'" in *Infinite Thought: Truth and the Return to Philosophy*, trans./ed. Oliver Feltham and Justin Clemens (London: Continuum, 2003), 131.

2   Félix Guattari and Antonio Negri, *Communists Like Us: New Spaces of Liberty, New Lines of Alliance*, trans. Michael Ryan (New York: Semiotext[e], 1990), 7, 19.

3   Ibid., 55.

4   Jean-Luc Nancy and Jean-Christophe Bailly, *La Comparution (politique à venir)* (Paris: Christian Bourgois, 1991), 62. In English, "*La Comparution*/The Compearance: From the Existence of 'Communism' to the Community of 'Existence,'" trans. Tracy B. Strong, *Political Theory* 20:3 (1992): 377.

5   Nancy, *La Communauté désœuvrée* (Paris: Christian Bourgois, 1986), 177. In English, *The Inoperative Community*, ed. Peter Connor (Minneapolis: University of Minnesota Press, 1991), 71 (translation modified).

6   Nancy and Bailly, *La Comparution*, 100/393 (translation modified).

7   Badiou, *Théorie du sujet* (Paris: Seuil, 1982), 115, qtd. in *La Comparution*, 63 n. 5/394 n. 5 (translation corrected).

8   Compare Daniel and Gabriel Cohn-Bendit, *Le gauchisme, remède à la maladie sénile du communisme* (Paris: Seuil, 1968), and Lenin's classic *Left-Wing Communism, an Infantile Disorder*, trans. Julius Katzer, in *Lenin's Collected Works*, vol. 31 (Moscow: Progress Publishers, 1966), 17–118.

9 Alain Badiou and François Balmès, *De l'idéologie* (Paris: François Maspero, 1976), 67. Ernesto Laclau early on discusses the hypothesis of communist invariants, which according to him are actually neither communist nor invariant, in *Politics and Ideology in Marxist Theory: Capitalism, Fascism, Populism* (London: New Left Books, 1977), 167–72. If Laclau finds Badiou and Balmès's argument wanting, though, this can also be explained at least in part by the fact that he seeks to produce an opposition similar to the masses/state opposition, this time in the Gramscian terms of people/power bloc.

10 Badiou and Balmès, *De l'idéologie*, 67.

11 Ibid.

12 Ibid., 69. Gilles Deleuze and Félix Guattari salute the originality of this dialectic of masses and classes in *A Thousand Plateaus: Capitalism and Schizophrenia*, trans. and foreword by Brian Massumi (Minneapolis: University of Minnesota Press, 1987). Like Laclau, however, they have serious reservations: "But it is difficult to see, first of all, why masses are not themselves historical variables, and second, why the word is applied only to the exploited (the 'peasant-plebeian' mass), when it is also suitable for seigneurial, bourgeois masses, or even monetary masses" (537 n. 20).

13 Badiou and Balmès, *De l'idéologie*, 74.

14 Ibid., 75.

15 Ibid., 96, 79.

16 Ibid., 83.

17 Ibid., 84.

18 Paul Sandevince (pseudonym for Sylvain Lazarus), *Qu'est-ce qu'une politique marxiste?* (Marseille: Potemkine, 1978), 6. For a more detailed account of Badiou's Maoist organization, UCFML (Union des Communistes de France marxiste-léniniste), see my article "Post-Maoism: Badiou and Politics," *positions: east asia cultures critique* (forthcoming).

19 Badiou, *Théorie du sujet*, 62.

20 UCFML, *Sur le maoïsme et la situation en Chine après la mort de Mao Tsé-Toung* (Marseille: Potemkine, 1976), 3.

21 Badiou, *Théorie du sujet*, 198.

22 Ibid.

23 UCFML, *Questions du maoïsme: De la Chine de la Révolution Culturelle à la Chine des Procès de Pékin* (Paris: Potemkine, 1981), 10.

24 UCFML, *Sur le maoïsme et la situation en Chine après la mort de Mao Tsé-Toung*, 1–2.

25 Badiou, *Peut-on penser la politique?* (Paris: Seuil, 1985), 56.

26 Ibid., 56, 60.

27 Ibid., 55.

28 UCFML/Groupe Yénan-Philosophie, "Etat de front," *La situation actuelle sur le front philosophique* (Paris: François Maspero, 1977), 12.

29 Ibid.

30 Badiou, "Le flux et le parti (dans les marges de l'*Anti-Œdipe*)," *La situation actuelle sur le front philosophique*, 31–32. In English, "The Flux and the Party: In the Margins of *Anti-Oedipus*," trans. Laura Balladur and Simon Krysl, *Polygraph* 15–16 (2004): 75–92.

31 Badiou, *Théorie du sujet*, 60, 30. In *Logics of Failed Revolt: French Theory after May '68* (Stanford: Stanford University Press, 1995), Peter Starr devotes much of his argument to the paralyzing effects of this kind of dualism and the search for "third way" solutions

among members or fellow travelers of Tel Quel. Unfortunately, he does not deal with a single text by Badiou. Kristin Ross, in her more recent *May '68 and Its Afterlives* (Chicago: University of Chicago Press, 2002), also fails to study the long and complex prehistory behind Badiou's notion of the "event," mentioned in her introduction, which otherwise is one of the most loyal thoughts transmitted to us from May 1968.

32 Badiou, *Peut-on penser la politique?* 11.

33 Daniel Bensaïd, "Alain Badiou and the Miracle of the Event," in *Think Again: Alain Badiou and the Future of Philosophy*, ed. Peter Hallward (London: Continuum, 2004), 101.

34 Badiou, *L'Etre et l'événement* (Paris: Seuil, 1988), 232–33. A much earlier use of the expression *speculative leftism* can be found in Jacques Rancière, *La leçon d'Althusser* (Paris: Gallimard, 1974): "The double Althusserian truth after May 1968 finds itself shattered between two poles: the speculative leftism of the all-powerful ideological apparatuses and the speculative zdanovism of the class struggle in theory, which interrogates each word in order to make it confess its class" (146; see also 110 n. 1 regarding the search for an "absolute beginning" as the sign of an ultraleftist interpretation of the link between Althusserianism and Maoism).

Peter Hallward

The Politics of Prescription

The assassinations of Salvador Allende and
Amílcar Cabral in 1973 mark the end of the last
truly transformative sequence in world politics,
the sequence of national liberation associated
with the victories of Mao Tse-tung, Mohandas
Gandhi, and Fidel Castro. It may be that this
end is itself now coming to an end, through the
clarification of what Mao might have called a
new "principal contradiction"—the convergence,
most obviously in Iraq and Haiti, of ever more
draconian policies of neoliberal adjustment with
newly aggressive forms of imperial intervention,
in the face of newly resilient forms of resistance
and critique.[1]

Political philosophy is confronted today by
only one consequential decision: either to anticipate this end of an end and develop its implications, or else to ignore or deny it and reflect
on its deferral. The first option is the path of
prescription and hope, of disruptive innovation
and retrospective justification; the second is split
between cautious reformism and postrevolutionary despair.

In its liberal-democratic guise, the reformist
fork of this second path remains the dominant
discourse of the day. It continues to believe that

The *South Atlantic Quarterly* 104:4, Fall 2005.

the course of historical change remains broadly in line with forms of rational improvement, or at least that alignment with the general way of the world offers a reasonable chance of peaceful coexistence and mutual respect. The "ordinary language philosophizing" still popular among some Anglo-American thinkers, for instance, provides what one of its more versatile practitioners calls "a way of tapping the resources of the self in a way which will allow the philosopher to recall, explore, and display the nature, extent and security of her alignments with the world and with the human community."[2] One way or another, variations on this theme of alignment and its cognates (communication, community, consensus, toleration, recognition, and so on) continue to inform much of the recent work of thinkers like Jürgen Habermas, William Connolly, Stanley Cavell, Charles Taylor, and Richard Rorty.

Many of their more inventive continental rivals, by contrast, have sought an elusive refuge from the world through strategies of deferral or withdrawal. Such is the general movement of the postrevolutionary alternative, a trajectory illustrated nowhere more dramatically than through the austere and ardent example of Guy Lardreau. Faced in the mid-1970s with frustration of the avowedly impossible demands of absolute revolt, with the reduction of a "cultural" to a merely "ideological" revolution, Lardreau has subsequently explored the compensations of a negative philosophy: "Negative philosophy is ineluctably worth more than any affirmation for, affirming nothing, it has no interest in betrayal, and it never lies."[3] Each in their own way, many of Lardreau's contemporaries have charted a similar course. Contaminated by fascism, notions of decision and resolution were abandoned in favor of a generalized indecision. Contaminated by imperialism, the category of the universal was dissolved in favor of the fragmentary, the particular, or the contingent. The pursuit of clarity and distinction was eclipsed by a determination to bear witness to an apparently more fundamental obscurity or paralysis — thought confronted by situations in which it is impossible to react (Gilles Deleuze), demands that cannot be met (Emmanuel Levinas), needs that can never be reconciled (Jean-François Lyotard), promises that can never be kept (Jacques Derrida).

Nonetheless, there is nothing to stop us from anticipating a way out of this impasse. Prescription is first and foremost an anticipation of its subsequent power, a commitment to its consequences, a wager on its eventual strength. Against alignment with the way of the world, against withdrawal from engagement with the world, it is time to reformulate a prescriptive practice of politics.

════════

1. *A prescription involves the direct and divisive application of a universal principle (or axiom).* For instance: if we uphold the axiom of equality, we can prescribe the rejection of slavery, and with it the organization of a force capable of transforming the relations that sustain the plantation economy. If we uphold the axiom of the worker, we can prescribe the restriction of corporate power, that is, the organization of forces capable of reversing the subordination of politics to profit. If we uphold the axiom of territorial integrity, we can prescribe a relation of resistance to foreign aggression, and with it the mobilization of a force capable of repelling invasion.

After Joseph Jacotot, Jacques Rancière's approach to education offers an especially instructive example of this more general point. If we assume the axiom of equality, if "equality is not a goal to be attained but a point of departure, a supposition to be maintained in all circumstances," then we can prescribe an approach to learning that is indifferent to differences of knowledge, mastery, or authority. We can subtract the process of learning from the progress of explanation, the process of education from training or "preparation." We can isolate the process of learning from the cultivation of ability. We can teach things we know little or nothing about. We can grasp even the most difficult of ideas, since "the same intelligence is at work in all the productions of human art."[4]

Prescription is *direct* because its element is the urgency of the here and now. Prescription ignores deferral; it operates in a present illuminated through anticipation of its future. A prescriptive politics sidesteps the authorized mediation of public inquiries, sociological studies, or NGOs — the recent rise of charitable or "humanitarian" NGOs as privileged points of commentary and concern is itself one of the more striking signs of the ongoing depoliticization of contemporary conflicts.[5]

Prescription is *divisive* because its application divides adherents from opponents, but *universal* insofar as its assertion depends on a properly axiomatic principle. From Kant, the politics of prescription retains an indifference to difference, interest, consensus, adaptation, or welfare;[6] against Kant, the prescribing of politics proceeds only in the element of partisan division, through engagement with strategic constraints that cannot be justified in terms of unconditional duty or respect for the law. Unlike Kantian morality, unlike any singular or immediate articulation of the individual and the universal, relational prescription operates in a version of the domain that Étienne Balibar (after Alexandre Kojève, Gilbert Simondon, Jacques Lacan, Pierre Bourdieu, et al.) calls the "transindividual."[7]

Alain Badiou is the great contemporary thinker of axioms. In each case, what Badiou calls a "truth-procedure" proceeds as the assertion of an axiomatic principle, one subtracted from the mediation of existing forms of knowledge, recognition, or community. As a rule, "the real is only encountered under the axiomatic imperative."[8] An axiom neither defines nor refers to some entity external to itself. Instead, it posits a purely implied term and then stipulates the way that its implicit term can be manipulated, such that this manipulation exhausts all that can be said or deduced about this term.[9] Badiou's axiomatic orientation thereby suspends the supervision of language games, deflates the pathos of romanticism, interrupts the management of consensus or communication. In its axiomatic integrity, every

> political decision tears itself away from any dialectic of the subjective and the objective. No, it is not a matter of leading to action a consciousness of what there is, of changing, through reflection and operation, necessity into liberty. There is no passage here from the in-itself to the for-itself. The beginning, under its eventual injunction, is pure declaration.[10]

In strategic terms, the importance of Badiou's intervention in the field of contemporary philosophy is second to none. But a prescription is not reducible to an axiom, and what remains relatively underdeveloped in Badiou's work is its properly prescriptive or relational aspect. An axiom is intransitive; it governs the terms (points, sets, citizens, and so on) it implies without exception. A prescription applies what an axiom implies, in the concrete medium of relational conflict. Consider, as a representative example, the axiom "Everyone who is here is from here"—a principle that often recurs in recent issues of *La Distance politique*. Versions of this principle continue to guide one of the few militant political projects in France today, the movement of the *sans papiers*. Such an axiom acquires a prescriptive force, however, only through the slow transformation of *here*, through a process that engages with the entrenched forms of discrimination (the division of labor, the distribution of resources, the location of housing, the access to education and to the media of expression in the public sphere, etc.) that serve to isolate immigration as a political "problem." Badiou has made no small contribution to many of these issues. For him it remains axiomatic, nonetheless, that every political sequence proceeds at a "pure" distance from the domain of the social, *subtracted* from the domain of social relationships and economic constraints. If political equality must be "precisely an axiom and not a goal," if it must be "postulated rather than willed," then Badiou concludes that "the effect of the egalitarian axiom is to undo relationships [*liens*] and to desocialize thought."[11]

A more prescriptive approach will acknowledge, instead, that only confrontation of these constraints and transformation of these relationships offers any lasting political purchase on a situation. The distance presumed by such confrontation remains a relational (or "impure") distance. A version of the axiom of equality no doubt inspired the American mobilization for civil rights, just as it does contemporary struggles against racism and neocolonialism: the whole problem, clearly, is how to make an antiracist prescription *consequential* in a situation that has long since accommodated itself to the explicit principle of equality. To uphold this prescription is to participate in the step-by-step transformation of what Nikhil Singh has recently described as the ramified "spatial apartheid" of a structurally racist socioeconomic order.[12] The axiom of equality is a fundamental point of departure, and it refers to no more primordial value (humanity, altruism, compassion, etc.), but it remains formal and nonrelational; a prescriptive political practice, by contrast, undertakes the concrete transformation of those relations that sustain inequality, exploitation, or oppression.

An axiom, we might say, is a principle we posit in such a way as to take it subsequently for granted. A pure point of departure, it is by same token "forgotten" in the prescriptive pursuit of its consequences. But if equality is always a postulate, justice remains an achievement: in each particular case, the presumption of equality will have been subsumed in the struggle against injustice.

---

2. Politics is the aspect of public or social life that falls under the consequences of a prescription. Politics is not reducible to the art of the possible. Prescription is indifferent to calculations of the possible or the feasible, along with the "progressive" temporality associated with making-possible. Politics, then, is a condition that sometimes happens to the social. Not everything is political. Prescriptions are targeted and specific. The personal is not political, and there is no "politics of the everyday" that does not, precisely, convert the latter into its opposite. Prescription converts hitherto inconsequential, multivalent, and multipolar relations into consequential (and thus bipolar) ones.

The thinker so often credited today with our most compelling concept of the political, Carl Schmitt, is in fact guilty of a disastrous and systematic confusion of the political and the social. Schmitt's notorious distinction of friend from enemy is as much social as it political. The existential element of this distinction is "extreme peril" and war, and only the *political* sovereign can decide on war, at a distance from all "normative ties."[13] On the other hand, the normless intensity of "real combat with a real enemy" presumes and reinforces the *social* homogeneity of the combatants. The "political enemy need not be morally evil or aesthetically ugly . . . but he is, nevertheless, the other, the stranger; and it is sufficient for his nature that he is, in a specially intense way, existentially something different and alien, so that in the extreme case conflicts with him are always possible."[14] Schmitt's fascistic glorification of violent struggle does nothing to mask his dependence on the specified identity of particular communities or ways of life. Even the state-political order that Schmitt nostalgically associates with the old *nomos* of the earth, the *jus publicum Europaeum* that allowed for the civilized containment of European interstate war from the mid–seventeenth to the late nineteenth centuries, is patently based on the extension, in global terms, of an aristocratic social order: conflict between dueling European states could remain within respectfully lawful limits so long as civilized Europe preserved an absolute barrier between itself and the territory of non-European barbarity, where no rules apply.

The problem with Schmitt's concept of the political, in other words, is that it is not prescriptive *enough*. Politics divides, but not between friends and enemies (via the mediation of the state). Politics divides the adherents of a prescription against its opponents.

═══════

3. A prescriptive politics presumes a form of classical logic—the confrontation of two contrary positions, to the exclusion of any middle or third. The targeted transitivity of a prescription compels a response that can only take one of two forms: for or against. A prescriptive politics refuses any "third way." When an issue becomes political, when it ceases to be a matter of merely social interest or cultural expression, it polarizes between yes or no. This brutal simplification of the issue is characteristic of any political sequence. Prescriptive (as opposed to moral or pragmatic) positions against slavery or colonial domination, for example, must initially preserve what Frantz Fanon diagnosed as the "manichean" division of colonial society.[15] Such was the guiding insight of the great anticolonial movements of the 1940s and 1950s, the presumption common to Gandhi, Cabral, C. L. R. James, Nelson Mandela, Aimé Césaire (and subsequently abandoned by most contributions to *post*colonial theory) — that between colonizer and colonized there was no third term, no progress, development, or *évolution*, no "human contact," but only what Césaire listed as "intimidation, oppression, the police, taxation, theft, rape, contempt, distrust."[16]

If Marx remains the dominant point of reference for any prescriptive conception of politics, it's not because he supposedly bound the fate of political prescription to a determinist science of history or economics but because he offers the most profound and instructive analysis of the essential dualism of political struggle. Against any nostalgic reference to the evasive complexity of early modern society (with its multiple and overlapping social classifications), Marx proposes a transformative conception of politics as a stark struggle between "two great hostile camps, two great classes directly facing each other."[17] Marx's analysis of capitalist production allows for the isolation of a *single* operator of socioeconomic distinction, the process of exploitation that separates two and only two terms: exploited from exploiter, proletariat from bourgeoisie. This remains the most urgent and most valuable lesson of *The Communist Manifesto*, and it is the reason why its third and final section, titled "Socialist and Communist Literature," retains a more than polemic force. In the crucible of prescriptive conflict, the complex social distinctions and mediations explored in Hegel's *Philosophy of Right* (and revived by contemporary theorists of diversity and recognition) are subsumed along with all other forms of nonpolitical complexity, "all religious and political illusions."[18] As Lenin will insist when he comes to answer "One of the Fundamental Questions of the Revolution," vacillation is itself "the most painful thing on earth," and when the conditions for decisive action are right, then there can be "no middle course."[19]

In the divisive present of a prescription, the political is always that aspect of public life that, in view of a specific simplification, falls for a certain time under the decisive logic of a "last" or final judgment. The refusal to recognize the implacable dualism of a prescription is itself an *orthodox* ideological reaction; an insistence on compromise, on negotiation, on piecemeal "democratic" reform, has long been the privileged vehicle for the reproduction and reinforcement of the status quo.

One prescription, two positions; the logic of prescriptive antagonism evokes the old "union of contraries" if and only if this unity persists as the "effective gap" between two.[20] That "one divides into two" has never meant that a whole splits into halves; it means that the antagonistic relation of the two is itself one. To the one of domination corresponds the two of the dominant and dominated.

―――――

4. Prescription is oriented by its anticipation of clarity and distinction. A decision will have been right, a project will have held true: the temporality of prescription must initially be conjugated in that future anterior championed by Maximilien Robespierre and Fanon (along with Jean-Paul Sartre, Lacan, Badiou, et al.). Lacan's early formulation remains one of his most illuminating: even in the ordinary intersubjective relation of speech, "I utter what was only in view of what will be. . . . What is realized in my history is not the past definite of what was . . . but the future anterior of what I shall have been for what I am in the process of becoming."[21] As Badiou reminds us, however, the "anticipatory certitude" that alone can guide any extraordinary "process of becoming" itself depends on the courage and confidence that a decisive intervention, in the element of present uncertainty, demands of its subject.[22]

The temporality of anticipation (to say nothing of its joining with resolution) need not be abandoned to the Heideggerian tradition. In keeping with the rationalist tradition, a prescriptive politics accepts that since everything begins in obscurity and confusion, clarity, where it exists, will come to exist as the *result* of an assertive distinction. A prescription applied to an issue that is already clear is obviously either redundant or digressive. Though nothing could be simpler than a prescription, a prescription applies only in the element of dissensus and uncertainty. To prescribe is not to edify or instruct. A prescription emerges as a distillation of what will have been obvious.

The "obvious" principle of territorial sovereignty applies only in the prescription of an active and divisive resistance against occupation or assault — for instance, in Vietnam, Gaza, or Falluja (whereas the imperial position has always been "Abandon your resistance; accept the occupation as a preliminary condition of entering into negotiations for an attenuated form of future occupation." Likewise, the axiom of civic equality posited by the French Revolution was never less obvious or more consequential than when it guided, between 1791 and 1794, a prescriptive campaign against colonial slavery—a campaign that was itself shaped by the astonishing mobilization, in the face of united metropolitan opposition, of the slaves of Saint-Domingue. Despite his relatively slow response to this particular mobilization, Robespierre himself, of course, endures as one of the great proponents of anticipatory clarification. If the revolution requires the death of the monarch, to cite one of his more notorious speeches, this is not because Louis should be judged and deemed guilty of this or that offense but because, as will have become obvious, the revolution has *already taken place*, and those who would carry it forward will find its continuation incompatible with royalty.[23]

A prescriptive practice always works on the edge of the unknown, without the authority or authorization of established knowledges. If Slavoj Žižek is right to say that Lenin is once again a decisive political reference today, it's precisely because of his forceful insistence on the relative autonomy of strategic anticipation, of an intervention that only retrospectively allows for the full clarification of its conditions of possibility.[24] Prescription is always specific to a situation; its work of simplification always involves the careful investigation of particular configurations and opportunities: only after the abortive July uprising and the deflection of General Kornilov's revolt does the Lenin of 1917 come to acquire a firm sense of the difference between the "mature" and the "immature."[25] Against more cynical versions of materialism, the Lenin who reads Hegel's *Logic* after the disaster of 1914 understands that the critical political relation is indeed *between* the real and the ideal, that "the idea of the transformation of the ideal into the real is *profound*."[26] Around the same time, against Nikolai Bukharin and the dogmatic pursuit of direct proletarian revolution, Lenin will realize that the weakest link in the chains of exploitation is often to be found in literally marginal places—in the pursuit of national or anticolonial autonomy, for instance, as so many local contributions to a tendentially universal struggle against the highest stage of capitalism.[27]

In his current work, Badiou usefully describes the decisive moments of subjective mobilization in terms of the critical "points" a militant body (party, organization, movement) encounters. You encounter a point of the situation when you are obliged to choose between the continuation of a prescription and preservation of the status quo.[28] A truth proceeds *point par point*, where each point tests the development of subjective resources or "organs" capable of upholding the consequences of its commitment to transform a situation, the development of a subject's capacity to "live for an Idea."[29] Guided by an anticipation of the ideal, to prescribe is always to force the issue, in the absence of any guarantee. Prior to the imposition of its retrospective clarity, its eventual self-evidence, a prescriptive move will always appear as a step too far. Sartre explained this perfectly well: first you decide, then you justify the decision by providing it with defensible motives or reasons. First you commit, then you explore the limits of what this commitment allows you to do. The progressive-regressive method: first you act and then, in the new light of this action, you reconstruct the circumstances that led you to act.

This point calls for three immediate qualifications.

The first is that this retrospective justification of the decision is nevertheless an essential aspect of the process that validates a decision, that will allow its consequences to hold true. A decision is clearly no decision at all if its outcome can be deduced by criteria that preexist the taking of that decision; on the other hand, if a decision isn't made right through the consequential development of these criteria, then it will turn out just as clearly to have been the wrong decision. A decision begins in uncertainty but only endures as decisive, precisely, if it *lasts*. Needless to say, there is nothing intrinsically progressive or emancipatory about the logic of prescription per se.

Second, though a decision anticipates its criteria, this anticipation does not itself *create* them ex nihilo. It is essential to avoid the trap that tempts both Sartre and Žižek: the logic whereby any genuinely decisive act is "authorised only by itself."[30] Derrida wrestles with this same temptation in inverted form—the dissolution of decision through its passive exposure to an "im-possible" event, to a wholly secret and unrecognizable advent in a domain stripped of *all* anticipation or expectation.[31] The obvious danger here was pointed out (and exaggerated) by Maurice Merleau-Ponty: if a decision proceeds purely ex nihilo, immediately, in the element of the void as such, then it risks remaining voluntarist and abrupt—that is, inconsequential.[32]

Third: we must not forget that once they have become obvious, the implications of a prescription will be and will remain obvious! Those who dwell on the incalculable and the unrecognizable advent of an event would do well to remember this point.

≡≡≡≡

5. *Prescription thus enables the relative autonomy of its effects, the strategic subtraction of cause from effect.* This is perhaps the most profound point of convergence between Deleuze, Rancière, and Badiou: an incorporeal effect is not reducible to its bodily cause; a political intervention exceeds its socialized place; a subjective formalization is carried but not mediated by its militant body. The whole point is that the relation between prescriptive mobilization and its historical conditions or "causes" will remain forever undecidable, pending the moment of prescription itself. There can be no question of reviving, even as the preliminary phase of a more complex mediation, a notion of thought and discourse as "the direct efflux of material behaviour."[33] The most we can say is that while we never choose the circumstances in which we make our own history, some circumstances are more provocative than others.

This is not the place to go back over the vast literature concerning relative autonomy and "determination in the last instance." But clearly we can cut short the recent farewells to the working class without simply returning to the messianic singularity of the proletariat. The pressures that tend toward global proletarianization neither dissolve into the cheery pluralism of new social movements nor converge into the unity of one Historical destiny: there is no eliding the conjunctural dimension of specific prescriptions. Suffice it to say that Louis Althusser's great contribution to the renewal of political thought endures to this day, insofar as he broke once and for all with every reductive or mechanical conception of antagonism and in so doing opened the door to a more ramified but still unapologetically partisan analysis of complex social configurations "structured in dominance."

Nevertheless, Althusser bequeathed his remarkable students the legacy of two problematic notions that none of them, arguably, have yet managed fully to resolve: on the one hand, the essential complexity (if not inertia) of a historical process without subject or goal; on the other hand, the essential simplicity (if not abstraction) of a politics in which "the masses make their own history."[34] The effort to lend a non-evolutionary dynamism to the former led Balibar to develop an unwieldy theory of structural transition before turning to ever more equivocal, ever more "ambiguous" configurations of the political, divided between the competing claims of autonomy, heteronymy, and the heteronymy of heteronymy—this last a non-negation of the negation that promises little more, in the face of the supposed menace of ethnic ultraviolence, than the tired resources of citizenship and civility.[35]

The effort to sustain a militant version of the latter led Badiou to stress an ever more ephemeral, ever more "vanishing" movement of the masses before committing himself to a void-based philosophy in which a strictly inaccessible inconsistency offers the sole foundation of any transformative truth.[36] And in a sense, the effort to invert both principles still guides the work of Althusser's most emphatic student-turned-critic, Rancière, for whom politics subsists only in the transient and necessarily inconclusive suspension of domination, of the sanctioned distribution of functions and places. Rancière's critique of Althusserian mastery leads him to embrace the antimastery at work in "the invention of that unpredictable subject which momentarily occupies the street, the invention of a movement born of nothing but democracy itself"—a movement that depends on nothing beyond its "constitutive fragility," that "identifies and localises what has its being only in the gap of places and identities."[37]

Better than Althusser, Rancière understood that the "masses make history" only when, as in the particular circumstances theorized by Mao, the inventive military potential of the peasants and the proletariat is stronger than that deployed by foreign and feudal armies.[38] If today the end of the end of this advantage may define the horizon of politics, this end also commits us, more for strategic than for moral reasons, to the renewal of nonmilitary forms of struggle. Of the great anticolonial leaders it is perhaps Gandhi, rather than Mao, who has the most to teach our new anticolonial generation.

———

6. Through anticipation, prescriptive intervention thus proceeds at a relative distance from socioeconomic causation. There has long been no need for the renewal of warnings, routine since the Second International, against the symmetrical perils of economic determinism and reckless voluntarism. In the context marked by our post-Marxist (or anti-Althusserian) eclecticism, it is perhaps more important to resist the kind of "short-circuit" whereby— even in Balibar's own recent work, for instance—the political and the economic dissolve into a single play of forces, such that relations of exploitation do not so much condition a political sequence as appear themselves as immediately political. It is a short step from here to the direct political investment of the social characteristic of a Deleuzian approach—a move that accounts for the obscurity of its political impact. In a recent interview in which he draws on Deleuze's notion of affective connection and Charles Sanders Peirce's notion of abductive participation, Brian Massumi offers a suggestive account of how such a politics seeks merely to "navigate" movement, rather than direct or interrupt it. "It's about being immersed in an experience that is already underway. It's about being bodily attuned to opportunities in the movement, going with the flow. It's more like surfing the situation, or tweaking it, than commanding or programming it."[39]

For Antonio Negri, likewise, the critical distinction has always been between a productive or constituent materialism (Machiavelli, Spinoza, Marx) as distinct from a merely critical idealism (Descartes, Hobbes, Rousseau, Hegel). The external vantage point claimed by the latter has supposedly been absorbed, along with everything else, through the completion of capitalist "real subsumption," the absolutization of bio-power. Each in their own way, Negri, Derrida, Žižek, and Giorgio Agamben all accept this absolutization as the condition of an effectively *desperate* politics, a condition that solicits the equally absolute affirmation of an unmediated creativity (Negri), of a potentiality that subsists in the annulment of actuality (Agamben), of a decision withdrawn from activity (Derrida), of a radical act uncontaminated by reflection (Žižek).

A prescriptive politics, by contrast, busies itself with the invention of newly effective, newly *deliberate* ways of intervening in a situation. A consequential theory of prescription must conceive it as the process that allows for the relatively autonomous constitution of a militant subject, at a qualified distance from the social, economic, and psychological manipulation of affects and flows. A political subject prescribes its own boundaries. The prescriptive subject exists in its militant and emergent interface with the world rather than in any specified psychological (let alone cultural or biological) location. Prescriptive autonomy, in other words, necessarily presumes *some* kind of qualitative leap in the constitution of the subject, a leap adequate to enable its relative freedom from causal or presubjective determination. Without such freedom we cannot say that people make their own history; we can merely contemplate the forms of their constraint. And however radical or indignant such contemplation, by itself it will always fall short of the political as such—a point overlooked, in much of his work, by Pierre Bourdieu.[40]

———

7. *The "leap" of subjectivation is directed on the basis of a preliminary anticipation or "hunch."* Rather than invent its own criteria, an anticipation draws on the inheritance of previous prescriptions and learns from the forms of

resistance or opposition that it faces. Unlike Sartre and Žižek, Lenin himself conceives of his anticipatory intervention precisely as a sort of premo-
nition that can withstand the test of clarity and distinction in their strictest
sense, that is, the criteria formulated by a *science* of historical materialism.
As everyone knows, Leninist intervention is not so much "authorized by
itself" as it is informed by a sober discernment of the weakest link; Maoist
intervention, likewise, is guided by the careful effort to distinguish the principal contradiction that governs a particular strategic conjuncture.[41] (It is
precisely the simplicity of this distinction, of course, along with its strategic
effect, that begins to get lost with Althusser's emphasis on the complexity
of *over*determination, to say nothing of the sort of loose polydetermination
privileged by Ernesto Laclau and Chantal Mouffe.)[42]

Rather than subscribe to Žižek or Badiou's claim that a radical act or
imposition of a principle is what "induces" its subject effectively ex nihilo,
then, we might do better to say that a prescription serves to *crystallize*
hitherto inconsequential aspects of a subject in a newly consequential form.

===

*8. A consequential prescription requires an effective foothold in the situation it
transforms.*[43] Guided by its hunch or anticipation, prescriptive subjectivation
is also dependent on the crystallization of historical conditions of *pertinence*.
The axiom of territorial integrity is not pertinent in every political situation; it would be fatal, on the other hand, to assume that a supposedly global
condition of postnational mobility has rendered it universally impertinent.
As Edward Said knew all too well, to take only the most obvious example, it
is no accident that the armored bulldozer remains the chief weapon of the
Israeli occupation.[44]

A prescription concerning immigration cannot proceed, today, on the
basis of a utopian rejection of international borders (although it can and
must concern the "reception" of immigrants here and now: the quasi-
criminalization of refugees, the exploitation of immigrant workers in the
domestic economy, the segregation of their communities, etc.). Prescriptions about working conditions will advance less in the abstract terms of
a campaign against "capitalism" or "globalization" than through combat-
ive opposition to particular neoliberal policies or the elimination of precise forms of corporate power—for instance, through direct measures like
those advanced by Via Campesina or Brazil's Landless Workers Movement
in their campaigns for food sovereignty, fair trade, and land redistribu-

tion. Again, the key to the decisive campaign against slavery, according to the most detailed study of the "Haitian revolution from below," lay less in resolute leadership at the top than in the "self-sustained activities of the masses," activities that proved powerful enough to transcend the various regional, occupational, and cultural tensions working against their long-term cooperation. These activities were themselves conditioned by structural changes to the plantation economy during its last decades of rapid commercial expansion, and these changes, together with the conjunctural impact of the revolution in France and new divisions within the slave-owning sector, lent the 1791 mobilization against slavery a strategic pertinence that François Mackandal's rebellion, for instance, had lacked back in 1757.[45]

Upheld as a strategic imperative, a prescription says *shall* rather than *ought*. Prescription is not a matter cf abstract moral reflection, of aspecific obligation, of "objective" rights and wrongs: it is a matter, under the constraints of a given situation, of practical consequence and material invention, of relational struggle, of mobilization and countermobilization.[46]

---

9. A prescriptive conception of politics presumes that its conditions of possibility are transcendental in the conventional sense — unconditional, transhistorical, indifferent to questions of context or pertinence. Conditions of pertinence must not be confused with conditions of possibility. Such confusion leads to claims that the subject is merely an effect — that the subject cannot act or that the subaltern cannot speak. It is essential, if we are to affirm the end of the end of politics, that we do not suture conditions of possibility to the actions they allow. We must depoliticize (and dehistoricize) the conditions of possibility of politics. The point is not that the human being is a political animal but that the human is capable of doing more than any sort of being. And this capacity includes a capacity for prescriptive politics that is itself irreducible to any biological "nature" or social (gregarious, communicative, altruistic, etc.) disposition.

It is no accident, notwithstanding dramatic differences in outlook and orientation, that the most forceful proponents of a prescriptive politics tend to ground its conditions of possibility in autonomous, "auto-poetic," and extrapolitical faculties or capacities — Noam Chomsky in a mental-cognitive faculty, Gandhi in a spiritual faculty, Sartre in a faculty of imagination or negation, Rancière in a discursive capacity, Badiou in a capacity for unabashedly "immortal" truth. It is precisely the autonomy of such capacities that is at issue in the divergence, for instance, between Chomsky and his more conservative student Stephen Pinker, a divergence that is as much scientific as it is political. For Pinker our "language instinct" evolved more or less smoothly as an adaptive solution to the pressures imposed by natural selection; for Chomsky language comes to function at an essential distance from any coordination with nature, that is, at a distance from principles other than those of a critical autonomy itself. It is this distance that underlies our ability to *think* rather than simply *behave*.

≡≡≡

10. *Prescription can proceed only in the imperative mode of a "logical revolt."* In its indifference to community, compromise, or consensus, every prescriptive practice has an authoritarian or intransigent aspect. To avoid or dilute the moment of a "dictatorship of the prescription" is to evade the prescription itself. By definition, a prescriptive mobilization binds its adherents in a common dedication: a dedication that exceeds its deferral to authorized representatives, that is irreducible to the exercise of merely individual choice or to the reproduction of sociocultural norms.

In today's circumstances, a "democratic *politics*" designates first and foremost a contradiction in terms.[47] Democracy defines a particular administrative or procedural regime, not the dimension of politics itself. The imperial advocates of "political democracy" have themselves always recognized the true meaning of this phrase whenever it applies to situations polarized by significant conflict or resistance—from Guatemala (1954) and Vietnam (1956) to Haiti and Iraq (2004).[48] An election is a routine organized for the stable validation of an evolving status quo; an election that threatens to do otherwise is cancelled or postponed, pending the extermination of insurgents. The Algerian sequence that began with the annulment of an unacceptable vote in 1992 and ended with the electoral "stability" of April 2004—a sequence marked by some 100,000 deaths—will no doubt remain a model for the imminent democratization of the Middle East.

≡≡≡

11. *Prescription is vigilant but not "observant."* Prescription does not wait and see. Prescription is not inspection. By the same token, prescription is adamantly opposed to the ethical subsumption of politics, a "politics" based on the compassionate response to the spectacle of suffering, on respect for

the other and the consensual management of established human rights. In particular, prescription is in no sense a response to the pitiful visibility of others, and still less a response to their invisibility. In the absence of a prescription, what can be "seen" of politics is not political subjects but only victims and terrorists, the two sides of the same humanitarian coin. Imperial observers of recent events in Abidjan or Port-au-Prince have seen only anarchy and fear, not principle or resistance.

Since principles are invisible, there can no question of a "politics of recognition." Equality isn't something you can recognize or infer. If we prescribe the right of all inhabitants of a territory to a say in the government of that territory, then we will not require them to appear worthy of this right. They will not have to pass preliminary tests of citizenship and entitlement. Politics has no dress code. "Really existing citizenship," however, remains profoundly marked by its conventional valorization of the noncitizen, and in particular, in our postcolonial era, of the descendants of those noncitizens par excellence: the natives, *les indigènes*. In the last couple of decades France, the country that once prescribed the universal bias of citizenship, has repatriated this "civic" distinction of *colon* and *indigène* from its original deployment in Algeria and Senegal as part of a long campaign to filter the remnants of republican universality through newly exclusive norms. To be a citizen of French Algeria, of course, was always to be the recipient of discriminatory protections and benefits, at the direct expense of indigenous noncitizens. To be a French citizen today is first and foremost to accept the discriminating embrace of the republican state, secured against threats both at home and abroad. Rather than postcolonial, the recent global extension of such a mind-set might be better described, to adapt Cécile Winter's phrase, as simply "colonial without colonies," *colonial sans colonies*.[49] After Ariel Sharon, after George W. Bush, Nicolas Sarkozy has learned this lesson well. The result is complicity in what Naomi Klein is right to call the ongoing Likudization of the world.[50]

═══════

12. Prescription is indifferent to the manipulations of passionate attachment. Like any decisive commitment, politics is always affective. But even the most affective prescription can be sustained only at a critical distance from the "passionate" or "emotional." Neither pity nor fear has any place in politics.

A prescription posits a positive (and divisive) principle as primary, whereas an emotional nonpolitics is based on a negative (and unifying) prejudice or antiprinciple. The logic of consensual social or nonpolitical order, the logic of what Rancière calls *police* as opposed to politics, always relies on the manipulation of a paranoid *ochlos*—the "frightening rallying of frightened men." Police consolidation promises security through a stable distribution of places and roles, through the fearful exclusion of threats and outsiders; the political *demos*, then, begins only with that divisive "movement whereby the multitude tears itself away from the weighty destiny which seeks to drag it into the corporeal form of the ochlos. . . . Democracy only exists in a society to the degree that the demos exists as the power to divide the ochlos."[51]

In other words, a prescriptive politics must remember the critical lesson taught by the early Sartre, a lesson most starkly framed in his *Sketch for a Theory of the Emotions*: it is one thing to experience affects or feelings; it is quite another to participate in the "magical" manipulation of passions or emotions. It is one thing cautiously to acknowledge an opponent as dangerous or threatening; it is another to collaborate in the performance of fear or hate. Affects are rational responses to the reality they confront; emotions, by contrast, are theatrical routines we invent to justify a given alignment with the world. In each case, liberation from the emotional spell we cast upon ourselves "can only come from a purifying reflection or from the total disappearance of the emotional situation."[52]

Indifferent to the way we feel, indifferent to the way things look, a prescriptive politics avoids complacent reflection on our "modern social imaginary" for the same reason that it deflates premodern dreams of "turning the world upside down." The renewal of a prescriptive politics will have required the refusal of both cynicism and distraction.

Notes

1 See in particular Gordon Lafer, "Neoliberalism by Other Means: The 'War on Terror' at Home and Abroad," *New Political Science* 26.3 (September 2004): 323–46; Naomi Klein, "Baghdad Year Zero: Pillaging Iraq in Pursuit of a Neo-Con Utopia," *Harper's Magazine* 309 (September 2004): 43–53; Peter Hallward, "Option Zero in Haiti," *New Left Review* 27 (May 2004): 23–47; Stan Goff, "The Haitian Intifada," *FromTheWilderness*, January 10, 2005, available online at: www.fromthewilderness.com/free/ww3/011005_haitian_intifada_pt2.shtml. Accessed January 11, 2005.

2 Stephen Mulhall, *Stanley Cavell: Philosophy's Recounting of the Ordinary* (New York: Oxford University Press, 1994), 19.

3 Guy Lardreau, *L'Exercice différé de la philosophie: À l'occasion de Deleuze* (Lagrasse: Verdier, 1999), 88.

4 Jacques Rancière, *Le Maître ignorant* (Paris: Fayard, 1987), 229, 33.
5 As Arundhati Roy notes, "The greater the devastation caused by neo-liberalism, the greater the outbreak of NGOs." See Arundhati Roy, "Public Power in the Age of Empire," *Socialist Worker*, October 2004 (European Social Forum Special Issue), available online at www.socialistworker.co.uk/article.php4?article_id=2910. Accessed February 15, 2005.
6 Practical reason involves "a respect for something entirely different from life, something in comparison and contrast with which life with all its agreeableness has no worth at all" (Immanuel Kant, *Critique of Practical Reason*, ed. Mary McGregor [Cambridge: Cambridge University Press, 1997], 88).
7 Étienne Balibar, *The Philosophy of Marx*, trans. Chris Turner (London: Verso, 1995), 30–32, 121; cf. Balibar, *Politics and the Other Scene*, trans. Daniel Hahn (London: Verso, 2002), 27.
8 Alain Badiou, *Court Traité d'ontologie transitoire* (Paris: Seuil, 1998), 135.
9 For a more detailed discussion of this point see Hallward, "Depending on Inconsistency," *Polygraph* 17 (Spring 2005): 7–21.
10 Badiou, "Sur le livre de Françoise Proust, *Le Ton de l'histoire*," *Les Temps modernes* 565/566 (1993): 239.
11 Badiou, *Abrégé de métapolitique* (Paris: Seuil, 1998), 126; Badiou, *Infinite Thought* (London: Continuum, 2003), 77–78.
12 Nikhil Singh, *Black Is a Country* (Cambridge, MA: Harvard University Press, 2004), 221.
13 Carl Schmitt, *Political Theology: Four Chapters on the Concept of Sovereignty*, trans. George Schwab (Cambridge, MA: MIT Press, 1985), 12.
14 Schmitt, *Concept of the Political*, trans. George Schwab (Chicago: University of Chicago Press, 1996), 48, 26–27.
15 Frantz Fanon, *Les Damnés de la terre* (Paris: Folio, 1991), 81.
16 Aimé Césaire, *Discours sur le colonialisme* (Paris: Présence Africaine, 1955), 19.
17 Karl Marx and Friedrich Engels, *The Communist Manifesto* (Woodbridge: Merlin Press, 1998), 2.
18 Ibid., 3.
19 Vladimir Lenin, *Revolution at the Gates: A Selection of Writings from February to October 1917* (London: Verso, 2002), 110, 121.
20 Badiou, *Théorie du sujet* (Paris: Seuil, 1982), 42; cf. Pierre Macherey, "Un se divise en deux," *Histoires de dinosaure* (Paris: PUF, 1999), 69–73. What remains at stake in such division is a central concern in the ongoing work of Bruno Bosteels and Alberto Toscano.
21 Jacques Lacan, "The Function and Field of Speech and Language in Psychoanalysis," in *Ecrits: A Selection*, trans. Alan Sheridan (New York: Norton, 1977), 86; cf. Lacan, "The Subversion of the Subject," in ibid., 306.
22 As Badiou explains in his critique of Lacan's "Logical Time," a courageous "haste, not inferable from the symbolic, is the mode in which the subject exceeds [the symbolic] by exposing himself to the real" (Badiou, *Théorie du sujet*, 272). For an illuminating discussion of this point, one that links Badiou's conception of courage with the Kantian notion of "enthusiasm," see Dominiek Hoens and Ed Pluth, "What If the Other Is Stupid? Badiou and Lacan on 'Logical Time,'" in *Think Again: Alain Badiou and the Future of Philosophy*, ed. Peter Hallward (London: Continuum, 2004), 182–90.

23 Maximilien Robespierre, "Sur le procès du roi: 13 December 1792," in Robespierre, *Pour le bonheur et pour la liberté: Discours*, ed. Yannick Bosc, Florence Gauthier, and Sophie Wahnich (Paris: La Fabrique, 2000), 193–94.

24 Žižek, "Between the Two Revolutions," in Lenin, *Revolution at the Gates*, 3–6. In a moment of crisis it is "sheer idiocy, or sheer treachery," Lenin knows, to postpone action pending the explicit approval of sanctioned authority (Lenin, "The Crisis Has Matured," in *Revolution at the Gates*, 139).

25 See in particular Lenin, "Letter to Comrades," in *Revolution at the Gates*, 157.

26 Lenin, "Annotations on Book I (Being) of Hegel's *Science of Logic*," in Lenin, *Collected Works*, vol. 38, available online at www.marxists.org/archive/lenin/works/1914/cons-logic/ch01.htm#LCW38_114. Accessed February 15, 2005.

27 See Lenin, *The Right of Nations to Self-Determination* (1914), chapter 10.

28 Points indicate moments in which subjects "confront the global situation with singular choices, with decisions that involve the 'yes' and the 'no.'" In the example that Badiou develops in the first section of *Logiques des mondes*, the mobilization of Spartacus against Roman slavery, these punctual decisions include answers to the questions: "Is it really necessary to march south, or to attack Rome? To confront the legions, or evade them? To invent a new discipline, or to imitate regular armies? These oppositions, and their treatment, measure the efficacy of the slaves gathered together as a fighting body, and ultimately they unfold the subjective formalism that this body is capable of bearing. In this sense, a subject exists, as the localization of a truth, *insofar as it affirms that it holds a certain number of points.* That is why the treatment of points is the becoming-true of the subject, at the same time as it is the filter of the aptitudes of bodies." (I quote from the draft manuscript of *Logiques des mondes*, forthcoming 2006; the translation is by Alberto Toscano.)

29 Badiou, *Logiques des mondes*, statement 63.

30 Žižek, *Ticklish Subject*, 380; cf. Žižek, "Between the Two Revolutions," in Lenin, *Revolution at the Gates*, 8; Badiou, *Infinite Thought*, 173.

31 See, for instance, Jacques Derrida, *Gift of Death*, trans. David Wills (Chicago: University of Chicago Press, 1995), 77; *Voyous: Deux essais sur la raison* (Paris: Galilée, 2003), 198, 203.

32 Maurice Merleau-Ponty, *Adventures of the Dialectic*, trans. Joseph Bien (Evanston, IL: Northwestern University Press, 1973), 98–99.

33 Karl Marx and Friedrich Engels, *The German Ideology*, part 1A, sec. 4, available online at www.marxists.org/archive/marx/works/1845/german-ideology/ch01a.htm. Accessed February 15, 2005.

34 See Louis Althusser, *Lenin and Philosophy*, trans. Ben Brewster (New York: Monthly Review Press, 1972), 20–22; *Essays in Self-Criticism*, trans. Grahame Locke (London: NLB, 1976), 46–47.

35 See in particular Balibar, "Three Concepts of Politics," in *Politics and the Other Scene* (2002), 23–35.

36 See in particular Badiou, *Théorie du sujet*, 81–82, 190; Hallward, "Depending on Inconsistency," 14–15.

37 Rancière, *On the Shores of Politics*, trans. Liz Heron (London: Verso, 1995), 61; *The Names of History*, trans. Hassan Melehy (Minneapolis: University of Minnesota Press, 1994), 98.

38 Rancière, *La Leçon d'Althusser* (Paris: Gallimard, 1974), 39–41.

39 Brian Massumi, "Navigating Movements," *21C Magazine* 2 [2003], available online at www.21cmagazine.com/issue2/massumi.html. Accessed February 15, 2005.

40 Cf. Bruno Latour, "La Gauche a-t-elle besoin de Bourdieu?" *Libération*, September 15, 1998; Rancière, *Le Philosophe et ses pauvres* (Paris: Fayard, 1983), 266–71.

41 Mao Tse-Tung, "On Contradiction," in *Selected Works of Mao Tse-Tung*, vol. 1 (Beijing: Foreign Languages Press, 1967), 331–36.

42 These are among the questions that have been discussed in detail during sessions of the Althusser reading group organized by Ozren Pupovac, Alberto Toscano, and Nina Power (London, 2004–5); see also Bruno Bosteels, "Alain Badiou's Theory of the Subject: The Re-Commencement of Dialectical Materialism," *Pli (Warwick Journal of Philosophy)* 12 (2002): 200–229.

43 In Badiou's jargon, this foothold corresponds to the "eventual site" that shapes the foundation of a situation.

44 Cf. Edward Said, "Epilogue," in *The Politics of Dispossession: The Struggle for Palestinian Self-Determination, 1969–1994* (London: Vintage, 1995), 416; *The Question of Palestine* (New York: Vintage, 1992), 244.

45 Carolyn Fick, *The Making of Haiti: The Saint Domingue Revolution from Below* (Knoxville: University of Tennessee Press, 1990), 228, 241–47.

46 To associate the term *prescription* here with forms of militant, divisive, but universalizable anticipation is to distance it, of course, from many of the connotations usually associated with prescriptivist approaches to moral philosophy—for instance, from A. J. Ayer's emotivism, or from R. M. Hare's emphasis on the prudent, consensual, and ultimately utilitarian management of preferences. By definition, a politics of prescription can conform to no abstract "golden rule" (see in particular Hare, *Freedom and Reason* [Oxford: Oxford University Press, 1963]).

47 Cf. Badiou, "Democratic Materialism and the Materialist Dialectic," *Radical Philosophy* 130 (March 2005).

48 Cf. Seumas Milne, "If the U.S. Can't Fix It, It's the Wrong Kind of Democracy," *The Guardian*, November 18, 2004. For a particularly instructive example of this more general trend, see Greg Grandin's book on Guatemala after Arbenz, *The Last Colonial Massacre: Latin America in the Cold War* (Chicago: University of Chicago Press, 2004).

49 Cécile Winter, "Quelques Remarques après quatre années de travail du Collectif Politique Sida en Afrique" (unpublished ms., September 2004).

50 Naomi Klein, "The Likudization of the World," *Globe and Mail*, September 9, 2004, p. A25.

51 Rancière, *Shores of Politics*, 32.

52 Jean-Paul Sartre, *Sketch for a Theory of the Emotions*, trans. Philip Mairet (London: Routledge Classics, 2002), 53. In his important new book on the ideological history of fear, Corey Robin makes a broadly similar point: whereas premodern thinkers from Plato through to Hobbes evoke fear only as a rational aversion to dangers that might threaten positive political principles, the distinctively modern approach to fear configures it as a manipulable reaction to an apolitical if not purely phantasmatic evil, a reaction based on a supposedly self-evident emotional experience (Robin, *Fear: The History of a Political Idea* [Oxford: Oxford University Press, 2004]).

Notes on Contributors

SRINIVAS ARAVAMUDAN is associate professor of English and director of the John Hope Franklin Humanities Institute at Duke University. His teaching and research interests include Enlightenment political theory, comparative imperialisms, and the history of the novel. He is the author of *Tropicopolitans: Colonialism and Agency, 1688–1804* (1999), and his book *Guru English: South Asian Religion in a Cosmopolitan Language* is forthcoming from Princeton University Press.

BRUNO BOSTEELS is associate professor in the Department of Romance Studies at Cornell University and editor of *Diacritics: A Review of Contemporary Criticism*. His teaching and research interests include Latin American literature, contemporary philosophy, and political theory. His book *Badiou and Politics* is forthcoming from Duke University Press, as is his translation of Badiou's *Can Politics Be Thought?* He is currently finishing another book, *After Borges: Literature and Antiphilosophy*.

MALCOLM BULL is a Fellow of St. Edmund Hall, Oxford, and a member of the editorial committee of *New Left Review*. His books include *Seeing Things Hidden* (2000); he is currently writing a book against Nietzsche.

ANNE F. GARRÉTA is an associate professor in the Department of Literature at the University of Rennes 2 (France), and a regular visiting professor in the Literature Program at Duke University. Her most recent research on subjects including queer theory, fiction theory, and Rousseau has appeared in *Yale French Studies* and at the Presses Universitaires de Rennes.

PETER HALLWARD is professor of modern European philosophy at Middlesex University. He is the author of *Absolutely Postcolonial* (2001) and *Badiou: A Subject to Truth* (2003), and the editor of a special issue of the journal *Angelaki* on recent French philosophy. His book *Deleuze and the Philosophy of Creation* is due out next year from Verso.

FREDRIC JAMESON is professor of French and comparative literature and director of the Institute for Critical Theory at Duke University. He is the author of *Marxism and Form, The Political Unconscious, Postmodernism, or, the Cultural Logic of Late Capitalism*, and *A Singular Modernity*.

STATHIS KOUVÉLAKIS currently teaches in the French department of King's College London. He is coeditor of *Actuel Marx* and cochair of the International Marx Conference. Along with Slavoj Žižek and S. Budgen, he has coedited the forthcoming collection *Toward a Politics of Truth: Retrieving Lenin* (Duke University Press).

WARREN MONTAG teaches English and comparative literature at Occidental College in Los Angeles. He is the author of *Louis Althusser* (2003) and *Bodies, Masses, Power: Spinoza and His Contemporaries* (1999). He is currently working on a book on Adam Smith.

ALBERTO MOREIRAS is Anne and Robert Bass Professor of Romance Studies and Literature and director of the Center for European Studies at Duke University. His most recent book is *The Exhaustion of Difference: The Politics of Latin American Cultural Studies* (2001). *Piel de lobo. Morfología de la razón imperial* is forthcoming in 2005. He is a coeditor of the *Journal of Spanish Cultural Studies.*

STELLA SANDFORD is Senior Lecturer in Modern European Philosophy at Middlesex University, London. She is the author of *The Metaphysics of Love: Gender and Transcendence in Levinas* (2000) and the forthcoming *Plato and Sex* (2006) and *How to Read de Beauvoir* (2006).

TERESA M. VILARÓS is associate professor of Romance Studies and Bass Fellow at Duke University and a founding coeditor of the *Journal of Spanish Cultural Studies.* She has written extensively on modern and contemporary literature and film and on the Spanish political transition. She is the author of *El mono del desencanto: Una crítica cultural de la transición española (1973–1993)* (Madrid: Siglo XXI, 1998) and of *Galdós: Invención de la mujer y poética de la sexualidad* (Madrid: Siglo XXI, 1995). Her work in progress includes "Banalidad y biopolítica," a reading of Spain in the sixties.

Contents of Volume 104

One Hundred Years of
The Souls of Black Folk: A Celebration

Originally published in 1903, *The Souls of Black Folk* is W. E. B. DuBois's biting critique of the racist and nationalist ideologies that animated the political culture of post-Reconstruction, Jim Crow America. This special issue celebrates and considers the influence of *Souls* during the last one hundred years. Featuring the work of a new generation of DuBois scholars, it suggests that a full appreciation of *Souls* requires reading it both as literary art and as political theory.

SUBSCRIPTION INFORMATION

Three issues annually
Institutions: $145 / Individuals: $37
Students: $25 (photocopy of valid student ID required)
Single issues: $15

Canadian orders: Please include 7% GST and $9 postage. Orders outside the U.S. and Canada: Please include $12 postage.

To place your order using a credit card, please call toll-free 888-651-0122 (in the U.S. and Canada) or 919-688-5134; or e-mail subscriptions@dukeupress.edu.

For more information, visit **www.dukeupress.edu/publicculture.**

PUBLIC CULTURE
Society for Transnational Cultural Studies

Contributors:
Anne E. Carroll
Vilashini Cooppan
Robert Gooding-Williams
Sheila Lloyd
Charles Nero
Cheryl A. Wall
Alexander Weheliye

Robert Gooding-Williams and Dwight A. McBride, special issue editors
Volume 17, number 2 Spring 2005

DUKE
UNIVERSITY PRESS